CAMBRIDGE LII

Books of enduring scholarly value

# Egyptology

The large-scale scientific investigation of Egyptian antiquities by Western scholars began as an unintended consequence of Napoleon's invasion of Egypt during which, in 1799, the Rosetta Stone was discovered. The military expedition was accompanied by French scholars, whose reports prompted a wave of enthusiasm that swept across Europe and North America resulting in the Egyptian Revival style in art and architecture. Increasing numbers of tourists visited Egypt, eager to see the marvels being revealed by archaeological excavation. Writers and booksellers responded to this growing interest with publications ranging from technical site reports to tourist guidebooks and from children's histories to theories identifying the pyramids as repositories of esoteric knowledge. This series reissues a wide selection of such books. They reveal the gradual change from the 'tomb-robbing' approach of early excavators to the highly organised and systematic approach of Flinders Petrie, the 'father of Egyptology', and include early accounts of the decipherment of the hieroglyphic script.

# The Great Pyramid

The publisher and author John Taylor (1781–1864), who took an interest in various antiquarian matters, published this work in 1859. Using the measurements taken by the seventeenth-century archaeologist John Greaves and by the French savants who had examined the Great Pyramid at Giza during Napoleon's Egyptian expedition, he deduced the existence of a 'pyramid inch' (fractionally longer than the British inch), which was one twenty-fifth of the so-called 'sacred cubit' and was derived from ancient astronomical and time-measurement observations; and as a convinced Christian, he concluded that the British inch was therefore divinely inspired. His work was very influential and had a considerable following (the astronomer Charles Piazzi Smyth's 1864 book on *Our Inheritance in the Great Pyramid* is also reissued in this series), but was later debunked by the more accurate surveys and measurements of Flinders Petrie, whose interest in Egypt was partly aroused by reading this book.

# The Great Pyramid

*Why Was It Built? And Who Built It?*

JOHN TAYLOR

CAMBRIDGE
UNIVERSITY PRESS

# CAMBRIDGE
## UNIVERSITY PRESS

University Printing House, Cambridge, CB2 8BS, United Kingdom

Cambridge University Press is part of the University of Cambridge.
It furthers the University's mission by disseminating knowledge in the pursuit of
education, learning and research at the highest international levels of excellence.

www.cambridge.org
Information on this title: www.cambridge.org/9781108075787

© in this compilation Cambridge University Press 2014

This edition first published 1859
This digitally printed version 2014

ISBN 978-1-108-07578-7 Paperback

# THE GREAT PYRAMID.

THE PYRAMID COFFER IN THE KING'S CHAMBER.

*To face title page.*

# THE GREAT PYRAMID.

## Why was it Built? & Who Built it?

BY

## JOHN TAYLOR,

AUTHOR OF

"JUNIUS IDENTIFIED," "AN ESSAY ON MONEY,"

"THE STANDARD AND MEASURE OF VALUE,"

ETC.

" OLD TIME, himself so old, is like a child,
And can't remember when these blocks were piled,
Or caverns scooped, but, with amazed eye,
He seems to pause—like other standers-by—
Half thinking, that the wonders, left unknown,
Were born in ages older than his own."—CLARE.

LONDON:

LONGMAN, GREEN, LONGMAN, AND ROBERTS.

—

1859.

LONDON :
PRINTED BY WERTHEIMER AND CO.
CIRCUS PLACE, FINSBURY.

# PREFACE.

IN the following work I have made an attempt
to recover *a lost leaf in the World's History*.
There was no need that the information which
it contains should form any portion of the
Hebrew Scriptures, since all the particulars
relating to man's salvation are complete without it; and as to the heathen records, the
earliest of the Greek historians did not live till
more than 1500 years after the Great Pyramid
is supposed to have been built.

The materials out of which this volume is
composed, were obtained chiefly from the Great
Pyramid itself, in the accounts given of it by
various writers, from the earliest times to the
present day. Many brief but interesting me-
morials have descended to us from Greek
and Roman sources; but the most important,

because the most minute, descriptions of the
Great Pyramid, are those which have been
given to the world in modern times by the
writers of England and France. So complete,
indeed, is the knowledge now obtained, that it
leaves scarcely anything to be desired.

I have confined my observations to the Great
Pyramid alone. It was not only the largest
of the three most important structures, called
the Pyramids of Gizeh, but was, probably,
the most correct and exact of them all in
its proportions. It is, happily, also the
most perfect of the three; and its minutest
details, internal and external, have been recorded with scrupulous fidelity. The uncer-
tainty which has prevailed as to the purpose
for which the Pyramids were originally built,
was no doubt one of the causes of that extreme
care which each writer took, to remark and
narrate every little peculiarity he could discover in their construction: this, while it
prevented him from establishing any theory
of his own, necessarily led to the accumulation

of a multitude of facts, which are at length found capable of harmonious adjustment.

The Drawing of *The Pyramid Coffer in the King's Chamber* is taken from Sir Robert Ainslie's Views in Egypt, 1804; and that of *The Discovery of the Casing Stones* is copied from Colonel Howard Vyse's work on the Pyramids, published in 1840.

JOHN TAYLOR.

LEONARD PLACE,
 KENSINGTON.
 *September*, 1859.

## ERRATA.

Page  39, Note, for "τετραγονου," read "τετραγωνου."
    145, third line from the bottom, for "3128," read "3126."

# TABLE OF CONTENTS.

## EXTERIOR OF THE GREAT PYRAMID.

### CHAPTER I.

### CHAPTER II.

## Chapter III.

## Chapter IV.

## Chapter V.

## Chapter VI.

## Chapter VII.

## Chapter VIII.

## Chapter IX.

## Chapter X.

## INTERIOR OF THE GREAT PYRAMID.

## Chapter XI.

*b*

## Chapter XII.

## Chapter XIII.

## Chapter XIV.

## Chapter XV.

## Chapter XVI.

## Chapter XVII.

THE FOUNDERS OF THE GREAT PYRAMID.

## Chapter XXI.

## Chapter XXII.

## Chapter XXIII.

## Chapter XXIV.

## Chapter XXV.

CHAPTER XXVI.

CHAPTER XXVII.

CHAPTER XXVIII.

CHAPTER XXIX.

CHAPTER XXX.

## Chapter XXXI.

## Chapter XXXII.

## APPENDIX.

### ADDITIONAL SCRIPTURE MEASURES OF LENGTH.

THE CASING STONES.

*To face page 1.*

# THE GREAT PYRAMID:

ETC., ETC.

—————

## EXTERIOR OF THE GREAT PYRAMID.

### CHAPTER I.

*The Pyramids of Gizeh commonly supposed to be Sepulchres —
Some have thought them a Standard of Measure — The latter
Opinion hitherto unsupported by Proof — Colonel Howard
Vyse's Discoveries in favour of it.*

### 1.

WITH few exceptions, all the writers who have
described the Pyramids of Gizeh, have supposed
them to be meant for the burial-places of kings.
Among the earliest who have entertained this opinion,
are Strabo and Diodorus Siculus, who say that the
kings who built the two largest intended them for
their own sepulchres, though they were not buried in
them. Among the latest, Dr. Robinson, in his recent
"Biblical Researches," observes, "There seems now
little room to doubt that they were erected chiefly, if
not solely, as the sepulchres of kings:" and then he
exclaims, — "Vain pride of human pomp and power!
Their monuments remain unto this day, the wonder of
all time; but themselves, their history, and their very

B

names, have been swept away in the dark tide of oblivion!" The Rev. A. P. Stanley, one of the most recent writers on the subject, evidently inclines to the opinion that the Pyramids were the tombs of kings. He describes the three largest of them as forming "the most sacred and frequented part of that vast cemetery which extends all along the western ridge for twenty miles behind Memphis;" and he says the Sphinx, "the giant representative of royalty" fitly "guards the greatest of royal sepulchres;" being "as much greater than all other sphinxes as the Pyramids are greater than all other temples or tombs."—"The Pyramids! What a lesson to those who desire a name in the world does the fate of these restless, brick-piling monarchs afford. Their names are not known; and the only hope for them is, that by the labours of some cruelly industrious antiquarian, they may at last become more *definite objects of contempt.*" *

2.

But at the commencement of the present century a different opinion for a time prevailed. The men of science who accompanied the French expedition into Egypt, took great pains to obtain the exact measure of the three largest Pyramids, and came to the conclusion that not only were they founded on certain geometrical principles, but that they were intended to perpetuate the memory of the standard by which they were constructed. M. Jomard imagined that the present Egyptian cubit is contained 400 times in each side of the base of the Great Pyramid, and the common cubit 500 times; as also that the side of the base is the 480th part of a degree of the meridian proper to

* Helps' Conquest of Peru.

Egypt. The measurements, however, which were made failed to substantiate any of these conjectures.

"It was contended," says Dr. Peacock, "by Paucton, in his *Métrologie*, that the side of the Great Pyramid was the exact $\frac{1}{500}$th part of a degree of the meridian, and that the founders of that mighty monument designed it as an imperishable standard of measures of length. Absurd as this notion apparently is, it was patronised by the celebrated Bailli, with his usual fondness for extravagant hypotheses, who conjectured that both in it, and in the *coudée nilométrique*, or *cubit of the nilometer*, was to be found the invariable standard of measures derived from the magnitude of the earth. It was somewhat unfortunate for both these suppositions, that the length of the side of the Great Pyramid was found to be 716½ French feet, instead of 684⅕, and the cubit of the nilometer, 20·54 inches, instead of 19·992, as it should have been."[*]

Similar opinions had been entertained at a much earlier period, at which time the recorded measures of the base differed considerably from those of M. Jomard. "Early in the 17th century," says Mr. De Morgan, "there arose a disposition, among those who inquired into the subject, to seek a mystical origin of weights and measures, on the supposition of some body of exact science once existing, but now seen only in its vestiges: a disposition which is not yet entirely extinct. Some speculated on the Pyramids of Egypt, and tried to establish that the intention of building those great masses was, that a record of measures founded on the most exact principles, might exist for ever. But more turned their attention to the measurement of the earth;

[*] Arithmetic, by the Rev. George Peacock, D.D., in *Ency. Metrop.*

and, by assuming nothing more difficult than that a degree of the meridian, a thousand times more accurate than that of Eratosthenes, was in existence hundreds if not thousands of years before him, it was easy enough to make out that the whole system of Greek, Roman, Asiatic, Egyptian, etc. measures was a tradition from, or a corruption of, this venerable piece of lost geodesy. There runs through all these national systems a certain resemblance in the measures of length: and, if a bundle of faggots were made of foot rules, one from every nation ancient and modern, there would not be any very unreasonable difference in the lengths of the sticks."*

### 3.

Paley says, " He who *proves* discovers." The above extracts from the works of two of the ablest mathematicians of the present day, will serve to shew quite as well as any more laboured proof, that the investigations of the French *savans*, though made with the greatest exactness, did not enable them to support their conjectures with respect to the Pyramids. In the opinion of the scientific world they failed to prove their case; and, after a lapse of fifty years, the theory which they tried to establish is held to be as far from verification as it was at the commencement of their inquiries.

### 4.

Some information, of great value, has, however, been communicated to the world on this subject, within the last twenty years. In 1840, the late General (then Lieut.-Col.) Howard Vyse rendered an important

---

* Arithmetical Books from the invention of printing to the present time. By Aug. De Morgan, A.M. 1847, p. 6.

service to science by publishing the results of his investigation into the present condition of the Pyramids. His researches have added greatly to the extent and accuracy of our previous knowledge. He did not measure the length of the base of the Great Pyramid with greater care and precision than those who immediately preceded him, but he corroborated their measures; and he introduced a new element of certainty into the discussion, by discovering two of the *casing-stones* in their original position, which enables their evidence to be brought to bear on the relative proportions of the height of the Pyramid to its base. We acknowledge, with pleasure, our obligations to this noble-minded man, who prosecuted his inquiries with great ardour, and must have incurred a heavy loss by presenting his country with that splendid work which he published at his own expense. If he has contributed, as we believe he has, to the elucidation of the purpose for which the Pyramids were built, that circumstance alone will constitute a monument to his memory more lasting than brass or marble.

## Chapter II.

*Earliest Measure of the Base of the Great Pyramid, by John
Greaves—His Description of the Great Pyramid—Measure of
the Base by De Monconys, Thévenot, etc.—Measure of the Base
by Davison—Measure of the Base by the French Savans—Discovery of the Casing-stones by Colonel Howard Vyse —
M. Caviglia's Discovery of the Pavement—Colonel Vyse's Description of the Casing-stones — Vyse and Perring's Measure of
the Great Pyramid — Angle of the Casing-stones—All the Different Measures of the Base reconciled.*

### 5.

IT cannot be denied, that our knowledge of the
length of the base of the Great Pyramid is derived
from many different and apparently conflicting accounts;
but these various statements, when properly considered,
corroborate each other.   Those of greatest authority
are found to range themselves under the following
numbers :—693, 728, 746, and 764 English feet.   We
have no doubt that each of these measurements was
correct at the time it was made; and all, properly considered, contribute to prove that the last number of the
series is the most perfect of any.

Mr. John Greaves, Savilian Professor of Astronomy
in the University of Oxford, was the earliest of all
persons, of modern times, who attempted to make
an exact measurement of the Great Pyramid.   He left
London for this purpose in the spring of 1637, and
"took with him a radius of ten feet, most accurately
divided into 10,000 parts, besides some other instru-

ments, for the fuller discovery of the truth." While
he was employed in making his measure of the
Pyramids, he caused the length of the English foot " to
be observed by all nations, in one of the rooms under
the said Pyramid, with his name, *J. Gravius,* under it":
that is, he engraved his measure of the English foot on
the walls of the room called the King's Chamber, in the
Great Pyramid, as a perpetual memorial of the foot he
took with him, which was exactly copied from the
standard as it existed in Guildhall. If some modern
traveller would take the like pains to make a faithful
copy of this foot, or ascertain its precise relation to the
French *mètre,* he would confer a great favour on those
who are interested in studies which require the
strictest comparison of ancient with modern measures.
Our present foot is, perhaps, a little different from that
which was recorded in the Pyramid two centuries ago.

### 6.

Greaves took extraordinary precautions to ensure
accuracy in the measures which he made of the Great
Pyramid; and we have every reason to believe that his
account is correct: we give it therefore in his own
earnest and graphic words. "The first and fairest of
the three greater Pyramids is situated on the top of
a rocky hill, in the sandy desert of Libya, about a
quarter of a mile distant to the west from the plains of
Egypt, above which the rock riseth 100 feet or better,
with a gentle rising ascent. Upon this advantageous
rise, and upon this solid foundation, the Pyramid is
erected; the height of the situation adding to the
beauty of the work, and the solidity of the rock giving
the superstructure a permanent and stable support.
Each side of the Pyramid, computing it according to

Herodotus, contains in length 800 Grecian feet; and in Diodorus Siculus' account, 700. Strabo reckons it less than a furlong; that is, less than 600 Grecian feet, or 625 Roman: and Pliny equals it to 883. That of Diodorus Siculus, in my judgment, comes nearest to the truth, and may serve in some kind to confirm those proportions, which in another discourse I have assigned to the Grecian measures. For, measuring the north side of it, near the basis, by an exquisite radius of ten feet in length, taking two several stations, as mathematicians use to do when any obstacle hinders their approach, I found it to be 693 feet, according to the English standard: which quantity is somewhat less than that of Diodorus. The rest of the sides were examined by a line, for want of an even level, and a convenient distance to place my instruments, both which the area on the former side afforded.

" The ascent to the top of the Pyramid is contrived in this manner : — From all sides without we ascend by degrees; the lowermost degree is near four feet in height and three in breadth. This runs about the Pyramid in a level; and at the first, when the stones were entire, which are now somewhat decayed, made on every side of it a long but narrow walk. The second degree is like the first, each stone amounting to almost four feet in height, and three in breadth ; it retires inward from the first near three feet; and this runs about the Pyramid in a level, as the former. In the same manner is the third row placed upon the second ; and so in order the rest, like so many stairs, rise one above another to the top, which ends not in a point, as mathematical pyramids do, but in a little flat or square."*

* Pyramidographia, 4to. 1646, p. 72.

7.

The next early measurements, which make any pre-
tensions to accuracy, were chiefly put forth by the French
nation. M. de Monconys, about the year 1647, made
the side of the base of the Great Pyramid, 682 French
feet (728 English). M. Thévenot, in his voyage to the
Levant, in 1657-8, also made it 682 French feet.
Melton, an Englishman, whose work was published in
the Dutch language, and who travelled between 1660
and 1667, makes it 682 French feet. Cassini, in the
"Memoirs of the Academy of Sciences in Paris,"
writing in 1702, says, " M. de Chazelles made an actual
measurement of the base of the Great Pyramid with a
line, and found it to be 690 French feet; but as it
stands on an uneven plot of ground, raised in the centre
of the side of the structure, it will be necessary to
subtract something from this length to arrive at the
proper base." He proposes to reduce the measure by
ten feet on this account; but we may, with as much
reason, deduct eight feet, and this will bring M. de
Chazelles' measure, made in 1693, into accordance with
the others which were made about the same time.
Cassini next mentions the measure which Gemelli
received in 1693, from an eminent mathematician,
Fulgentius of Tours, a Capuchin Friar, which was 682
French feet. He also says, that M. Jaugeon received
the same measure from M. de Nointel, the French
Ambassador to the Sublime Porte, which he communicated to the Academy of Sciences. It is impossible
to avoid suspecting that these several authorities for
one and the same measure derived their information
from some one common source, and that the most they
did was to see that it was verified by their own mea-

surement. To this source also we may attribute the
measure of Mr. Graves, an Englishman, who, as we
are informed by Major Rennell, made the base of the
Great Pyramid 728 English feet (682 French feet).

### 8.

The next measurement was made, in 1763, by Mr.
Nathaniel Davison, the British Consul at Algiers. He
found the side of the base of the Great Pyramid to
contain 746 English feet. Mr. Davison resided eighteen
months at Alexandria, and as many at Cairo, and from
the latter place frequently visited the Pyramids. He
was the first explorer of the chamber in the Great
Pyramid, which is over the King's Chamber, and is
now known as Davison's. In a letter to Professor White,
written from London in 1779, Davison makes a conjecture which has since been verified. " From some of
the original covering still remaining at the top of the
second great one, it is more than probable that the
steps of which the sides of the other now consist, were
covered in the same manner, with stones of such a form
as to make a smooth surface from top to bottom, with
a profile somewhat resembling this figure." He then
makes a diagram, exactly like the profile of one of the
casing stones discovered by Colonel Howard Vyse.

### 9.

Davison's measure received, in 1798, a most satisfactory confirmation from the labours of the French
*savans*. They further established the observation of
M. de Monconys and M. de Chazelles, that the Pyramid
was constructed so that its sides should face the cardinal
points of the compass. Having measured the apparent

base of the Great Pyramid twice, viz., from east to west, and again from west to east, with a good measuring chain, — receding for that purpose one hundred feet towards the north, but still keeping on a line parallel with the base, M. Jomard found the length of the Pyramid, from one visible angle to the other, to be 227·32 *mètres* (= 745·8 English feet); thus remarkably verifying Davison's measurement made thirty-five years before. A year after this, while Le Père, the architect, and Colonel Coutelle, were carefully surveying the platform on which the Pyramid was founded, they discovered, at the north-east angle, a wide shallow socket cut in the rock, in which indentation a corner-stone might have been placed. The socket was nearly square, being in English measure 11 feet 6 inches long, by 9 feet 9½ inches wide, and 8 inches deep. They then searched at the north-west angle, and found there also a socket of exactly the same dimensions as the other. Between the farthest extremities of these two indentations, they measured the base again with the greatest care and circumspection, and found it to be 232·747 *mètres* (= 763·6 English feet). Thus the latter measurement, made a year after the other, by a method, if possible, still more exact, not only confirmed the accuracy of the one preceding it, but rendered the result of the two operations, as the writers well observe, "*inattaquable.*"

### 10.

"——Last scene of all
That ends this strange eventful history,"—

the Casing-stones themselves were discovered in 1837, by Colonel Howard Vyse; and thus was placed beyond all doubt the inference which had been drawn by Le Père and Coutelle as to the probable use of the socket,

and the conjecture which had been formed by Davison
as to the Great Pyramid having been covered by a
*revêtement*. The following is an extract from Colonel
Vyse's Journal. "May 12. After having gone round
the several works, I was sent for about two o'clock to
the Great Pyramid, as the casing-stones at the base had
been discovered. The size and angle of the building
could therefore be exactly determined, and all doubts
were removed respecting a *revêtement*. Two of the blocks
were in their original position, nearly in the centre of
the Pyramid; and those adjoining them must have
been covered by the mound of rubbish for a considerable
time before they were removed, as the exact space which
they had occupied was left in it, like a perfect mould.
Why they were thus taken out sideways, and by what
means, without disturbing any part of the mass above
them, it is difficult to say."

## 11.

A narrow excavation into this mound had been
carried on by M. Caviglia, in the centre of the northern front, to within about thirty-eight feet of the
base, whereby the rock, and what was supposed to be
a step, had been uncovered. "This work," says
Colonel Vyse, "had been commenced on too small a
scale, and only at the bottom; and the materials had
not been removed to a sufficient distance; consequently,
as the mound was composed of very large blocks,
and upwards of 40 feet high, the removal of it was
attended with great difficulty on approaching the
building, and was not completely effected. It should
have been carried on at the top, and on both sides, as
well as at the bottom." M. Caviglia had excavated to a
distance of 43 feet when he reached the rocky found-

ation, and he was 11 feet nearer the base, when he
arrived at the supposed step, which proved to be a
pavement. M. Caviglia's services ceased on the 12th
of February, and on the 24th, Colonel Vyse made an
arrangement with a Reis, from Kerdasse, to remove the
stones and rubbish from the centre of the northern front
in fifteen or twenty-five days, as the work might turn
out, for 2,000 piastres; but the Colonel broke off this
engagement, fearing it would lead to disputes between
the villages, and probably interfere with the other
works; and on the 28th, he continued the excavation
on his own account. On the 31st of March, he found
that the supposed step was the commencement of a
pavement, " and as it was in the form of a step like that
at the second Pyramid, it was considered that a similar
entrance might exist, and that it might possibly conduct
to the famous tomb mentioned by Herodotus. The
pavement was, therefore, carefully examined, but the
stones were found to be laid upon the solid rock. They
had the finest joints, but were perfectly plain, without
the slightest indication of sculpture or of painting, or
appearance of an entrance."

12.

Six weeks after this the casing-stones were discovered.
" They were quite perfect, had been hewn into the
required angle before they were built in, and had then
been polished down to one uniform surface; the joints
were scarcely perceptible, and not wider than the thickness of silver paper; and such is the tenacity of the
cement with which they are held together, that a fragment of one that has been destroyed remained firmly
fixed in its original *alignement*, notwithstanding the
lapse of time, and the violence to which it had been
exposed. The pavement beyond the line of building

was well laid and beautifully finished; but beneath the edifice it was worked with even greater exactness, and to the most perfect level, in order probably to obtain a lasting foundation for the magnificent structure to be built upon it. I consider that the workmanship displayed in the *King's Chamber*, in this *pavement*, and in the *casing-stones*, is perfectly unrivalled; and that there is no reason to doubt that the whole exterior of this vast structure was covered over with the same excellent masonry."

The stones which compose the body of the Pyramid were quarried from the rock on which it stands. It is a free limestone, and abounds with fossil remains. The casing-stones were brought from a rock on the opposite side of the river, about nine miles off, called the Mokattam quarry. This rock is a compact limestone, which contains few fossils, and is termed by geologists *Swinestone*.

### 13.

The dimensions of the Great Pyramid, according to Mr. Perring, the surveyor employed by Col. Howard Vyse, are as follows :—

|  | Feet. | Inches. |
|---|---|---|
| The former base with the casing-stones . | 764 | 0 |
| The present base . . . . . | 746 | 0 |
| Former height, including the casing-stones | 480 | 9 |
| Present height, perpendicular . . ˙ | 450 | 9 |
| Former height, inclined . . . . | 611 | 0 |
| Present height, inclined . . . . | 568 | 3 |
| Width of the pavement in front of the casing-stones in the centre of the northern side . . . . . . . | 33 | 6 |
| Thickness of the paving-stones . . | 1 | 9 |

The tiers of stones vary in depth from 4 feet 10 inches at the bottom, to 2 feet 2 inches toward the top.

The platform on the top is about 33 feet square,
above which are four or five stones belonging to the
upper layers.

| | Acres. | Roods. | Poles. |
|---|---|---|---|
| Former extent of the base . . | 13 | 1 | 22 |
| Present extent of the base . . | 12 | 3 | 3 |

### 14.

Each of the casing-stones was in depth 8 feet 3
inches at the bottom, 4 feet 3 inches at the top,
4 feet 11 inches in perpendicular height, and 6 feet
3 inches in sloping height.

#### PROFILE OF ONE OF THE CASING-STONES.

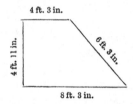

The angle of the face of the casing-stones, as taken
by Mr. Brettell, Civil Engineer, was found to be 51° 50′.

Thus was solved a most important problem, which had
long engaged the attention of men of science, especially
in England and France; and exactly two hundred
years after Greaves had made the first skilful effort, by
the use of well-appointed instruments, to measure the
base of the Great Pyramid, and to determine the height
of that vast structure, both objects were satisfactorily
accomplished by the discovery of the casing-stones *in
situ*. At the same time, *all the previous measures were
confirmed*. This unlooked-for result may be easily de-
monstrated, whether we accept the English or the
French measure for our basis.

| | English Measure. | | French, in English feet. | | |
|---|---|---|---|---|---|
| | Ft. | In. | Ft. | In. | |
| Base | 764 | 0 | 763 | 8 | |
| Deduct | 17 | 8 | 17 | 8 | for the casing-stones |
| Leaves | 746 | 4 | 746 | 0 | for the measure in 1763. |
| Deduct | 17 | 8 | 17 | 8 | for the lowest tier of stones. |
| Leaves | 728 | 8 | 728 | 4 | for the measure in 1693. |
| Deduct | 17 | 8 | 17 | 8 | for the second tier. |
| Leaves | 711 | 0 | 710 | 8 | of which no record is left. |
| Deduct | 17 | 8 | 17 | 8 | for the third tier. |
| Leaves | 693 | 4 | 693 | 0 | for the measure in 1637. |

### 15.

Commencing with Greaves's estimate, which was taken with such care that we can hardly believe it to have been incorrect, we find that if the sand were at that time not cleared away from the three lowest tiers of stones, the measure of the base would be 693 feet, as in this diagram :—

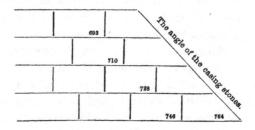

At the end of that century, if only one tier remained buried, the measure would be, as De Monconys, Thévenot, and so many others found it, 728 feet. In the middle of the next century, the sand from that tier

being removed, Davison now made the base 746 feet;
and this measure was confirmed by Jomard and others
at the end of the same century.   Lastly, a year or two
afterwards, the space occupied by the casing-stones—
and in 1837, the casing-stones themselves—being discovered, the full measure of 763·6 or 764 feet was confirmed, and accordingly all the earlier measures were
rendered probably true at the time they were taken.

## CHAPTER III.

*Various Heights ascribed to the Great Pyramid — Height deter-
mined by the Angle of the Casing-stones — Why the Founders
fixed on that Angle for the Face of the Great Pyramid — Herodotus makes use of Square Measure — The Great Pyramid a Demonstration of the Diameter of a Sphere to its Circumference—
Height of the Pyramid the Radius of the Sphere—Its Height
the tenth of a Roman Mile—Various Estimates of the Roman
Foot—The Measure of the Earth by Eratosthenes—His Error
in taking Proportion for Actual Measure—Various Estimates
of a smaller Roman Foot.*

### 16.

THE various estimates of the height of the Great
Pyramid differ more widely than those of the base,
and would have been incapable of adjustment, had not
the angle of the casing-stones afforded a means of ascertaining the height with the greatest exactness.   Even
the number of tiers of stones of which the Pyramid
consists was not counted with any accuracy before
Greaves's time.   Pierre Belon, whose work was published in 1555, reckoned them about 250.   George
Sandys, about 1610, makes them 255, and each step
above 3 feet high, wherein he greatly errs.   Greaves
makes the number 208, which is also the number
assigned by De Monconys, Thévenot, Melton, Fulgentius of Tours, and Dr. Veryard.   In 1801, Grobert,
who measured every step, makes the number 208,
while Davison, forty years earlier, found only 206.   But
it is in the supposed height, that the various authorities chiefly differ.   Greaves, in his first edition, comes

the nearest to the truth, when he reckons the perpendicular height at 481 feet, and in his "Observations," published from his MSS. after his death, states it to be 490 feet. Grobert's measure is 478 English feet. Le Père and Coutelle's is 479½ English feet. Vyse and Perring's 480¾, and Sir Gardner Wilkinson's (if the casing were entire) 502 feet.

### 17.

The angle of the casing-stones being 51° 50', and the base 764 feet, would give for the perpendicular height, supposing the Pyramid ended in a point, 486 feet. Or, if we take the French measure of the base, 763·6 English feet, the same angle will give for the perpendicular height, 485·85 English feet.

### 18.

What reason, it may be asked, can be assigned for the founders of the Great Pyramid giving it this precise angle, and not rather making each face an equilateral triangle? The only one we can suggest is, that they knew the Earth was a sphere; that they had measured off a portion of one of its great circles; and by observing the motion of the heavenly bodies over the earth's surface, had ascertained its circumference, and were now desirous of leaving behind them a record of that circumference as correct and imperishable as it was possible for them to construct. They assumed the Earth to be a perfect sphere; and as they knew that the radius of a circle must bear a certain proportion to its circumference, they then built a Pyramid of such a height in proportion to its base, that its perpendicular would be equal to the radius of a circle equal in circumference to the perimeter of the base. To effect this they

would make each face of the Pyramid present a certain
ascertained angle with reference to its base (supposing a
vertical section made of it), which angle would be that
of 51° 51′ 14″, if modern science were employed in
determining it. We can hardly imagine that the
founders of the Pyramids were able to make so exact an
estimate; but if they had such an object in view as
that which we have supposed, in building the Great
Pyramid, the angle of its face with its base would bear
some near relation to the angle of 51° 51′ 14″. Now
the actual angle of the casing-stones was found to be
51° 50′. Can any proof be more conclusive than this,
that the reason we have assigned for the construction
of the Great Pyramid was the true reason which in-
fluenced its founders? How the thought occurred to
them we cannot tell; but a more proper monument for
this purpose could not have been devised than a vast
Pyramid with a square base, the vertical height of which
Pyramid should be the radius of a sphere in its circumference equal to the perimeter of that base. It was
impossible to build a hemisphere of so large a size. In
the form of a Pyramid, all those truths might be declared
which they had taken so much pains to learn; and in
that form the structure would be less liable to injury
from time, neglect, or wantonness, than in any other.
The ascertained measure of a degree of the earth's circumference might be engraven upon its surface in large
and deeply incised characters; and by the aid of a
College of Curators, whose perpetual support should be
a charge upon the land, the founders might hope that
they had made as permanent a provision as the structure
itself or the nature of man would permit, for communi-
cating from generation to generation, to the latest
posterity, those facts and that explanatory knowledge
which they desired to impart.

Of the three largest Pyramids, which stand very near each other, the second is said to be inclined to an angle of 52° 20', the third to an angle of 51°. The largest, or Great Pyramid, which is supposed to have been the last built, has the angle of 51° 50'. The angle required, if it were built for the purpose we have attributed to it, would be 51° 51' 14''. It is scarcely possible, that a work so stupendous should have been polished down to an uniform surface with less deviation from the prescribed angle. The workmen must all have been remarkably skilful, and have constantly wrought with a quadrant in their hands, to fulfil their presumed instructions so nearly as they did.

### 19.

Herodotus says of the Great Pyramid, "It is made of polished stone, jointed with the greatest exactness, and none of the stones are less than 30 feet."\* When he uses this language, he is evidently speaking of the Pyramid when it was covered with the casing-stones. They are made of a kind of marble which is capable of taking a high polish, and the joints of those which Vyse and Perring saw were scarcely perceptible, being not thicker than silver paper. That not one of these stones was less than 30 feet is, no doubt, as true as the rest of the description. As casing-stones, this measure can only be understood with reference to their superficies, and with regard to this it may have been correct. The *width* of the casing stones *in situ*, measured by Mr. Brettell, is not given, but judging from their appearance in the frontispiece to the first volume of Colonel Vyse's work, we should not suppose it to be less than

---

\* Λιθου δε ξεστου τε και ἁρμοσμενου τα μαλιστα· ουδεις των λιθων τριηκοντα ποδων ελασσων. ii. 124.

five feet, and this would make each contain at least 30 feet in superficial measure. Mr. Perring says the courses of stone varied in perpendicular height from 4 feet 10 inches to 2 feet 2 inches : the smallest, there-fore, would have a sloping height of 2 feet 10 inches, which in 12 feet of length would shew a surface of more than 30 square feet, admitting even that Herodotus meant Greek feet, which a little exceed the English.

### 20.

We have seen that the Great Pyramid was formed on a principle which would render its perpendicular height and its perimeter, in their *proportion* to each other, equal to that which the radius of a sphere bears to its circumference ; and as this proportion, if our theory be true, would be half that of the diameter of a circle to its circumference, which is stated in the *Table of Constants* to be that of 1 to 3·1415927, we may reasonably expect that the Great Pyramid, in its actual measure as it is now recorded, would exhibit some approach to this *proportion*. In that case, the diameter of the circle will be twice the perpendicular height of the Pyramid, and will be expressed by 1 as *unity*, while the circumference of the circle, or the perimeter of the pyramid, will be represented by 3·1415927 of the same number, or some near approach to it. Otherwise, the circumference must be denoted by 1, and the diameter by a number con-taining the fractional parts.

### 21.

In the vertical height, or radius of the Great Pyra-mid, as deduced from the angle of the casing-stones, we have the number of 486 English feet, which, when doubled, makes the diameter 972 feet. The base of

764 feet, multiplied by 4 gives a perimeter or circumference of 3056 feet.  Taking the diameter as *unity*, we
have 1000 feet of ·972 parts of the English foot, equal to
11·664 inches; of which feet there are in the circumference 3144.  The true proportion in a sphere would
be 3141·5927, about two and a half feet less than the
actual measure.  Is it possible that the founders of
the Great Pyramid should come so near to the right
proportion of the diameter of a circle to its circumference, in the construction of the Pyramid, without
intending to express it as nearly as they were able?

## 22.

But what feet are these which bear the relation of
·972 to the English foot when it is estimated at 1·000?
If they are not that which may be called the Roman
foot, they come very near it.  As the length of the
Roman foot is a subject which has attracted the attention of men of science of all countries for several centuries, it is desirable that the reader should know what
are the results at which they have arrived.

Our first authority is Greaves, whose measures were
made two centuries ago, when the monuments on which
they are founded were less injured than they are now
He took with him a standard measure of length
adjusted with great exactness to the standard at Guildhall, and made all his measures with extreme care.
His words are as follows :—" In the year 1639, I went
into Italy to view, as the other antiquities of the
Romans, so especially those of weights and measures ;
and to take them with as much exactness as it was
possible, I carried instruments with me made by the
best artizans; where my first inquiry was after that
monument of T. Statilius Vol. Aper, in the Vatican

Gardens, from whence Philander took the dimensions
of the Roman foot, as others have since borrowed it from
him.  In the copying out of this upon an English foot
in brass, divided into 2000 parts, I spent at least two
hours (which I mention to shew with what diligence I
proceeded in this and the rest) so often comparing the
several divisions and digits of it respectively one with
another, that I think more circumspection could not
have been used; by which I plainly discovered the
rudeness and insufficiency of that foot.  For besides that
the length of it is somewhat too much (whatsoever
*Latinius*, out of an observation made by *Ant. Augustinus,
Sighicellus, Pacatus, Maffœus, Statius, Ægius,* and
*Fulvius Ursinus,* pretends to the contrary), there is never
a digit that is precisely answerable to one another.
Howsoever, it contains 1944 such parts as the English
foot contains 2000."*  This measure, therefore, gives
·972 to 1·000 of the English foot.

The value of Greaves' testimony to the length of this
foot is not impaired by the censures which he has cast
upon its accuracy, on account of its *digits* being not all
precisely answerable to each other; since if the entire
measure were correct, the subdivisions are easily
adjusted, and in fact require only to be marked to shew
their number, and not to give the true measure of each.
Still less is his persuasion that another foot is the more
correct standard of the two, to be allowed to have any
weight in an enquiry like the present.  His evidence in
regard to the magnitude of this foot is the more to be
depended upon for its fidelity, because it is that of a
prejudiced witness.  By his measure, as above, he
makes it ·972 parts of the English foot, or 11·664
English inches.

* Greaves's Works, p. 208.

## 23.

That "the Roman foot was equivalent to ·29624 of
a mètre has been placed beyond doubt by Cagnazzi's
researches." This remark is made in a note to Niebuhr's
History of Rome, by Hare and Thirlwall.* The
measure given is equal to ·9719 of the English foot,
or 11·663 inches. The "Metrologies Constitutionelle
et Primitive" assigns ·296296 of a mètre to the
Roman foot (ii. 339); being ·9721 of the English foot,
or 11·665 inches. In Stuart's estimate of the Heca-
tompedon at Athens, the Roman foot is made equal to
·971 of the English, or 11·652 inches. From a recent
measurement of the same temple made by Mr. F. Penrose, it is stated to be ·97286 of the English foot, or
11·673912 inches. Raper says that the sculptured foot
on the monument of *M. Ebutius* in the *Villa Mattei*, as
measured by Revillas, was ·97222 of the English foot.*
Comparing these statements with the pyramid measure
of 486 English feet for the perpendicular height, according to the casing stones, which gives a length of ·972
of the English, or 11·664 inches, for the Roman foot—
or with the French measure of the same, which makes
the height 485·85 English feet, and the length of the
Roman foot ·9717 of the English, or 11·660 inches—
we find a strong corroboration of our opinion, that
there was, at an early period, a Roman foot of these
dimensions; though the evidence is not sufficiently
clear to warrant us in saying that the inference we have
drawn is so positive that it cannot be controverted.
The subject will, however, receive further elucidation as
we proceed with our enquiry.

* Second Edition, vol. ii. p. 407.
† Raper's Enquiry, 4to, p. 11. 1760.

## 24.

A smaller Roman foot than this was in use at a later period, of which we find mention in the following extract from Pliny, as translated by Philemon Holland : " Eratosthenes, who was skilful in all kinds of learning, but especially in this, wherein he excels all other persons, and is by all esteemed a great authority, sets down the entire compass of the Earth at 252,000 stades, which measure, by the Roman computation, makes 31,500 miles. A startling conclusion ! but yet so well supported by skilful reasoning that we should be ashamed not to believe him."* This passage throws much light on our subject, though in some respects the measure which it records is erroneous.

Whence, we may ask, did Eratosthenes get his notion of the compass of the Earth being equal to 252,000 Greek stades, or 31,500 Roman miles ? Was it from the measure of the Great Pyramid ? In its perimeter of 3056 feet (the English measure) are 3150 feet of ·970 ; and in that of 3054 (the French measure) are 3150 feet of ·96965 : the medium is ·9697. Five hundred of these feet, in the perpendicular height of the Great Pyramid, are equal to 484·85 English feet, which is the tenth of a Roman mile : but, unless there are 10,000 Roman miles in the diameter of the Earth, there cannot be 31,500 miles in its circumference ; and 10,000 Roman miles exceed the due proportion by 1428 miles, or *one-seventh* part.

* Universum autem hunc circuitum, Eratosthenes, in omnium quidem literarum subtilitate, et in hac utique præter cæteros solers, quem cunctis probari video, ducentorum quinquaginta duorum millium stadium prodidit. Quæ mensura Romanâ computatione efficit trecenties quindecies centena millia passuum. Improbum ausum : verum ita subtili argumentatione comprehensum, ut pudeat non credere. — Plinii Hist. Nat. l. ii. c. 112 ; Hardouin, fol. 1723.

Cassini says, " Les pilotes de la Mediterranée donnent
75 milles à un degré.  Ceux de l'ocean n'en donnent
que soixante."  The former measure is the Roman
mile ; the latter is the geographical mile : but 360
degrees, of 75 miles each, are no more than 27,000
Roman miles.  The estimate of Eratosthenes exceeds
this measure by one sixth.  Seventy-five miles of 4848·5
English feet allow 363,637·5 feet to the degree, and make
the circumference of the Earth equal to 130,909,500
English feet, or 27,000 Roman miles.

### 25.

But, though Eratosthenes was wrong in assigning
31,500 instead of 27,000 Roman miles to the compass
of the Earth, he was very nearly correct in stating the
*proportion* which the circumference of a sphere bears to
its radius, when he represents it by a ratio of 10,000
to 31,500.  By his use of these figures, correctly if
viewed in relation to the Great Pyramid, but erroneously if viewed in relation to the Earth, he shows
that his knowledge was not derived from a new measure
of the Earth, but from the proportions recorded in the
Great Pyramid.  By his measure of 31,500 miles of
4848·5 English feet, the compass of the Earth is made
equal to 152,727,750 feet.  Deducting *one seventh* for his
error, leaves 130,909,500 English feet for the circumference.  He made a similar mistake in the number
of Greek stades, which should be reduced *one seventh*;
that is, from 252,000 to 216,000, to preserve the same
proportion.

### 26.

Thus, there is positive evidence of the existence of
another Roman foot equal to ·9697 of the English, in use
probably at a later time than the one containing ·972

parts of the English foot. How does this comport
with our authorities? We answer that they not only
countenance the larger measure, but justify also the
smaller.

Greaves's preferable foot here comes into play. In
continuation of our former quotation, he proceeds thus:
" My next search was for the foot on the monument of
*Cossutius*, in *hortis Colotianis*, from whence it has since
received its denomination (though it be now removed),
being termed by writers *Pes Colotianus*. This foot I
took with great care, as it did well deserve, being very fair
and perfect; afterwards collating it with that Roman
foot which Lucas Pætus caused to be engraven in the
Capitol on a white marble stone. I found them exactly
to agree; and therefore I did wonder why he should
condemn this with his pen (for he makes some objec-
tions against it) which, notwithstanding, he hath
erected with his hands, as appears by the inscription in
the Capitol, CURANTE LU. PÆTO. It may be, upon
second thoughts, he afterwards privately retracted his
error, which he was not willing to publish to the world.
Now this of foot Cossutius is 1·934, such parts as the
English foot contains 2·000."* This measure leaves ·967
of the English foot, or 11·604 inches, for the Roman
foot.

According to Dr. Hussey's Essay (p. 228) Barthélémy
and Jacquier obtained, as a result from ancient foot-
measures, 130·6 French lines, or ·9671 of the English.
Scaccia, 131 lines, or ·9696 of the English; Zach, from
28 foot-measures, 130·8 lines, or ·9681 of the English;
Revillas, from distances measured in the streets and
neighbourhood of Rome, 130·8 lines, or ·9681 of the

* Greaves's Works, by Birch, p. 209.

English ; Ideler, 131 lines, or ·9696 of the English.
Sir George Shuckburgh, from an average of several measures, made the Roman foot ·9683 of the English ; Raper,
from a measurement of the most ancient buildings in
Rome, ·970; and Bernard ·970. Dr. Hussey, " from
all the measures most to be depended on," draws an
average of ·9708. Dr. Smith adopts the same measure.
Mr. De Morgan gives that of ·968 of the English, but
adds, " eminent authorities of late prefer ·971 English
feet," or 11·65 inches. The medium of Greaves's two
feet of ·972 and ·967 is ·9695; and this is also the
medium of Mr. De Morgan's two feet of ·968 and ·971.
Thus we have abundant evidence, ancient and modern,
to prove that the measure of ·9697 adopted by Eratosthenes, from the Great Pyramid, was that of the
smaller Roman foot. But it is also perfectly true that
there was a larger Roman foot in existence at an
earlier period, equal to ·972 of the English foot, which
larger foot was called the Italian. And both the larger
and the smaller are shewn to have had their origin in
the Great Pyramid.

CHAPTER IV.

*Various Estimates of the Greek Foot—The Ptolemaic, a smaller
Greek Foot — The Foot of Drusus and that of Diodorus
Siculus—The Circumference of the Earth in lat. 30° expressed
by this Foot — Modern Estimates of the Circumference in
lat. 30°—Modern Estimates of the Circumference in lat. 45°—
The Diameter of the Earth in lat. 30° expressed by the English
Inch—All such Measures, in round numbers, Primitive Measures—The Circumference of the Earth in lat. 30° connected
with the Measure of the Great Pyramid.*

27.

THERE were two Greek feet, which held the same
relation to each other that the two Roman feet
appear to have done. The larger Greek foot is that
which Stuart derived from the measure of the Heca-
tompedon at Athens, 1·0115 English feet, or 12·138
inches; and which Mr. F. Penrose finds to be equal to
1·01336 English feet, or 12·16 inches. The smaller is
that which results from Eratosthenes' measure of
252,000 Greek stades; viz., 1·0101 English feet, or
12·12 inches.

The stade of this foot contains 606·06 English feet.
Eight are equal to a Roman mile of 4848·5 English feet.
Of these stades there are 216,000, instead of 252,000, in
the circumference of the Earth, when taken at 130,908,960
English feet. In this number of feet we find 360 degrees, each containing 363,636 English feet, and consisting of sixty geographical miles, of ten Greek stades

to the mile, agreeably to the observation of Cassini; but in the rest of his remarks, as stated in the note, we cannot concur.*

28.

Eratosthenes was born in the year B.C. 276, in the reign of Ptolemy Philadelphus, about eight years after the death of Euclid. He was placed over the library at Alexandria by Ptolemy Euergetes, and died about B.C. 196, at the age of eighty. If he were not himself the discoverer of the Roman foot of ·9697, it is highly probable that it was introduced into Alexandria while he was living there, either in the reign of Ptolemy Philadelphus, who was a great encourager of learning and science, or in that of his successor. The smaller Greek foot, from its having been produced under the Ptolemies, was called the *Ptolemaic*; as the larger of the Roman feet was called the *Italian*, to distinguish it from the smaller, called the *Roman* foot.

29.

Sir Isaac Newton says, in his "Dissertation on Cubits,"† that "the oldest feet of which any account has been transmitted to us are the *Roman*, the *Ptolemaic*, and the *Drusian* foot, at Tongeren, in Germany, the last

---

* "Les milles anciens d'Italie aux milles modernes sont comme 60 à 75 ; car les anciens donnent 25 milles à la distance de Bologne à Modene ; et les modernes ne comptent que 20 milles d'une de ces deux villes à l'autre. Dont ceux de la Mediterranée se servent des milles anciens qui sont encore aujourd'hui en usage en diverses provinces d'Italie, et ceux de l'Ocean se servent des milles modernes qui sont en usage en d'autres provinces. La mesure moderne a cette commodité, qu'elle prend une minute pour mille, au lieu que l'ancienne donne a chaque minute un mille et un quart."—p. 23.

† Greaves's Works, by Birch, vol. ii. p. 419.

of which is equal to 13½ *unciæ* of the Roman foot." If we add to the Roman foot of ·9697 one inch and a half, making 13⅛ inches, the sum gives 1·0909 of the English foot for this foot of Drusus.

The Drusian foot is the same as that which is mentioned by Diodorus Siculus. He says of the Great Pyramid: "It is in shape four-sided, and each side of the base contains seven plethra," or 700 feet.* Seven hundred feet of 1·0909 are equal to 763·63 English feet. The measure of Mr. Perring makes the base 764 feet; the measure of M. Le Père and Col. Coutelle, 763·6 English feet. The same measure is deduced from the Roman foot ·9697, of which 3150 are equal to 3054·5 English feet in the perimeter of the Great Pyramid, giving 763·62 for each side.

### 30.

Of these feet, as recorded by Diodorus Siculus, there were 444·5 in the perpendicular height of the Great Pyramid, and 2800 in its perimeter. These numbers present nothing remarkable; and so far as the pyramid is concerned, they appear to teach us nothing. But a further circumstance of the highest interest is connected with this foot : it reveals to us the measure of the circumference of the Earth, as it had been ascertained by the founders of the Great Pyramid. The foot of 1·0909 is contained 120 millions of times in the compass of 130,908,000 English feet. This is the number of feet contained in the measure of the Earth by Eratosthenes, when the excess of *one-seventh* has been deducted from it. It is also that measure of the circumference of which 363,636 feet constitute a degree.

'Η μεν γαρ μεγιστη τετραπλευρος ουσα τῳ σχηματι, την επι της βασεως πλευραν εκαστην εχει πλεθρων ἑπτα.

## 31.

It would be an extraordinary circumstance that this
should be the measure of a degree obtained both from
the Roman and the Ptolemaic foot, and from the foot
recorded by Diodorus Siculus, all of which are traceable
to the Great Pyramid, if it were not also the measure
of a degree of the meridian in the latitude of the Great
Pyramid. Let us inquire what is the probable value of
the degree in that latitude, that by comparing it with
the above-mentioned figures we may bring our theory
of the purpose for which the pyramids were constructed
to the strictest test possible.

Nouet, who accompanied the French expedition into
Egypt, calculated the latitude of the Great Pyramid,
and found it to be 29° 59' 49''. Perring says that the
pyramids extend from 29° 16' 56'' to 30° 2' 30'' (the
middle term of which is 29° 39' 43''), and that they
occupy a space of fifty-three miles, measuring from north
to south. If the pyramids were constructed with the
view of being made subservient to the measure of a
degree of the meridian, or any portion of it, such measure must have been made between 29° and 30° N.L.

In Pinkerton's tables the degree is calculated as equal
in lat. 29° to 363,676 English feet; and in lat. 30°, to
363,724 English feet. Jomard makes the degree
proper to Egypt 363,532 English feet; but by another
estimate he states it to be 363,684 English feet. The
measure of the degree recorded, as we have seen, in the
Great Pyramid itself, is 363,636.

## 32.

It is not possible to conceive a nearer approximation,
in measures of this kind, than is presented by these

numbers.   If we compare the various estimates, made
by scientific persons in their respective countries, of the
degree in latitude 45°, which is regarded as the standard
of all measures in France, they do not more nearly coincide with each other, than do the above measures of the
degree in Egypt, taken at an interval, it may be, from
first to last, of 4,000 years.

The degree in latitude 45° is stated to be, in English
feet.

|  |  |  |  | English Feet. |
|---|---|---|---|---|
| By the Table of Constants | - | - | - | 364,543 |
| By Pinkerton's Tables - | - | - | - | 364,546 |
| By the French Mètre - | - | - | - | 364,652 |
| By the American Measure - | - | - | - | 364,630 |

In these modern calculations, the greatest difference is
109 English feet; in the ancient it is only 104.   But
in reality the difference in the latter case is much less;
because the pyramid measure of 363,636 feet ought to be
compared with the *average* of Pinkerton's two estimates,
and the *average* of Jomard's two estimates.   It is below
Pinkerton's 64 feet, and above Jomard's 28 feet.

### 33.

We come now to the *English foot,* which is closely
connected with the Egyptian foot, as recorded by
Diodorus Siculus.   If we deduct *one-twelfth* from the
foot of 1·0909 it leaves the English foot *without any
remainder !*

This circumstance is sufficient to shew a certain connexion of the English foot with the measures of the
Great Pyramid; but besides this there is direct evidence
of the *inch* of the English foot being a recognised element of measure made use of by the founders of the

pyramids, when they had ascertained the circumference
of the Earth, and determined the proportion due to its
diameter.    That proportion is at present found by
dividing the circumference, viz., 120,000,000 of Egyptian
feet of 1·0909 English, by 3·1415927 which would
allow for the diameter about 38,200,000 Egyptian feet;
but this number seems incapable of furnishing any principle of unity as a measure of the diameter. The amount
in inches of the Egyptian foot is about 458,400,000,
which is a measure equally impracticable.

But what was denied to the Egyptian foot was made
attainable by the English inch. In 38,200,000 Egyptian
feet of 1·0909 are contained 41,672,380 English feet,
and this number of feet is equal to 500,068,560 English
inches.    The circumference of 120 millions of Egyptian
feet of 1·0909 is equal in English feet to 130,908,000,
and to 1,570,896,000 English inches.    If we double this
number we have 3,141,792,000; and if we divide
130,908,000 by the number 3·141792 (instead of by
3·141592) it will give us 41,667,000 English feet, or
500,000,000 inches for the diameter.    Thus the proportion of the diameter to the circumference of a circle was
considered by the founders of the Pyramid as 1 to
3·141792; and the diameter of the Earth was represented by them as equal to 500,000,000 English
inches, or 41,667,000 English feet, since its circumference was equal to 1,570,896,000 inches, or 130,908,000
feet.

### 34.

When we find, in so complicated a series of figures
as that which the measures of the Great Pyramid, and of
the Earth, require for their expression, round numbers

present themselves, or such as leave no remainder, we may be sure we have arrived at primitive measures. The 500 Roman feet in the perpendicular height of the Great Pyramid are of this kind; and so are the 700 feet of Diodorus Siculus in the side of the base. Still more remarkably is this latter measure shewn to be a primitive one by the circumstance that the circumfer- ence of the Earth is equal to 120,000,000 of these feet. But not the less primitive is the English inch, without which the diameter of the Earth could not have been expressed *as unity* according to the measure of its cir- cumference in Egypt. The English foot is allied to the Egyptian foot, of which it forms *eleven-twelfths* : but it is not derived from it. Both are original measures, the one being founded on the circumference of the Earth, the other on the diameter.

### 35.

A peculiar property of the English foot in connexion with the measure of the base of the Great Pyramid is, that when we divide unity by 764 (the number of feet in the side of the base) the quotient gives the number of feet in the circumference of the Earth as it was measured in the latitude of the Great Pyramid. This may be deemed nothing more than a numerical coincidence; but when we recollect that this foot alone expresses this relation, and that the measure by which it is expressed may possibly have had its origin at this time, and may even have been called into existence to denote this pro- portion, it seems to be a peculiarity which deserves notice. If we divide 1 by 764, or in other words, reduce $\frac{1}{764}$ to a decimal, we are presented with a series of figures which represent very approximately the number of feet in the circumference as it was estimated by the founders of the Pyramid. Thus —

$$\frac{1}{764} = \cdot00,130,890,052 = \frac{130,890,052}{100,000,000,000}.$$

That is, *one* English foot bears the same ratio to the side of the Pyramid, that the circumference of the Earth bears to *one hundred millions* of English feet.

## Chapter V.

*The Measure of the Great Pyramid according to Herodotus—*
*The Plethron of Herodotus, Square Measure—The Square of*
*each Face equal to the Square of the Height—The Aroura*
*equal to the Area of the Eighth Pyramid—Comparison of the*
*Aroura with the Plethron—Description of the Great Pyramid*
*by Herodotus perfect — The Square of the Height slightly*
*differs from the Square of each Face—Pliny's Measure of the*
*Great Pyramid correct; his Foot the Royal Span—The Royal*
*Cubit, or Cubit of Memphis—Sir Isaac Newton on the Use of*
*this Cubit in the Great Pyramid—Recent Corroboration of his*
*Views.*

### 36.

THE measure of the Great Pyramid, as recorded
by Herodotus, is generally taken to mean
linear measure, but his words admit of a different construction; and, as they are inapplicable to any supposed
foot, or other linear measure, which can be found in the
side of the Great Pyramid, or in the diameter or circumference of the Earth, we will not attempt to explain his observations with reference to length, but
treat them as if they were intended to represent superficial measure, in which respect they will be found to
bear out all his assertions.

### 37.

Having informed us that " twenty years was the time
employed in the construction of the Great Pyramid,"
he adds, " of this Pyramid, which is four-sided, each
face is, on every side, 8 plethra, and the height is

equal."* The plethron is a name for 100 feet, either linear or square. As linear measure, it usually denotes the sixth part of a stade. "As square measure it represents 10,000 square feet; but it is also employed as the equivalent of the Latin *jugerum*, though this was about 28,800 square feet" (Scott and Liddell). By Herodotus the plethron is often employed to represent that quantity of land which in Egypt was called an *aroura*. As he speaks of each *face* of the Pyramid, it may be presumed that he intends here to make the term specify square or superficial measure as before (§ 19).

But if each face of the Pyramid contain eight plethra, and the height be equal, that height must contain eight plethra also. Linear measure being in this case entirely out of the question, we have to consider how the measure of eight plethra, if it be true of each *face* of the Pyramid, can be predicated of its *height*. There is only one way in which the two measures can be reconciled; and that is, by supposing that the historian meant to say that the number of *square feet* in the measure of *each face*, and the number of *square feet* in the measure of the *height*, are equal, each containing eight plethra. But in this case we must understand him as speaking of the *square* of the height.

### 38.

Referring to the measure of 764 feet for the base, in connexion with the angle of 51° 50′ for the casing-stones, we find the sloping height of each face is 618 feet. This gives, for the contents of each face of the Pyramid, 236,076 square feet. The same measure

---

* Τη δε πυραμιδι αυτη χρονον γενεσθαι εεικοσι ετεα ποιευμενη· της εστι παντακη μετωπον ἑκαστον οκτω πλεθρα, εουσης τετραγονου, και ὑψος ισον.—II. 124.

and angle make the perpendicular height 486 feet, and
this gives, for the contents of a square of that height,
236,196 square feet. These numbers come very near
each other. The difference is 120 square feet.

### 39.

But each face of the Pyramid contains, as Herodotus
says, eight plethra. He is speaking of Egyptian
measures. Now that square measure which he calls
a *plethron*, and the Egyptians an *aroura*, is the square of
100 royal cubits. To denote that space, and give a
practical measurement of it, one of the smaller pyramids appears to have been constructed. It is the middle
one of the three which stand on the east side of the
Great Pyramid, in a line with each other, and occupy a
space rather more than half the length of the base of
that pyramid. They are called, by way of distinction,
the *Seventh*, *Eighth*, and *Ninth* Pyramids. The middle
one, which is the least dilapidated, is described by
Colonel Howard Vyse as an extremely well-constructed
work. " The blocks," he says, " were as beautifully
polished, and as firmly set, as those in the Great
Pyramid; and the masonry of the two monuments had
a great resemblance, which was remarkable, as the
Eighth is generally supposed to have been the tomb of
the daughter of Cheops," the reputed founder of the
Great Pyramid. By this connexion, we are given to
understand that equal care was bestowed upon each of
them.

### 40.

Mr. Perring's measurement of the original base of
this Pyramid makes it a square of 172 feet 6 inches.
Its perpendicular height was found to be 111 feet; and
its inclined height 140 feet. He estimates the square of

the base as equal to 3,295 yards, that is, equal to 29,655 square feet. The angle was 52° 10'.

Comparing these numbers with those which are contained in the dimensions of the Great Pyramid, as stated by Herodotus, the following results are obtained. Each face of the Great Pyramid contains 236,076 square feet—the square of the height contains 236,196. Eight arouræ or plethra of 29,655 square feet would be equal to 237,240. In 236,076 are eight plethra of 29,510 square feet. In 236,196 are eight plethra of 29,525 square feet. These results afford satisfactory proof that the measure of Herodotus was intended to represent superficial measure.

### 41.

Thus, in a few graphic words, Herodotus has given us a most correct idea of the form and size of the Great Pyramid. He has shewn us its precise *form*, by saying that it was a four-sided pyramid. He has stated its *magnitude*, when he tells us that each face contained eight plethra, each being the square of 100 royal cubits. He has described the exact *angle* which the face makes with the base, when he informs us that the square of the perpendicular height is equal, in content, to the square of each face. We require no more than these few particulars to enable us to pourtray it of its proper height, and of its proper width at the base, and, consequently, to assign to each face of the Pyramid its proper angle.

### 42.

An interesting question meets us here. Were the founders of the Pyramids acquainted with this property of the Great Pyramid, which the Egyptian priests appear to have communicated in no very clear terms to Herodotus? Or was it the discovery of a later age? The priests, we should think, or the interpreters, whom Herodotus met with, deserve no credit for this discovery: they were apparently incapable of discriminating truth from falsehood in their statements; and as mere traditionists they would be as likely to hand down this truth from the earliest times as any others. The founders, on the other hand, were equal to the task. Having ascertained the ratio which the radius of a circle bears to its circumference, they were competent to discover, and very likely to observe, that a pyramid which expresses that ratio, is of such proportions, that its slant face will be found to contain (they may have thought exactly) as many square feet as are contained in the square of its perpendicular height. And if they noticed this, they would, in all probability, leave it on record. The exact angle which the face makes with the base is, in the former case, that of 51° 51′ 14″, and, in the latter, that of 51° 49′ 46″. The difference is only 1′ 28″. The angle of the Great Pyramid itself is 51° 50′ or 1′ 14″ below the former, and 14″ above the latter angle.

### 43.

Pliny's measure of the Great Pyramid is correct, though most writers who have treated of it imagine it to be erroneous. Greaves says: "Certainly Pliny is much mistaken in assigning the measure of the side to be 883 feet, and the basis of the Pyramid to be but eight jugera, or Roman acres." He supposes that Pliny "writ twenty-eight jugera, instead of eight; or else in his proportion of the side to the area of the basis he hath greatly erred." Jomard, thinking that Pliny must have meant Roman feet, proposes to correct the imputed error by changing the number 883 to 833, but this only brings the foot up to about *five-sixths* of the Roman foot.

The statement of Pliny is to the following effect:—
" The largest Pyramid occupies eight jugera of surface within the equal distances of the four angles, by a measure of 883 feet on each side." Let us see whether his description is not likely to be correct, without any alteration. In 764 feet are 883 of ·865 of the English foot, or 10·380 inches. Now this measure is one of the most ancient in the world. It is properly a royal *span*, and not a foot, being the half of a royal cubit, made use of in the interior of the Great Pyramid, as will be presently shewn. Its exact estimate is 10·368 English inches.

The words of Pliny are: "Amplissima octo jugera obtinet soli, quatuor angulorum paribus intervallis, per octingentos octoginta tres pedes singulorum laterum." Greaves was mistaken in supposing that these words mean, that the *basis* of the largest Pyramid contained but eight jugera or Roman acres. Pliny says: "The largest occupies eight jugera *of surface* (*soli*) within the equal intervals of the four angles, reckoning eight hundred and eighty-three feet in each of its sides." The *eight jugera* are easily explained: they are the same as the *eight plethra* of Herodotus. The *jugerum* was a Roman term quite as applicable to the Egyptian measure of an *aroura*, as was the Greek term *plethron*, or the English term *acre*, by which Greaves explains the Latin word. Pliny says, there were eight *jugera* of *surface* within the compass of each face of the Pyramid; and Herodotus says the same, but he calls them *plethra*. Both, however, mean *arouræ*, as we have shown by reference to the eighth pyramid, the area of which contains the square of 100 royal cubits of 1·728 feet, or 20·736 inches each.

### 44.

The *Royal Cubit*, or cubit of Memphis, is equal to
two of the *royal spans* mentioned by Pliny, being in
measure 20·736 English inches. A cubit of this proportion is commonly met with in the measures of the
interior of the Great Pyramid, as is noticed by Greaves,
and commented upon by Sir Isaac Newton* in the
following terms : —

### 45.

" That the Pyramid was built by a cubit of this
magnitude appears from several dimensions of it.
The square passage leading into it, of polished marble,
was in breadth and height 3·463 of the English foot;
that is, two of the above-mentioned cubits of Memphis
[of 20·778 inches] ; and of the same breadth and height
were the four other galleries. In the middle of the
Pyramid was a chamber most exquisitely formed of
polished marble, containing the monument of the king.
The length of this chamber was 34·38 English feet, and
the breadth 17·19; that is, it was twenty cubits long,
and ten cubits broad, the cubit being supposed to be
1·719 of the English foot [or 20·628 inches]. The difference between this measure and the former is 125 in
10,000, or one-eighteenth of a foot; that is, about one-
seventh of an inch, an error of no importance, if we
consider the much greater irregularities observed by
Mr. Greaves in the best buildings of the Romans. The
roof of this chamber consisted of nine oblong and
parallel stones; the seven middle ones of which were of
the same breadth, but the two outermost were less by half
a breadth than the rest; and the breadth of them
altogether was equal to the length of the chamber, or
to twenty cubits [of 20·628 inches] ; so that the length

* See Greaves's Works, by Birch, p. 405.

of the middle stones was two and a half cubits. The
marble gallery which led into this chamber was six feet
and 87 of 100 parts of a foot; that is, four cubits of the
chamber in breadth [of 20·61 inches]. In the middle
of the gallery was a way of polished marble, 3·435 feet,
that is, two cubits broad [of 20·61 inches]; and on both
sides the way went two banks, like benches, of polished
marble likewise, 1·717 feet broad, and 1·717 feet deep;
that is, in breadth and depth one cubit [of 20·604
inches]. Who will therefore imagine that so many
dimensions, not at all depending upon each other,
should correspond by mere chance with the length of
the cubit assigned by us?" After enumerating many
other instances of the use of this cubit, he remarks
particularly, "that the whole length of that gallery,
with the hypothenuse of a rectangular triangle, whose
base was 15 feet, and height about 5 or 6, or perhaps 7
feet, being measured by a cord, was 154 feet. Subtract
the hypothenuse, and there will remain the length of
the gallery, 138 feet, that is, 20 times the breadth, or
80 royal cubits [of 20·7 inches]. Two other galleries
were likewise measured, and found to be in length 110
feet, that is, 64 royal cubits [of 20·625 inches]; and
another chamber was in breadth about 17 feet, that is,
10 cubits [of 20·4 inches]; and an *anti-cameretta*, or ante-
closet, was in length 7 feet, in breadth about 3½ feet;
that is, about 4 cubits long, and about 2 cubits broad
[of 21 inches]. And it is my opinion," concludes the
learned author, "that the Pyramid was built throughout
after the measure of this cubit."

### 46.

A singular corroboration of this opinion is found in
the following fact. The entrance to the Great Pyramid

does not lie quite in the perpendicular which would bisect the face of the triangle: on the contrary, a vertical meridian plane, touching the east side of the entrance, is, according to M. Jomard, 20·8 feet (English) east of the perpendicular bisecting the face of the Pyramid. The difference is equal, therefore, to 12 royal cubits of 20·8 inches each.*

* M. Jomard found a cubit of wood, measuring in English inches 20·4729 ; and there are three others in the Museum at Turin measuring respectively 20·5787, 20·6186, 20·6584. The largest of these is only *one-tenth* of an inch less than the Pyramid Standard of the Royal Cubit.

## Chapter VI.

*The Cubit of Karnak ; its Antiquity—Its Length, as preserved in the British Museum — Its Measure that of the five Square Passages on the Great Pyramid — A Cubit of this Measure referred to by Herodotus—Observations of Herodotus recently confirmed—The Karnak Cubit a Measure of Solomon's Temple ; the Royal Span the same—The Royal Cubit a Measure of the Second Temple.*

### 47.

THE *Cubit of Karnak* may be called the *Double Royal Cubit.* Its discovery was announced a few years ago, by Sir Gardner Wilkinson, in the following communication : — " Since writing the above, I have received from Mr. Harris, of Alexandria, an account of a measure which has been discovered at Karnak, on the removal of some stones from one of the towers of a propylon, between which it appears to have been accidently left by the masons at the time of its erection, at the remote period of the eighteenth dynasty. It is divided into fourteen parts, but each part is double in length those of Elephantine, and therefore consists of four digits, and the whole measure is equal to two cubits, being $41\frac{3}{10}$ English inches. This double cubit has the first division, in its scale of fourteen parts, subdivided into halves, and the next into quarters, one of these last being equal to one digit." The towers of the propylon, in which it was discovered, we are told in a note, were executed by Horus (or Amun-men) ninth king of the eighteenth dynasty, who reigned from 1408 to 1395 B.C.

### 48.

This measure is now in the British Museum, in the collection of antiquities in the upper room relating to Egypt. On measuring it with great exactness by a minutely graduated scale made use of at the Museum, we find it to be 41·46 English inches, a very little exceeding the measure mentioned by Mr. Harris. It is made of larch, and having been closed up in the building between two stones, so that the air could not get access to it, the wood is as sound as it was when it was first made use of, by the Egyptian workman, about 3250 years ago.

### 49.

Greaves describes the five square passages of the Great Pyramid, as being all of the same dimensions, viz., 41·556 English inches, or 3·463 parts of the English foot in height and breadth. Over one of these passages he observed " five lines cut parallel and perpendicular, exactly bounding the open space below, and dividing it into four equal parts." Whatever may have been the intention of the founders of the Pyramid, when they caused these lines to be cut, it is impossible to discover with certainty; but they appear as if they were meant to teach us that the open space below was divisible into four equal parts; and these parts agree with those which we have ascribed to the following measures, viz. :—

1. The Karnak Cubit of 3·456 English feet, or 41·472 inches.
2. The Royal Cubit of 1·728    ,,    or 20·736  ,,
3. The Span, or Half
    Royal Cubit of . . 0·864    ,,    or 10·368  ..

The whole space is equal to 4 royal spans, or 2 royal cubits, or 1 double royal cubit, the cubit of Karnak.

### 50.

A remarkable proof of the early existence, in Egypt, of a cubit of the proportions of the cubit of Karnak, or *double* royal cubit, is contained in Herodotus. The priests told him (ii. 13), that in the reign of Mœris, whenever the waters of the Nile rose to the height of eight cubits, all the lands were overflowed; since which time (says the historian) 900 years have elapsed, and now, unless the river rise to sixteen, or at least to fifteen cubits, its waters do not reach those lands. Herodotus read his history at the Olympic Games, in 445 B.C. The two dates of 900 and 445, taken together, carry us back to the year 1345 B.C., which is within fifty years of the period assigned by Sir Gardner Wilkinson to the erection of that building, within the masonry of which the cubit of Karnak was found. As eight of these cubits are exactly equal to sixteen of those which were in use in the time of Herodotus, this difficulty of the historian's is explained.

### 51.

" During the three years of the French occupation of Egypt," says a modern writer, "the floods of the Nile reached 17 cubits and 10 digits, which implied an actual rise of 7·58, 6·85, and 7·96 mètres for the three years. A rise of 8 mètres is considered as boding fine crops ; 7 mètres makes them indifferent; while a rise of 9 mètres is considered injurious to some places. French engineers find that the level of the soil does not rise more than 126 millimètres in a century from the muddy deposits" (*Athenæum*, March 24th, 1849). Eight

mètres are only sixteen inches less than the eight
cubits of Karnak, of which Herodotus speaks, as properly overflowing all the lands.

### 52.

The cubit of Karnak being thus traceable to a period
only 100 years later than the Exodus of the Israelites
from Egypt, it might be expected that we should meet
with some evidence of the use of this cubit among the
Jews. The following quotation from II. Chron. iii. 3,
supplies us with the means of supporting this conjecture.

"Now these are the things wherein Solomon was
instructed for the building of the House of God. The
length, by cubits *after the first measure*, was threescore
cubits, and the breadth twenty cubits. And the porch
that was in the front of the house, the length of it was,
according to the breadth of the house, twenty cubits,
and the height was an *hundred and twenty.*" Thus there
was a cubit *after the first measure*, which implies the
existence of another cubit, probably a smaller one; and
there was, at the same time, a measure, not called a
cubit, which must have been one-fourth of the first
cubit, if we give the words such an interpretation as is
in accordance with other parts of the sacred Scriptures
relating to the same subject. For in I. Kings vi. 2, we
read, "The house which king Solomon built for the
Lord, the length thereof was threescore cubits, and the
breadth thereof twenty cubits, and the height thereof
*thirty* cubits. And the porch before the temple of the
house, twenty cubits was the length thereof, according
to the breadth of the house, and ten cubits was the
breadth thereof before the house." The height in
II. Chronicles is 120 of some measure, which in I. Kings

is represented as equal to 30 cubits, and these cubits are described in II. Chronicles as being of the *first measure*, implying probably the *largest* measure. What can we infer, then, from these particulars, but that the 120 measures which have no name given them, are equal to 30 of these largest cubits? and as the fourth part of the cubit of Karnak was a span, these which bear the same relation to the largest cubit, must have been *spans*. Thus the *cubit of Karnak* and the *span of Pliny*, appear to have been measures in use among the Jews in the time of Solomon.

### 53.

But no mention is here made of the *royal cubit*, or cubit of Memphis. For that, we must have recourse to the description of the rebuilding of the temple in Ezra vi., where it is said, " In the first year of Cyrus the king, the same Cyrus the king made a decree concerning the house of God at Jerusalem; let the house be builded, the place where they offered sacrifices, and let the foundations thereof be strongly laid; the height thereof threescore cubits and the breadth thereof threescore cubits." The height, therefore, being now 60 cubits which before was 30 cubits, it must follow, either that the second temple was twice the height of the first, which no one will allow, or that the cubit by which the second was measured was *half the length* of that which was used for the first. It may appear, at first sight, an inconsistency, that if the one cubit were twice the length of the other, the second temple should be represented as being 60 cubits wide (in Ezra) while the first is said to be only 20 cubits wide (in Kings and Chronicles); but to explain this we must remember, that the houses of the priests were added to the latter measure, which were five cubits in breadth on *each* side. Thus the

*Jewish double cubit*, is proved to have been the same
with the *cubit of Karnak*; the *cubit of Ezra* the same as
the *royal cubit*, or cubit of Memphis; and the *span* in
the former case is the same measure as that which is
recorded by Pliny as having been contained 883 times
in the side of the Great Pyramid.

According to the dimensions here given, the Temple
of Solomon and the Second Temple will be found to
be more than twice the size which is usually allotted to
them.   In height and breadth they were each 103 feet
8 inches, and in length 207 feet 4 inches of our measure.   The most famous temple of the Greeks, that of
Theseus at Athens, did not exceed these dimensions; but
that of Diana at Ephesus, according to Pliny, was twice
this size.

CHAPTER VII.

*The Philetærian Foot—The Cubit of the Mekyas, or the Nilo-
meter—The Geometrical Foot—The Oriental Span is the Geo-
metrical Foot — The Oriental Cubit — The double Oriental
Cubit is the Pyramid Meter—The Stade of Aristotle—Major
Rennell's Error as to this Stade—The Egyptian Parasang,
and Egyptian Schœne—Various Greek Stades—Table of Greek
Stades—The Paris Foot, the Persian Arish, and the smaller
Turkish Peek.*

54.

THE *Royal, or Philetærian Foot,* is the foot of the
royal cubit. Deducting one third from 20·736
inches leaves for this foot 13·824 inches, or 1·152
English feet.

Epiphanius speaks of this foot as a measure of
7 stades to the Roman mile. Hesychius does the same.
The fragment of Heron alludes to this foot, when it
states that the Italian contains 13½ digits of that foot
of which the royal or Philetærian foot contains 16
digits. The digit of the Philetærian being ·864 inches,
the Italian foot is equal to 11·664 inches or ·972 English
feet. Hence it appears that the earlier and larger
Roman foot retained the name of the *Italian* foot, after
the smaller had been adopted as the *Roman.* Ideler
also thinks the Philetærian foot is that of which 7 stades
are equal to the Roman mile. It falls a little short of
that proportion; 600 feet of 11·52 being equal to
691·2 feet; and seven of these stades being equal only
to 4,838 English feet instead of 4,848; but this is a

less difference than might have been expected in two measures which have no direct connexion with each other. It amounts to the 200th part of an inch.

55.

Greaves took the measure of *another cubit* which he met with in use in Egypt, and found it to be 1·824 English feet, or 21·888 inches. This measure is said by D'Anville, Grobert, and others to be that of the *Nilometer*,* but Greaves himself does not say so. The cubit of the *Mekyas*, of the Island of Raouddah, was found by Le Père, from the mean length of sixteen marked on that monument, to be 239·7 lines in French measure, or 17·74278576 inches English, which is very nearly 17¾ inches.† We cannot reconcile these measures of the Nilometer with each other, but we can shew a means whereby the true measure may be recovered.

The cubit of Memphis, or royal cubit, consisted of seven palms, and the cubit of Karnak was twice that length, as the measure in the British Museum shows. But seven palms was an unusual length; common cubits in general containing no more than six palms. The royal cubit of seven palms was equal to 20·736 inches, and hence the common cubit of six palms would be equal to 17·7696 inches. This measure exceeds only by 27 thousandths of an inch the measure of Le Père. Thus we have ascertained, to a certainty, the length of the Nilometer cubit. But, at the same

---

* " Il l' a mesurée, comme nous, sur le monument ; il atteste avoir trouvé 1824 parties du pied de Londres, devisé en 1,000 parties....Ce qui ne diffère que d'une ligne de notre mesure."— *Grobert, Description des Pyramides de Ghize,* 4to. p. 156.

† Hussey's Essay, 1836, 8vo. p. 237.

time, we have shewn that the cubit, which Grobert
supposed to be identical with that of Greaves, viz.,
21·888 inches, could not have been larger than 20·736
inches, a difference of more than an inch and a tenth.
Unless, therefore, Greaves had some other and better
authority for his measure than that of the Mekyas, or
Nilometer, he has no foundation for it ; and even that
monument, unequal as its divisions were,* could not
have justified two such different measures as those of
Grobert and Le Père.

The cubit of the Nilometer is engraven on an octa-
gonal column of yellow marble, which was erected by
the Saracens in the square well into which the water of
the Nile flows, to mark its increase.   The present
column replaced one which had fallen down A.D. 716.
It is probable that on the ancient column was engraven
the measure of the cubit of Karnak, as well as that of
the royal cubit, besides the smaller cubit measured by
Le Père, which the Saracens made use of, and which
was equal to six of those palms of which the royal
cubit contained seven palms.

### 56.

Mr. De Morgan, in his " Arithmetical Books " (p. 9)
contends earnestly for a foot of some antiquity, which
he calls the *Geometrical Foot.*  The earliest work in which
he finds it mentioned is the *Margarita Philosophica,* the
first edition of which is dated 1503.   The several edi-
tions of this work, and of others published between

---

* Nous avons reconnu, en mesurant les coudées hors du
niveau existant, qu'elles étaient inégales.  Leurs phalanges et
les subdivisions étaient incorrectes ; la hauteur moyenne que
nous avons pu reconnaître, a été celle de *vingt pouces et six
lignes."—Grobert,* p. 155.

1503 and 1621, contain paper modules of the length of the digit, palm, and foot of this measure, from all which Mr. De Morgan obtains a mean result of 9·7 English inches; but he places greater dependance on " the statement of Clavius, whose term of active life was the latter half of the 16th century; and who says very distinctly that the mathematicians, to avoid the diversity of national measures, had laid down a system for themselves." This system is founded on the measure of the *barleycorn,* the foot being considered equal to the *breadth* of sixty-four barleycorns. " The constant reference to this barleycorn measure, which is seldom if ever omitted," induced Mr. De Morgan to "try what it would really make," and the average he arrived at gave a measure of 9·8 English inches. From all his enquiries and experiments he comes to this conclusion, " that the *geometrical foot* is anything the reader pleases between 9·7 and 9·9 English inches. The result from modern barley gives 9·8 as above shewn " (p. 9).

### 57.

This *geometrical foot* is indeed a very ancient measure; for it dates from the foundation of the Pyramids. We have before shown that the foot of Egypt is contained, as Diodorus Siculus states, 700 times in the side of the Great Pyramid; and that this foot is 1·0909 of the English foot, or 13·0908 English inches. Three of these feet are equal to 39·27 inches, the *fourth* part of which measure is a *span* of 9·8175 inches, or ·81814 of the English foot. This *span* is contained 160 millions of times in the circumference of the Earth, when it is estimated at 130,908,000 English feet, or 1,570,896,000 English inches. This *span* is therefore the *geometrical foot.*

58.

The *Common Oriental Cubit* is twice the measure of
this span, viz. : 1·6363 English feet, or 19·6356 inches.
It is contained 80 millions of times in the circumference of the Earth, as above estimated.

59.

The *Double Oriental Cubit* being, as we have said,
equal to three Egyptian feet, or 3·2727 English feet, or
39·2724 inches, is contained 40 millions of times in the
circumference of the Earth as measured in Egypt.
This measure may be called the *Pyramid meter*.

60.

We are told by Aristotle that the most ancient measure of the Earth's circumference was that adopted by
Thales and Anaximander (about B.C. 600), by which
measure it was divided into 400,000 *stades*. At what
time, and in what manner, this estimate was first made,
we are not informed, but the measures of the Great
Pyramid supply us with the information which has
been lost. If we assume the circumference of the
Earth to be that which is recorded in the Great
Pyramid, viz.: 130,908,000 English feet, it is equal
to 120,000,000 of Egyptian feet, which number,
divided by 400,000 stades, renders each stade equal
to 327·27 English feet, or 300 Egyptian feet. Thus
the *Egyptian stade* contained 100 Pyramid meters,
equal to 300 Egyptian feet. This, then, was the measure of the earth which Thales and Anaximander
adopted, and this was the measure of the *stade* which
Aristotle has recorded, viz., 327·27 English feet.

### 61.

But at the time that Aristotle made this statement,
it would seem an alteration had taken place which
reduced the number of stades in the circumference from
400,000 to 360,000. This is apparent from his estimating the degree as containing 1111 stades. The
remarks of Major Rennell on this statement of the
great philosopher are very curious. "The stade of
Aristotle, valued at 1111 to a degree, we regard,"
says Rennell, "*purely as an imaginary measure*, and conceive that it was founded on certain supposed dimensions of the globe; which dimensions having been
found erroneous in *excess*, the moderns have diminished
the *standard* of the whole, instead of lessening the
number of stades in a degree. We are, therefore,
surprised to find it employed, in the application to
actual geography, to very late times." Yet what
does this obnoxious stade prove to be? Divide
130,908,000 by 360,000 and the quotient is 363,630
for the degree, which again divided by 1111, leaves
for the stade 327·27 English feet, or the Egyptian stade
of 300 feet of 1·0909 English.

### 62.

We obtain much useful information from the establishment of this stade. It teaches us the length of the
Egyptian *parasang*, and the Egyptian *schœne*, on which
great difference of opinion has existed. Herodotus, in
describing Egypt, uses both these terms, and then he
adds, " The parasang is equal to 30 stades; and each
schœne, which is an Egyptian measure, is equal to 60
stades." The parasang being equal to 30 stades of

327·27 English feet, is therefore equal to 9818 feet, or
12,000 of those Oriental *spans,* which Mr. De Morgan
has denominated "geometrical feet." Each schœne,
comprising 60 stades, is equal to 19,636 English feet,
or 12,000 Oriental cubits.

Herodotus mentions the distance from Heliopolis to
the sea, as being 1500 stades. Rennell proposes to read
in this place, 1000; but if we estimate the Egyptian
stade at 327·27 English feet, the former number is correct. " The distance," says Rennell, " is 80 geographical miles direct, equal to 100 Roman miles; so that
the schœne should be 4 Roman miles; about 40 stades
instead of 60." Rennell is right in this estimate, but
wrong as to what the Egyptian stade ought to be. Fifteen
hundred stades of 327·27 English feet each are equal to
490,905 English feet. So also 80 geographical miles,
and 100 Roman miles, are equal to 484,850 English
feet. This proof is conclusive, and the more satisfactory, because it is drawn from Rennell's own admission.
The difference of 20 yards in a mile is not greater than
might be expected in two different measures, which have
no natural connexion with each other.

### 63.

There are *many Greek stades,* besides that of Aristotle,
but they are all founded on the same measurement of
the Earth's circumference, viz., 129,600,000 Greek feet,
equal to 130,908,000 English. The degrees into which
the circumference is divided are, in Greek feet, 360,000,
equal to 363,630 English feet. The length of each
stade varies with the number into which the circumference is divided, as in the following table of Greek
stades : —

TABLE OF GREEK STADES.

| No. of Stades in Circumference. | No. of Stades in Degree. | Amount of Stades in English Feet. | | Amount of Stades in Original Feet. |
|---|---|---|---|---|
| 400,000 . . . | 1111 . . . | 327·27 | = | 300 |
| 300,000 . . . | 833⅓ . . . | 436·36 | = | 400 |
| 250,000 . . . | 696 . . . | 523·63 | = | 480 |
| 240,000 . . . | 666⅔ . . . | 545·45 | = | 500 |
| 180,000 . . . | 700 . . . | 727·27 | = | 666⅔ |

The original feet in the above numbers are those of 1·0909 English.

| | | | | |
|---|---|---|---|---|
| 259,200 . . . | 720 . . . | 505·05 | = | 500 |
| 216,000 . . . | 606 . . . | 606·06 | = | 600 |

The original feet in these two numbers are those of 1·0101 English.

### 64.

The *Paris foot* is a measure of very great antiquity, and there are circumstances connected with it which give it a peculiar interest. We conceive it probable, that this measure was in existence when the Pyramids were founded, though it is not traceable to them.

Greaves, while he was at Constantinople, measured the *Persian arish*, and found it to be 3·197 of the English foot. He measured also the *greater Turkish pike*, or *peek*, which he found to be equal to 2·200 of the English foot. He then states the *lesser Turkish peek* to be, in proportion to the greater, as 31 is to 32. He makes no remark on these measures, and that circumstance gives them the greater value, since it is evident they were not made to support any preconceived theory. To an enquirer after the origin of the Paris foot, they are extremely interesting.

The Paris foot is, by the Table of Constants,

stated to be 1·0657654 of the English foot, or 12·789 inches.

When the Persian arish is said, by Greaves, to be 3·197 of the English foot, it is equal to 3 feet of 1·065667, 3 feet of 12·788 inches.

The smaller Turkish peek is, on the same authority, equal to 2 feet of 1·065675, or 2 feet of 12·7881 inches.

It is impossible that these affinities of 12·788, 12·7881, and 12·789 inches, between *Persian, Turkish,* and *Paris* measures can have been accidental. How, then, are they to be accounted for? As the Gauls overran all Asia Minor in the third century, B.C., and one body of them settled in Galatia, to which they gave their name, while another made their way to Babylon, some may fancy that to this cause the resemblance is owing; but we are inclined to think that these measures came originally from Tyre, and that they were brought by the Phœnicians to the shores of Gaul.

## Chapter VIII.

*The Sacred Cubit of the Jews—Altar of Burnt Offering in the
Second Temple measured by the Sacred Cubit—Mersennus on
the Sacred Cubit—The Sacred Cubit the Measure of the Earth
before the Flood—The Cubit and Palm, and Great Cubit of
Ezekiel—The Itinerary Cubit of the Tyrians—The Itinerary
Cubit of the Babylonians—Modern Itinerary Cubits.*

### 65.

THE *Sacred Cubit* is a measure of the very highest
antiquity, according to the account given of it.
Sir Isaac Newton says, "It is agreeable to suppose that
the Jews, when they passed out of Chaldea, carried
with them into Syria the cubit which they had received
from their ancestors. This is confirmed both by the
dimensions of Noah's ark, preserved by tradition in
this cubit, and by the agreement of this cubit with the
two cubits which, the Talmudists say, were engraven
on the sides of the city Susan, during the empire of
the Persians, and that one of them exceeded the sacred
cubit *half a digit*, the other a *whole digit*. Susan was a
city of Babylon, and consequently these cubits were
Chaldaic. We may conceive one of them to be the
cubit of the royal city Susan, the other that of the
city of Babylon. The sacred cubit, therefore, agreed
with the cubits of divers provinces of Babylon, as far as
they agreed with each other; and the difference was so
small, that all of them might be derived, in different
countries, from the same primitive cubits."*

* Dissertation on Cubits, in Greaves's Works, vol. ii. p. 425.

The sacred cubit may be called the *itinerary* cubit of the Jews, since it was used among them to measure distances. The Sabbath-day's journey, which was measured by this cubit, consisted of 2000 cubits. In Numbers xxxv. 4, the suburbs of the cities to be given to the Levites, were required to reach "from the wall of the city and outwards 1000 cubits round about." Yet, in the next verse, it is said, "Ye shall measure from without the city, on the east side 2000 cubits, and on the south side 2000 cubits, and on the west side 2000 cubits, and on the north side 2000 cubits; and the city shall be in the midst: this shall be to them the suburbs of the cities." The change in the number from 1000 to to 2000 is doubtless intended to be here, as we have shewn it to be elsewhere, employed as a means of reminding the Jews that the cubits spoken of were those of which one was twice the length of the other.

The conclusion to which Sir Isaac Newton comes, from several authorities which he quotes, is "that the Roman cubit consists of 18 *unciæ*, and the sacred cubit of 25⅔ *unciæ* of the Roman foot; and consequently these cubits are to each other, in round numbers, as 2 to 3 very nearly; and this proportion is used by Josephus, out of regard to the greater expedition in computing the bulk of the buildings. For, writing to the Romans, he everywhere puts 3 Roman cubits for about 2 sacred cubits, except in some of the most eminent dimensions of the temple, properly so called, and set down in Scripture; in which case, he thought proper to retain the sacred cubit [of the Talmudists]. This will appear by comparing the cubits of Josephus with the sacred cubits of the Talmudists in the following table." He then gives the table, which we need not quote.

66.

One instance selected from this table will be sufficient to show, that the proportion above-mentioned is
observed between these several cubits.  Josephus states
the breadth of the altar of burnt-offering to be equal
to 50 [Roman] cubits, or 33⅓ sacred cubits, or 32
Talmud cubits; and the height of the altar to be equal
to 15 [Roman] cubits, or 10 sacred cubits, or 10
Talmud cubits.  But in another instance (the height of
the 19 steps) where the height is the same as that of
the altar, the Talmud cubits are said to be 9½.  According to these proportions, therefore, and estimating the
Roman foot at 11·636, and the Roman cubit at 17·454
English inches, the breadth of the altar will be equal to
872½ inches, being 50 Roman cubits of 17·454 inches,
or 33⅓ sacred cubits of 26·2 inches, or 32 Talmud
cubits of 27·26 inches.

But was this the exact breadth of the altar of burnt-
offering? for upon the answer to this question depends
the accuracy of our estimate of the sacred cubit.  We
read in II. Chron. iv. 1, that "Solomon made an altar of
brass, 20 cubits the length thereof, and 20 cubits the
breadth thereof, and 10 cubits the height thereof."
The size of these cubits may be learnt from the description given of them in the chapter preceding this,
wherein the dimensions of the Temple are specified.
"The length by cubits, after the first measure, was 60
cubits, and the breadth 20 cubits."  Accordingly, the
breadth of the Brazen Altar which Solomon made was
the width of the Temple itself.  Now we know that the
cubit of the first measure was the length of the cubit of
Karnak, 41·472 inches; and, if so, 20 cubits are equal
to 829·44 inches, which is 43 inches less than the

measure which Sir Isaac Newton obtained from the
statement of Josephus.

But it may be asked, whether the earliest measure of
the Brazen Altar, when the first temple was built, was
that which it possessed in the time of Josephus ?  We
have shown that the Second Temple, as described by
Ezra, was of the same width as before; and, therefore,
the Brazen Altar, to be in proportion, must be of the
same breadth as before; but Ezra's cubits are royal
cubits, half the size of those which were made use of in
building Solomon's Temple, and, therefore, 40 and not
20 must be the breadth of the restored Brazen Altar.
Now the sacred cubits, of which Josephus speaks, were
of such a size that $33\frac{1}{3}$ were equal to the breadth of the
Brazen Altar.  If, then, we divide 829·44 inches by
$33\frac{1}{3}$ we shall find the precise value of the sacred cubit of
Josephus, which is 24·9 inches ; and the same number
divided by 32 will give the precise value of the Talmud
cubit, according to the same authority, which is 25·92
inches ; or one digit larger than the sacred cubit (p. 77).
These, then, are the correct measures of the two cubits,
instead of the former estimate, from Josephus, of 26·2
inches, and 27·26 inches.

## 67.

A remarkable corroboration, if any were necessary,
of the accuracy of our estimate may be found in the
following quotation, by Sir Isaac Newton, from Mersennus, who, in his Treatise *De Mensuris*, prop. 1. cor. 1,
writes thus :—" I find that the cubit upon which a
learned Jewish writer (which I received by the favour
of the illustrious Hugenius,* Knight of the Order
of St. Michael) supposes the dimensions of the Temple

* Huyghens.

were formed, answers to 23¼ of our inches; so that it
wants ¾ of an inch of two of our feet, and contains
two Roman feet and two digits of a grain, which is ¼ of
a digit." Upon this statement, Sir Isaac Newton makes
the following observation : — " The Paris foot, with
which Mersennus compared this cubit, is equal to 1·068
of the English foot, according to Mr. Greaves; and,
consequently, is to the Roman foot as 1·068 is to ·967.
In the same proportion, reciprocally, are 23¼ and 25·68.
That cubit, therefore, is equal to 25·68 *unciæ* of the
Roman foot, and, consequently, falls within the middle
of the limits 25·57 and 25·79 (Roman *unciæ*) with
which we have just circumscribed the sacred cubit; so
that I suspect this cubit was taken from some authentic
model preserved in a secret manner from the knowledge
of the Christians."* We would offer here one remark
on this estimate of the sacred cubit made by Mersennus,
viz., that ¾ of an inch in two Paris feet of 1·068 English
inches, when deducted from 25·68 inches, leaves for
the sacred cubit 24·88 English inches; and that " two
Roman feet and two digits and a quarter" of the
Roman foot, when estimated at 11·636 inches, give,
for the sacred cubit, 24·90 inches: so very near by
this measure is the sacred cubit brought to that which
we have obtained for it from the measures of the
Temple.

68.

Having found the probable length of the *sacred
cubit*, we have now to ascertain upon what principle it
was formed ; since it is evident, that all leading measures were constructed on a simple basis, being some
round number contained either in the diameter or
circumference of the earth, or in the vertical height or

* Greaves' Works, 8vo. vol. ii. p. 429.

perimeter of the Great Pyramid. We have not far to
seek. If the diameter of the earth were equal to 12
millions of the double royal cubit, or cubit of Karnak,
of 41·472 English inches, it would be equal to
497,664,000 inches; and, dividing this sum by 20
millions, we obtain the measure of 24·8832 inches
for the sacred cubit.

But this number of inches in the diameter of the
earth is not quite equal to that which is recorded in the
measure of the Great Pyramid, for the latter contains
500,000,000 English inches. Dividing this number by
20 millions we obtain the measure of 25 inches for the
sacred cubit.

The question may now be asked, which of these is
the right measure? We reply, the smaller is the sacred
cubit which measured the diameter of the earth before
the flood; the one by which Noah measured the ark, as
tradition says; and the one in accordance with which
all the interior works of the Great Pyramid were constructed. The larger is the sacred cubit of the present
earth according to the standard of the Great Pyramid
when it was completed. But the *name of sacred cubit*
properly belongs to the smaller, the more ancient of the
two.

### 69.

The sacred cubit is not again referred to till after the
return of the Jews from Babylon, when it is called the
cubit and palm. "Cubitus," says Buxtorf, "mensura
cubitalis, quæ communiter continebat quinque palmos,
in sacris autem sex, ut Hebræi docent, Ezek. xl. 5,
and xliii. 13." If we add accordingly one-fifth to the
royal cubit of 20·736 inches, it will make the sacred
cubit, or 24·883 inches. The Jews, having for two
generations passed their lives in Babylon, required to

be reminded, on their return to their native country, that the sacred cubit to which they had been accustomed in Babylon was equal to *six* of those palms of its own measure, of which the royal cubit, made use of in the measures of the temple, contained but *five* palms.

The cubit and palm, or sacred cubit, is the measure mentioned in Ezekiel as forming part of a " full reed of six great cubits," called in the Hebrew " *cubits of the armpit.*" The reed measure was equal, therefore, to 12½ feet, or 149 English inches. Our pole or perch contains 16½ feet or 198 inches, and is four feet, or 48 inches, longer than the " full reed " of Ezekiel.

### 70.

The sacred cubit, as we have seen, differs from *another cubit* by half a digit. We have evidence, in the Scripture, of the existence of this latter cubit. In the description of the pillars called Jachin and Boaz, which were cast by Hiram in the plains of Succoth, and set up in the porch of Solomon's temple, it is said (1 Kings vii.), " He cast two pillars of brass, of 18 cubits high a-piece;" but we read in 2 Chron. iii. — " He made before the house two pillars of 35 cubits high." This difference, as we have before observed in other cases, is designedly set forth to teach us that the one cubit was a little more than half the length of the other. Had it been twice the length we should have concluded that the larger cubits being the cubits of Karnak, the smaller were the royal cubits of Memphis. The number of inches in 18 cubits of 41·472 inches, is 746·496; and if we divide this number by 35, we obtain a cubit of 21·328 inches. As the sacred cubit is one-fifth more than the royal

cubit of 20·736, which becomes, with that addition,
24·883; so this cubit of 21·328 inches will require
the addition of one-fifth to make it proportionate to a
sacred cubit; and, with this addition, it is equal to
25·5936 inches. We have here, then, the *itinerary cubit
of the Tyrians,* for Hiram's father was "a man of
Tyre, a worker in brass." It resembles closely the
smaller *Turkish peek* of 25·574 inches, and is equally
the measure of two-thirds of the *Persian arish*; or the
measure of two *Paris feet,* which make together 25·576
inches.

### 71.

The larger cubit of the two which were engraven on
the walls of Susan was, therefore, not as Sir Isaac
Newton conjectured, a cubit proper to Babylon, but
to Tyre. The Babylonian cubit may have been the
same as the larger Turkish peek at Constantinople,
which Greaves states he found equal to 2·2 English
feet or 26·4 inches. We have a further indication of
this cubit in the Cairo cubit, which Greaves measured
and found to be 1·824 English feet, or 21·888 English
inches. Assuming the Cairo cubit to be a royal cubit,
and adding to it *one-fifth,* as was done in the case of the
royal cubit of Memphis, we obtain for the itinerary
cubit of Cairo the measure of 2·1888 English feet, or
26·260 English inches. The agreement of this cubit
with that of Babylon, and its difference from that of
Memphis, made use of in the interior of the Great
Pyramid, warrant us in conceiving that it was, as we
before suspected, the cubit of the Mizraim, the children
of Ham, when they originally came into Egypt, and
that it was brought by them from Babylon, at the
dispersion of the builders of Babel.

Thus there are four itinerary cubits, of very great

antiquity, which differ from each other in the following
proportions :—

| | | |
|---|---|---|
| The Sacred Cubit of the Jews is | . 24·883 | English inches. |
| The Itinerary Cubit of the Tyrians | . 25·576 | ,, |
| That of the Talmudists . . | . 25·920 | ,, |
| That of the Babylonians . . | . 26·260 | ,, |

From these itinerary cubits, we derive some information, which we have not hitherto obtained, relating
to the present measure of Germany, called the Rhinland
foot.  Considering the itinerary cubits above-mentioned
as equal to two feet each,—

| | | |
|---|---|---|
| The Jewish is equal to 2 feet of . | . 12·441 | English inches. |
| The Tyrian to 2 feet of . . | . 12·788 | ,, |
| The Talmud to 2 feet of . . | . 12·960 | ,, |
| The Babylonian to 2 feet of . | . 13·180 | ,, |

The first of these is the measure of the *Rhinland*
foot, as it was ascertained by *Snellius*, and before him
by Greaves, who makes it 1·033, or 12·396.  Thus the
foot of Germany is derived from the Jewish foot, which
was the half of the sacred cubit employed in the
measure of the Ark before the deluge, equal to 1·0368
English feet or 12·441 inches.

The second is the measure of the *Paris* foot, as we
have already shown, which is equal to 12·789 inches.

The third is not known ; but the fourth is the foot of
a cubit found by Greaves, in Egypt, which was not
derived from the measures of the Great Pyramid, but
was probably introduced by the Mizraim, from Babylon,
before the Pyramids were founded.  It is also the foot
of the larger Turkish peek found at Constantinople, as
the Paris foot is that of the smaller Turkish peek.

72.

The *sacred cubit* was the *itinerary cubit* of the Jews,
when that measure had more importance attached to it,
because it became the measure of a Sabbath-day's
journey, " which, by the unanimous consent of the
Talmudists and all the Jews (says Sir Isaac Newton),
was 2000 cubits. Hence the Chaldee interpreter
upon Ruth i. 6, says, ' We are commanded to observe
the Sabbath and good days, so as not to go above 2000
cubits.' Now, men of middling stature, in walking
moderately, go every step more than two Roman feet,
and less than two and a third, and within these
limits was the sacred cubit circumscribed." These
limits are, from the Roman foot of 11·636 inches,
23·272 inches on the one hand, and 27·151 on the
other, forming an average of 25·2 inches. The sacred
cubit of the Jews, it will be remembered, is 24·883
inches.

Pierre Belon, who visited the Pyramids between
1546 and 1549, or nearly 100 years before Greaves,
took with him no instruments to measure them with,
but made all his observations in general terms. " We
measured the base," he says, speaking of the Great
Pyramid, " which is 324 steps from one corner to the
other, stretching our legs a little." * At that time
Greaves' measure of 693 feet was most likely the correct measure, which divided by 324, leaves 25·667
inches, for each of Belon's steps, which were somewhat
extended. This step a little exceeds the midway length
between the two limits laid down by Sir Isaac
Newton, for the itinerary cubit of the Jews.

* " Nous avons mesuré sa baze, qui a trois cents vingt-quatre
pas d'un coing à l'autre, lesquels comptames, estendant un peu
les jambes," Edit. 1555. p. 202.

George Sandys, the traveller, began his journey in 1610. He probably was a taller man than Belon, since he made the length of the base of the Great Pyramid equal to 300 of his steps, which allows 27·72 inches to each. Dr. Veryard, in "Divers Choice Remarks, etc." published in London in 1701, makes the base equal to about 322 of his paces; but as the length was then generally admitted to be not less than 728 feet, his step becomes equal to 27·12 inches. These several estimates, though loosely made, are interesting as approaching very nearly to those which were obtained by more exact means.

Since the Sabbath-day's journey is restricted to the length of 2000 cubits, and the sacred cubit is taken at 24·8832 inches, the entire length is 4147·2 feet, or 1132·8 feet less than an English mile. In Acts i. 2, we are told that the apostles "returned into Jerusalem from the mount called Olivet, which is from Jerusalem a Sabbath-day's journey." On this passage, Dr. Hammond observes that Mount Olivet was, according to the Syriac interpretation, seven furlongs from Jerusalem. Taking the furlong at 606 English feet, or 600 Greek feet, the distance would be 4242 feet. The Sabbath day's journey, therefore, was not more than seven furlongs. When it is described as 1,000 cubits, the *pace* or *double step*, equal to 49.7664 inches is the measure intended.

The Sabbath-day's journey being equal to 4147·2 English feet, and the cubit of Karnak being equal to 41·472 English inches, it follows that the extent of the Sabbath-day's journey was 1200 measures of the cubit of Karnak.

## CHAPTER IX.

*Degrees, Minutes, and Seconds, in the Table of Constants—These Divisions Ptolemaic Measures—Only one Measure of the Earth made by the Ancients—Radishes, Onions, and Garlic: their Symbolic Import—Quadrature of the Circle in Early Times— Its Proportion according to Archimedes—Its Proportion according to the Hindoos—Modern Proportion; how far it differs from the Ancient—French Metre; its Difference from that of the Great Pyramid—French and English Measures of Length compared with Ancient Measures.*

### 73.

IT is not easy to determine at what period those divisions into *degrees, minutes,* and *seconds,* which now mark the line of the Earth's measure, were first employed. They were in existence apparently under the Ptolemies, when Eratosthenes recorded his measures. But at an earlier period, when Thales and Anaximander are said to have divided the circumference of the Earth into 400,000 parts, these divisions could hardly have been known.

Even if this notation had been traceable to an earlier period, it would not have constituted a division strictly according to *time.* Commencing with seconds and minutes, it does not proceed to hours and days, but immediately introduces an arbitrary scale of 360 degrees, which has no other relation to *time* than as it happens to agree with the then reputed number of days in the year.

Whether the founders of the Pyramids had any more

E

accurate knowledge on this subject, and whether they committed it to the keeping of that inscription which they engraved on the face of the Great Pyramid can only be conjectured. It was evidently not suspected to form any part of that record which by the priest's authority was interpreted to Herodotus.

We might fairly suppose, however, that the founders of the Pyramids, who had learnt that the Earth was a sphere, revolving on its axis in the course of 24 hours, and who had measured a portion of one of its great circles as it passed under the stars in their diurnal motion, would naturally divide the line of such circle by the same intersections as those which marked the progress of time; and we have some reason to think that they acted on this principle.

"The same stars, in their diurnal revolution, come to the meridian, *successively*, of every place on the globe, once in 24 sidereal hours; and since the diurnal rotation is uniform, the interval, in sidereal time, which elapses between the same star coming upon the meridians of two different places, is the measure of the difference of longitudes of the places."* It follows, therefore, that if they knew this, and divided the whole circumference by the number of hours in the day, the hours by the minutes, and the minutes by the seconds, we might probably find some foundation for their having acted on this principle.

### 74.

The *modern division* of the circumference of the Earth is expressed by certain figures in the *Table of Constants*, which without some explanation are not easy to be understood. The circumference of 360 *degrees* is repre-

* Herschel's Astronomy.

sented by 1,296,000; the radius reduced to *seconds*, by
206264·8; and the radius reduced to *minutes*, by
3437·74677. These groups of figures are looked on as
those of *proportion* only, and as having no reference to
any actual measure. But they come so near the truth
as to indicate some veritable measurement at some time
or other of the circumference and diameter of the Earth;
and if we consider them in that light, we shall probably
discover by what people, and at what time, this calculation was first made.

Let us commence with the Pyramid record of the
Earth's circumference, which is 130,908,000 English
feet. The number 1,296,000 is formed of 360 times
360, or 360 degrees of 360,000 feet. There are
129,600,000 feet of a certain kind in this new measure
of the Earth's circumference; and if no actual measurement again took place, but the Pyramid record was
preserved, we shall find what feet these are, if we divide
130,908,000 by 129,600,000. This foot is equal to
1·01 English, or 12·12 English inches. Now this is
the Ptolemaic foot, or smaller Greek foot, corresponding, if we deduct one twenty-fifth part, to the Roman
foot of ·9696 English, or 11·636 inches.

The radius of the Earth, in the *Table of Constants*,
when reduced to seconds, is expressed by the figures
206264·8. If we consider these to be Ptolemaic feet,
and multiply the number by 1·01, we obtain for the
actual measure of the Earth's radius 20,832,744
English feet, and for that of the diameter 41,665,489.
These numbers are very near the true amount. The
diameter of the Earth, according to the measure taken
at the Pyramids, is 41,666,667 English feet, or
500,000,000 inches. Thus our opinion is confirmed
that the figures made use of, in the *Table of Constants*,

to denote the proportion of the Earth's radius to its circumference, have reference to some actual measure, and that they are correct if taken as Ptolemaic feet.

### 75.

The inference to be drawn from these various particulars is, that until those measures were obtained which are the glory of the present age, no other actual measure was ever made of the Earth's circumference, than that which was effected by the founders of the Pyramids. Later mathematicians have displayed much ingenuity in re-arranging the old materials, and forming them into new and more convenient combinations, but they did not accomplish a new measurement of the meridian, however much their writings may seem to prove the contrary.

Here, then, we have an undoubted fact, on which to establish our theory, that as early as the reign of the Ptolemies, a division of the Earth's circumference was made on the principle of the division of *time*. The great circle was divided into 12 months, and each month into 30 days, making a total of 360 days, each called a *degree*. Each degree was again divided into 60 *minutes*, and each minute into 60 *seconds*, making together another division equal to 3600. Add to these numbers the space of 100 feet,* as equal to each second, and the total is 129,600,000. This division, though not strictly that of time, proceeds on the same principle as far as it goes.

Earlier, however, than this, there was another division of a more arbitrary character; which had no reference to time. About 600 years before the Christian

---

* Speaking loosely, a degree is about 70 statute miles ; and a second, about 100 feet.—*Herschel's Astronomy*, p. 117.

era, Thales and Anaximander divided the great circle into 400,000 parts. Each of these parts would contain, taking the entire circumference at 130,908,000 English feet (the measure at the Pyramids) 327,270 English feet, or 100,000 Pyramid measures, which may be called meters, of 3·2727 English feet each. This division was probably the same as that which existed in the time of Herodotus. It has no reference to time.

## 76.

Yet we think it may be shewn, that the division made by the founders of the Pyramids had some kind of rela▪ tion to time. " There was signified on the Pyramid, by means of Egyptian characters," says Herodotus, " how much was expended on *radishes, onions*, and *garlic*, for the labourers; and, as I well remember, the interpreter, reading over the characters to me, said, that it amounted to one thousand six hundred talents of silver." *

By Egyptian characters we cannot tell, of course, what is meant. " The hieroglyphics of Egypt, as well as those of China," says Dr. Thomas Young, " appear clearly to have been, *at first, rude pictures* only of sensible objects. In the course of ages, the resemblance seems to have been forgotten in both countries, and *imitations* of the *imitations* only were employed; sometimes for denoting the same objects, and sometimes for expressing either the whole or a part only of the sounds of the names which were applied to them." † But whatever

---

* Σεσημανται δε δια γραμματων Αιγυπτιων εν τη πυραμιδι, ὁσα ες τε συρμαιην και κρομμυα και σκοραδα αναισιμωθη τοισι εργαζομενοισι. και ὡς εμε ευ μεμνησθαιτἀ ὁ ἑρμηνευς μοι επιλεγομενος τα γραμματα εφη ἑξακοσια και χιλια ταλαντα αργυριου τετελεσθαι.—ΙΙ. 125.

† Rudiments of an Egyptian Dictionary, p. 3.

these words meant in the mind of the interpreter, it is
probable, from the early age at which the inscription
was made, that he saw *a rude picture of some sensible
objects*, which appeared to him as well as to Herodotus
and to the people of that age and country generally, to
represent a *radish*, an *onion*, and a *clove* of *garlic*,—all of
them objects so well known, that we cannot suppose
the resemblance to have been misunderstood. What,
then, do we gather from these symbols? They are
evidently an indication of the existence, at that time,
of those divisions of the circumference of the Earth,
which we denominate by the terms *degrees, minutes,*
and *seconds,* and represent by ( ° ) for a degree, by ( ′ )
for a minute, and by ( ″ ) for a second; signs of a division drawn from *time,* but very nearly resembling
*onions, radishes,* and *garlic,* the *double stroke* for the *second*
having, in the lapse of ages, departed a little from what
may have been more like, at first, the *double head* or
*root* of a *clove* of garlic. That the *meaning* of the inscription was mistaken by the interpreter, we have no
doubt, and it is not wonderful when the *purport* of the
record was unknown. Such notions easily possess a
vulgar mind. In our own country, at this day, we hear
stories told quite as absurd, in explanation of circumstances with which they have as little connection, whenever we visit any of our own remarkable buildings.

Herodotus, however, does not appear to have been
satisfied with the statement of the interpreter; for he
shrewdly remarks : " If this were really the case, how
much *more* was probably spent in *iron tools,* and in
*bread,* and in *clothing* for the workmen," * articles of far

---

* Ει δ' εστι ούτως εχοντα ταυτα, κοσα εικος· αλλα δεδαπανησθαι εστι
ες τε σιδηρον τῳ εργαζοντο, και σιτια, και εσθητα τοισι εργαζομενοισι.
—II. 125.

more value than the radishes, onions, and garlic. He may not have suspected that the inscription had any reference to *measures*, though he was well aware that the three principal pyramids were objects of which it was important to ascertain the exact *measure*. Other writers of antiquity show the same regard for the discovery of the precise *measure* of each of the Pyramids. Aristides, the rhetorician, in speaking of them, says, that he had "partly procured such *measures* as might be had from writings, and partly with the priests had *measured* such things as were not obvious."* It is seldom that any public buildings are described by measure with so much exactness, unless it be understood that their dimensions are a matter of great importance.

### 77.

An article on the *Quadrature of the Circle* by Mr. De Morgan † states, "that Archimedes, in his book on the Mensuration of the Circle, is the first who made any approach even to a practical demonstration of the question. According to him a circle of 4970 feet in diameter would have a circumference lying between 15,610 and 15,620 feet, the truth being that such a circle would have a circumference of 15,613¾ very nearly. This measure of Archimedes gives 3·14286 for the approximate value of the ratio of the circumference to the diameter."

Again : "Among the Hindoos (Vija Ganita) are found the ratios of 3927 to 1250, and also the square root of 10 to 1. The first gives 3·1416 exactly, and is considerably more correct than that of Archimedes : the

* In a passage quoted by Greaves.
† In the Penny Cyclopædia.

second gives 3·1623 and is much less correct. The date of the first result is not known, but all agree that the writings in which it is found are anterior to any European improvement on the measure of Archimedes. The ratio given by Ptolemy in the Syntaxis is 3·141552, not quite so correct as 3·1416, but so near it, that those who doubt of the antiquity of Hindoo science will probably suppose the 3·1416 above mentioned to be a version of Ptolemy's measure."

### 78.

The measure of Archimedes above mentioned is expressed in numbers which lead us to suppose that he must have referred to some actual measurement of the Earth with which he was acquainted. Born at Syracuse B.C. 287, and having, in the early part of his life travelled into Egypt, where he is said to have studied under Conon, the Samian, a mathematician and astronomer, who lived under Ptolemy Philadelphus and Ptolemy Euergetes,—Archimedes must have been familiar with those discoveries of the philosophers at Alexandria, which are connected with the name of Eratosthenes. But as it was under Ptolemy Philadelphus, who reigned from B.C. 285 to 247, that the Septuagint translation of the Hebrew Scriptures was made, it is not improbable that the measures of the Jews also were well known to the mathematicians of Alexandria, and this may account for the knowledge which Archimedes seems to have had of the *sacred cubit* of the Jews. For when he describes the ratio of the diameter of a circle to its circumference as that of 4970 to 15,610 or 15,620, we find a measure set down for the *diameter* which is equal to 20 millions of cubits of 24·85 inches. Sir Isaac Newton, as we have

seen, estimated the sacred cubit as equal to 24·88
inches. Its exact measure is 24·883 inches (§ 68). In the
diameter of the Earth are 20 millions of these cubits.
If we take the circumference of the Earth as equal to
15,614 and divide it by 4970, the proportion is
3·14165.

### 79.

We acknowledge, in the second instance, the antiquity of Hindoo science, but we can carry back the
discovery here attributed to the Hindoos to a period
beyond any to which the records of that ancient people
reach. The ratio of 3927 to 1250, if doubled, is that
of 7854 to 2500, and doubled again is that of 15708
to 5000; but these numbers, as far as they extend, are
the very same that are found in the Pyramid measure
of the Earth's circumference. Doubled once more the
diameter is as 10,000 to 31,416. Thus the Hindoo
proportion is identical with that, as far as its numbers
go, which was expressed in English inches when the
Pyramids were founded (§ 33).

### 80.

The proportion of the circumference of a circle to its
diameter, as stated in the *Table of Constants*, is that of
3·1415927 to 1; which numbers are not supposed to
have any reference to an actual measurement of the
Earth, but to those of *proportion* merely, in which
respect they are regarded as forming the nearest approximation it is possible to make to the true ratio, within
the compass of that same number of figures: — they
may be extended indefinitely, and have been continued
to 250 places of decimals. But if we view this number

as an actual measure, the half of it is very nearly that
described by the Great Pyramid.

|  | English inches. |
|---|---|
| The Pyramid measure is equal to   .    .    . | 1,570,896,000 |
| The half of 3·1415927, is equal to   .    .    . | 1,570,796,350 |
| The difference is only   .    .    .    .    . | 99,650 |
| The measure of Archimedes gives   .    .    . | 1,570,825,000 |
| The measure of the Hindoos   .    .    .    . | 1,570,800,000 |
| The measure of Ptolemy .    .    .    .    . | 1,570,776,000 |

In other words, the proportion of the circumference of
the Earth to its diameter, supposing it to be a perfect
circle, is expressed by the figures 3·1415927 according
to the *Table of Constants*, the half of which number
(1,570,796,350) when it is regarded as composed of
English inches, is, within 100,000 inches, the same
measure of the circumference of the Earth at which it
was estimated by the founders of the Great Pyramid.

Thus the measure of a great circle of the Earth was
made in the earliest ages, probably 4000 years ago,
with so much accuracy, that it exceeded only by
8300 feet, that number which is employed in modern
times to denote the true proportion in the same latitude.

### 81.

At present we adopt the measure of the Earth taken
in lat. 45° instead of lat. 30°. The French *mètre* is
intended to represent the 40,000,000th part of the
circumference; the entire compass being equal to
1,574,831,600 English inches; the *mètre* to 39·3708
English inches. But so long as mathematicians continue to represent the *ratio of a circle to its diameter* by
the figures 3·1415927 to 1, so long will they render an
involuntary homage to the originality and accuracy of

the Pyramid measure, and the antiquity of the English inch.

| | English inches. |
|---|---|
| The French mètre is equal to . . . . | 39·37079 |
| And the Pyramid meter to . . . . | 39·27240 |
| The difference is only . . . . . | 00·09839 |

Accordingly a reduction of 1 in 400 from the French mètre is all that is required to bring the French mètre into conformity with the Pyramid meter. The reduction of $\frac{1}{12}$th from the Pyramid meter will equally bring it into conformity with the English yard. If the Pyramid meter were thus introduced into each system as an integral part of its measures, the two nations would have a common standard to which they could refer in their dealings with each other; while the minor divisions in each scale would remain under their present denominations for the convenience of the common people in each country.

### 82.

There can be little doubt that if it had been seen by the *savans* of France, at the commencement of the present century, how nearly their proposed mètre corresponded with the measure which had been established by the founders of the Pyramids in lat. 30°, they would not have sought to introduce another measure established on a similar portion of the meridian taken in lat. 45°. If they now adopt the Pyramid meter, which in forty inches is only *one-tenth* of an inch less than their own, they will have the satisfaction of knowing that they contributed to its discovery not less than the English, and have an equal right to consider it their own. They will also bring by this means their own measure of length into harmony with all other ancient measures of any authority, which must be a source of gratification to them, as well as a circumstance of infinite advantage to all who prosecute enquiries into the relative proportions of ancient and modern measures. The Roman, the Italian, the Greek, and the Ptolemaic Foot — the Foot of Drusus and of Diodorus Siculus, as well as that of the Pyramid yard or meter — the Philetærian Foot — the British Inch — the Geometrical Foot — the Karnak Cubit, or that of Solomon's Temple, the Royal Cubit, and the Royal Span or Foot of Pliny — the Cubit of the Nilometer — the Oriental Cubit and the Oriental Span — the Stade of Aristotle, and all the other Greek Stades, are but various arrangements of the same COMMON measure;

> " All are but parts of one stupendous whole,
> Whose body NATURE is —— "

though not in the sense in which the Poet understood that word. The several measures, by whatever name they may be called, are only parts of that one great *measure*, whose *body* is the EARTH, either in its *diameter* or *circumference*.

## CHAPTER X.

*Diameter of the Earth: its Decimal Proportions — Question of
John Quincy Adams answered — Measures of the present Earth
in Greek and English Feet — Probable Arrangement in Earlier
Times — Measures of the present and former Earth compared —
Difference caused by the Deluge — The Amount of that Differ-
ence — English Statute Mile, Drusian or Breton Mile, Welsh
Mile, Irish Mile, Romano-British Mile, Computed Mile.*

### 83.

THE late John Quincy Adams, at that time Secretary
to the United States, in his excellent " Report
upon Weights and Measures," published in 1821, by
order of the Senate, observes, that " when Méchain
and Delambre were employed by the National Assembly
of France to make an admeasurement of the arc of the
meridian to an extent which had never before been
attempted, and to weigh distilled water *in vacuo* with an
accuracy which had never before been effected ; Nature,
as if grateful to those exalted spirits, who were devoting
the labours of their lives to the knowledge of her laws,
not only yielded to them the object which they sought,
but disclosed to each of them another of her secrets.
She had already communicated, by her own inspiration,
to the mind of Newton, that the Earth was not a
perfect sphere, but an oblate spheroid, flattened at the
poles ; and she had authenticated this discovery by the
result of previous admeasurements of degrees of the
meridian in different parts of the two hemispheres.
But the proportions of this *flattening*, or, in other words,
the difference between the circles of the meridian and
equator, and between their respective diameters, had

been variously conjectured from facts previously known. To ascertain it with greater accuracy was one of the tasks assigned to Delambre and Méchain, for, as it affected the definite extension of the meridian circle, the length of the mètre, or aliquot part of that circle, which was to be the standard unit of weights and measures, was also proportionably affected by it. The result of the new admeasurement was to show that the flattening was of $\frac{1}{334}$; or that the axis of the Earth was to the diameter of the equator as 333 to 334. *Is this proportion to the decimal number of* 1,000 *accidental?* It is confirmed as matter of fact by the existing theories of astronomical mutation and precession, as well as by experimental results of the length of the pendulum in various latitudes. *Is it also an index to another combination of extension, specific gravity, and numbers hitherto undiscovered?* However this may be, the fact of the proportion was, on this occasion, the only object sought. This fact was attested by the diminution of each degree of latitude in the movement from the North to the Equator; but the same testimony revealed the new and unexpected fact, that the diminution was not regular and gradual, but very considerably different at different stages of the progress in the same direction; from which the inference seems conclusive, that the Earth is no more in its breadth than in its length, perfectly spherical, and that the northern and southern hemispheres are not of dimensions precisely equal."*

84.

The question here asked, *Is this proportion to the decimal number of* 1,000 *accidental?* receives its answer from the discoveries which have been made in the present work. It is not accidental, but the result of

* Report, etc., p. 51.

the measurement made of the Earth's diameter before
the deluge by the *Sacred Cubit* then in use, and of the
same measurement after the deluge by the corresponding cubit, the *Itinerary Cubit* of the Great Pyramid.
In the former case, as in the latter, the diameter of the
Earth being equal to 20,000,000 of cubits, containing
500,000,000 of inches, it could not but happen that if
these inches were the same which we now make use of
in England, our modern estimate would range itself, in
its proportions, closely round the decimal number of
1,000. We may see this proportion exemplified in the
following numbers taken from Herschel's Astronomy.

|  | Feet. | Inches. |
|---|---|---|
| Greater or equatorial diameter . | 41,847,426 | = 502,169,112 |
| Lesser or polar diameter . . | 41,707,620 | = 500,491,440 |
| Average diameter . . . | 41,777,523 | = 501,330,276 |

In these numbers the average diameter or axis of the
Earth is to the diameter at the Equator as 333·660760
is to 334·779408. The diameter at the Pyramids, or
axis of the Earth in lat. 30°, is 41,666,667 = 500,000,000
or 333·333334.

Thus the proportion which the numbers 333 to 334
bear to the decimal number of 1,000, is not the effect
of any accident, but the result of an actual measurement of the Earth's diameter, made with remarkable
care and wonderful accuracy in the earliest ages of the
world; and in this fact we find "an index to another
combination of extension, specific gravity, and numbers
hitherto undiscovered."

85.

According to the figures in the *Table of Constants* the
circumference of the present Earth is represented by
the following numbers:—1296000, which is the number
of 360 degrees expressed in seconds.

Supposing these figures to denote Ptolemaic Greek feet, each equal to 1·0101 English feet, we may arrange them, for comparison, in the following order :—

| (1) *Ptolemaic feet.* | | (2) *English feet.* |
|---|---|---|
| $\dfrac{100}{60}$ = 1 second | = | $\dfrac{101\cdot01}{60}$ = 1 second |
| $\dfrac{6,000}{60}$ = 1 minute | = | $\dfrac{6060\cdot6}{60}$ = 1 minute |
| $\dfrac{360,000}{360}$ = 1 degree | = | $\dfrac{363,636}{360}$ = 1 degree |
| 129,600,000 = 1 circumference | = | 130,908,960 = 1 circumf. |

According to the figures in the *Table of Constants*, the diameter of the present Earth is represented by the following numbers :—

| Radius reduced to seconds | . | . | 206264·8 |
|---|---|---|---|
| —————————— minutes | . | . | 3437·74677 |
| —————————— degrees | . | . | 57·295780 |

Regarding these figures also as denoting Ptolemaic Greek feet, and considering each foot as equal to 1·0101 English, we find them fall into the following arrangement :—

| (1) *Ptolemaic feet.* | (2) *English feet.* |
|---|---|
| $\dfrac{5,729\cdot578}{60}$ = 1 second | $\dfrac{5,787\cdot446}{60}$ = 1 second. |
| $\dfrac{343,774\cdot680}{60}$ = 1 minute | $\dfrac{347,246\cdot760}{60}$ = 1 minute. |
| $\dfrac{20,626,480\cdot800}{2}$ = 1 radius | $\dfrac{20,834,805\cdot600}{2}$ = 1 radius. |
| $\dfrac{41,252,961\cdot600}{12}$ = 1 diameter | $\dfrac{41,669,611\cdot200}{12}$ = 1 diameter. |
| 495,035,539·200 Greek inches | 500,035,334·400 = Eng. inches. |

In this arrangement, the same figures are employed
on the left hand which are given in the *Table of Constants*; and they are useful for comparison, as showing
that the Ptolemaic feet are correctly rendered into
English feet and inches in the present as in the preceding table. But the numbers which represent a
*second* are too large for such a division. It would be
more reasonable to assume that besides being reduced
into minutes and seconds there was a further reduction
made.

### 86.

The notation employed in the preceding statements,
to represent the diameter of the present Earth, is not
only too large: it is attended with too many fractions
to appear natural. There must have been some simpler
mode of representing the divisions into which the
diameter was cast when these forms were devised. We
may not be able to discover them in the construction of
the present Earth, but we can find some evidence of
their use in the Earth before the flood.

Commencing with 480 English feet, or 5760 English
inches, and assuming this for the present to be equal to
*one second*, we find the whole table resolve itself very
naturally into the following elements:—

| *English feet.* | | | | *English inches.* |
|---|---|---|---|---|
| 480 | = 1 second | = | | 5760 |
| 60 | | | | 60 |
| 28,800 | = 1 minute | = | | 345,600 |
| 60 | | | | 60 |
| 1,728,000 | = 1 degree | = | | 20,736,000 |
| 12 | | | | 12 |
| 20,736,000 | = 1 radius | = | | 248,832,000 |
| 2 | | | | 2 |
| 41,472,000 | = 1 diameter | | = | 497,664,000 |

As the *Sacred Cubit* is equal to 24·8832 English inches, so the radius of the former earth was equal to 10 millions of sacred cubits, and the diameter to 20 millions of the same, or 497,664,000 inches.

And as the *Cubit of Memphis* or the *Royal Cubit* is equal to 20·736 English inches, so was the radius of the former Earth equal to 12 millions of royal cubits, and the diameter to 24 millions.

But these larger measures leave the primary number of 480 feet or 5760 inches unaccounted for. The question may be asked, How came this number to be assumed in the first instance as the equivalent of what is here called *a second?* The answer leads us to remark that in all probability the analysis was at first based on a *series of times.* The cube containing 8 inches is the first of all cubes, being founded on the number 2. Beginning with this, and proceeding by a regular succession of *times* from a *second* to a *year,* we are brought at last to 10 millions of sacred cubits, and 12 millions of royal cubits, as the measure of the *radius* of the Earth, and by doubling these numbers we obtain the *diameter.*

From the centre of the former Earth, in this view of it, a cube containing 8 inches, extending in every direction 2 inches, began to radiate. Four of these cubes, equal to 8 inches, formed a *second,* 60 seconds a *minute,* 60 minutes an *hour,* 24 hours a *day,* 30 days a *month,* 12 months a *year,* which is equal to the *radius* of the Earth, or 248,832,000 inches. The diameter is twice this number, or 497,664,000 inches, in our present English measure, according to the following table :—

*Analysis of the Diameter of the former Earth.*

| (1) *The Radius.* | | (2) *The Diameter.* |
|---|---|---|
| Inches. | | Inches. |
| 8 | = 1 second | 16 |
| 60 | | 60 |
| 480 | = 1 minute | 960 |
| 60 | | 60 |
| 28,800 | = 1 hour | 57,600 |
| 12 | | 12 |
| 345,600 | = half a day | 691,200 |
| 2 | | 2 |
| 691,200 | = 1 day | 1,382,400 |
| 30 | | 30 |
| 20,736,000 | = 1 month | 41,472,000 |
| 12 | | 12 |
| 248,832,000 | = 1 year | 497,664,000 |

The *second* of the *diameter* is 16 inches in length, of which measure there are 360 in the 5760 inches, which are at present called a *second*.

### 87.

When the new Earth was measured in Egypt after the deluge, it was found that it exceeded the diameter of the old Earth by the difference between 497,664,000 inches and 500,000,000 inches; that is, by 2,336,000 inches, equal to 36·868 miles; and this increase was the reason why the former number of 5760 inches was enlarged to 5787·446. But how is this increase in the diameter of the present Earth, as compared with the former, to be explained?

### 88.

We read in the Book of Genesis, that "God said, Let there be a firmament in the midst of the waters, and let it divide the waters from the waters. And God made the firmament, and divided the waters which were under the firmament from the waters which were above the firmament; and it was so. And God called the firmament Heaven. And the evening and the morning were the second day.

"And God said, Let the waters under the heaven be gathered together into one place, and let the dry land appear; and it was so. And God called the dry land Earth, and the gathering together of the waters called he Seas."

Thus there were two grand reservoirs of waters at the time that the firmament was created: one above the firmament, or Heaven; and one below it. The one above the firmament, or Heaven, is not called by any particular name, but that which is below it is called SEAS.

The waters above the firmament are again particularly described in Gen. vii. 11. "In the six hundredth year of Noah's life, in the second month, the seventeenth day of the month, the same day were all the fountains of the great deep broken up, and the windows (or the 'floodgates') of heaven were opened. And the rain was upon the earth forty days and forty nights."

If from these words we infer that the fountains of the great deep were the waters below the firmament, those which came through the "windows" or the "floodgates" of heaven were as certainly above it. These waters were not like those in the SEAS, included in the body of the Earth: they were a part of the *planet*, and did not alter its *weight* or its relative position; but, while they were above the firmament, they were not incorporated with the body of the Earth. It was after the deluge that they were added to it, and with the Seas they then saturated with moisture the surface of this globe, and caused that addition to its diameter, especially in parts nearer the equator, which is the result of the rotation of the Earth on its axis.

### 89.

We cannot presume to determine the addition made by the deluge to the former bulk of the Earth. It is only the waters above the firmament which are to be taken into account; the seas being already included in the former Earth. But some conjectures may be hazarded on the subject, with the reasons on which they are founded.

So far as the *diameters* of the former and the present Earth are compared, they show an increase in the latter of 36·867 miles, or 18·4335 miles in the Earth's *radius*. This is the case if we assume the measure of the former Earth to have been that of a perfect sphere, or to have been made in the same latitude as that of the Great Pyramid. But we know too little of the nature of the former Earth to affirm any thing with certainty as to these two points.

The former Earth may have been more spherical for this reason, that the present system of rivers and fountains of waters was not at that period existing. It is stated that "the Lord God planted a garden eastward in Eden," and that " a river went out of Eden to water the garden, and from thence it was parted, and became into four heads;" but this river was not like our present rivers, one which watered the *earth*, for we are expressly told that " there went up a MIST from the earth, and watered the whole face of the ground." — Gen. ii. 6.

The "waters under the heaven being gathered together into one place," formed, we suppose, a great CENTRAL DEEP, from whence there issued in the garden of Eden the river, which being parted into *four heads*, supplied the MIST.

A sufficient argument for the truth of this opinion is found in the covenant which God made with Noah: " I do set my bow in the cloud, and it shall be for a token of a covenant between me and the earth. And it shall come to pass, when I bring a cloud over the earth that the BOW SHALL BE SEEN IN THE CLOUD; and I will remember my covenant, which is between me and you, and every living creature of all flesh; and the WATERS SHALL NO MORE BECOME A FLOOD to destroy all flesh."

When a mist went up from the earth, and watered the whole face of the ground, there was no cloud in the firmament,—when the waters were placed above the firmament, there could be no cloud there,— and when there was no cloud in the sky no rainbow could be seen there; but when the waters above the firmament were withdrawn, when rivers and fountains of waters intersected the whole face of the earth, and when vapours ascended from the earth and became clouds, then the BOW was seen, and by that same token the Lord God gave assurance "to every living creature for perpetual generations," that there should not "any more be a FLOOD TO DESTROY THE EARTH."

That there were mountains in the old world, in the midst of waters, we learn from St. Peter (II. Pet. iii. 5) who says: "By the word of God the heavens were of old, and the earth standing out of the water and in the water; whereby the world that then was, being over-

flowed with water, perished; but the heavens and the
earth which are now, by the same word are kept in
store, reserved unto fire against the day of judgment
and perdition of ungodly men."

Hence it seems probable that the seas in the compass
of the former Earth did not get incorporated with the
materials of which the Earth itself was composed, and
that they did not affect the sphericity of that Earth
in the same manner in which the present Earth is
affected by the waters which are intermingled with it.
Admitting this view of the case, let us now see how
much the Earth is increased in lat. 30° by the centri-
fugal force acting on the saturated surface of the Earth.

|  | Miles. |
|---|---|
| The greater or equatorial diameter . . . = | 7925·648 |
| The lesser or polar diameter . . . . . = | 7899·170 |
| The difference of the diameters . . . . = | 26·478 |
| The difference in lat. 30° . . . . . . . = | 17·652 |
| The average diameter . . . . . . . = | 7912·409 |

From this statement it appears that the increase in
the diameter of the present Earth is 26·478 miles at the
equator, and about 17·652 miles in the latitude of the
Pyramids. Deducting, therefore, 17·652 miles from
36·867 miles, we have 19·215 miles for the increase
made in lat. 30 in the diameter of the present Earth
by the accession of the waters above the firmament,
which is equal to an increase in the radius of the
Earth of 9·607 or 9½ miles. This increase is the com-
bined effect of all the waters, collectively, on the new
Earth : it represents accordingly the addition made to
the Earth's surface by the waters previously kept asunder from it by the intervention of the firmament.*

---

* Its effect would be proportionately represented on a globe of
16 inches diameter, by thickness of a card.—*See Herschel's Astro-
omy*, p. 12.

The granite peaks which may have risen in the old
world far higher than any mountains in the new Earth,
were not likely to exceed this limit of 9½ miles. The
highest mountains we have now do not reach 6 miles.
How high those were which are spoken of in Gen. vii. 19,
when "the waters prevailed exceedingly upon the earth,
and all the high hills that were under the whole heaven
were covered," we are not told; but we read that
"fifteen cubits and upwards did the waters prevail
and the mountains were covered." No creature on
the earth exceeded probably this measure of 15
cubits or 31 feet, for "all flesh died that moved
upon the earth, both of fowl, and of cattle, and of
beast, and of every creeping thing that creepeth upon
the earth, and every man: all in whose nostrils was the
breath of life, of all that was on the dry land, died."
Such creatures as survived were those which could live
in the turbid waters of the deluge, if there were any
such creatures.

## 90.

In the diameter of the former Earth, which is equal
to 41,472,000 feet, there are exactly 7200 miles of
5760 feet. No even number of any recognised mile is
to be met with in the diameter of the present Earth,
but it is found to contain in lat. 30° about 7234 of
these miles.

The mile of 5760 feet exceeds our present mile of
5280 feet by *one-eleventh* part, a circumstance which
affords some proof of their early affinity. The foot of
Drusus exceeds the English foot by *one-eleventh* part,
and the mile of 5760 English feet is composed of 5280 of
the foot of Drusus, each equal to 1·0909 English feet.

Some French writers inform us that the *Breton foot*

*of Antoninus* was the same as the foot of Drusus.* In that case it is probable that our earlier mile was equal to 5760 feet.

This opinion receives support from a peculiarity in the present table of the English mile, which shows that it was not always divided as it is at present:—

Inches.
12 = foot.
36 =     3  = yard.
198 =    16½ =     5½ = perch.
7,920 =   660  =   220  =  40 = furlong.
63,360 = 5280  = 1760  = 320 = 8 = mile.

The interruptions which occur in this table by the fractions of 16½ feet and 5½ yards are, of themselves, sufficient to assure us that the original table was not so constructed. The following is more likely to have been the primitive form :—

Inches.
12 = foot.
36 =     3 = yard.
216 =    18 =     6 = perch.
8,640 =   720 =   240 =  40 = furlong.
69,120 =  5760 =  1920 = 320 = 8 = mile.

In the Welsh language a *stang* (*ystang*) is " a *pole* or *perch* used in measure ; in some parts of South Wales it is 18 feet ; in others, 21 feet."—*Owen's Dict.* The perch of 18 feet forms part of the above table, and makes it probable that the Breton mile consisted of 5760 feet, or 1920 yards. This mile may be called the *Welsh mile.*

* Le double de ce pièd était la même chose que le pièd de Drusus, ou le pièd Breton d'Antonin.—*Metrol. Const. et Prim.* ii. 245.

F

The larger perch of 21 feet forms part of the following table :—

Inches.

12 = foot.

36 =      3 = yard.

252 =     21 =     7 = perch.

10,080 =   840 =   280 =   40 = furlong.

80,640 =  6720 =  2240 = 320 = 8 = mile.

This is the *Irish mile*. According to Kelly's Cambist, the Irish mile consists of 2240 yards or 6720 feet. Another Welsh mile or league is called *milltir :* it is composed as follows : 3 barleycorns make 1 inch.

Inches.

3 = palm.

9 =   3 = foot.

27 =   9 =   3 = pace.

81 = 27 =   9 = 3 = leap.

243 = 81 = 27 = 9 = 3 = land.

243,000 =                 = 1000 = mile.

In 243,000 inches are 20,250 feet of 12 inches, exceeding, by only 90 inches, 3 Irish miles.

The Act of the 35th of Eliz. defines the mile as consisting of 8 furlongs = 320 perches = 1760 yards = 5280 feet. The *previous* mile is said to have consisted of 7½ furlongs, 3 perches, and 2 palms of this new measure (exactly 5000 feet). But this was regarded as the length of the Romano-British mile, which it equalled in the number of feet, but somewhat exceeded in the length of each foot. Of this mile Sir John Maundevile says, " Aftre the auctoures of astronomye, 700 furlonges of erthe answeren to a degree of the firmament ; and the ben 87 myles and 4 furlonges. Now be that here multiplyed by 360 sithes, and than thei ben 31,500 myles, every of 8 furlonges, *aftre myles of oure contree.*" This was the number of miles which Eratosthenes ascribed to the circumference of the Earth in his erroneous estimate of the length of the Roman mile (§ 24.)

"Dr. Bernard, the most profound of English metrologists, found the mile of 5000 feet" says Mr. De Morgan, "sufficiently common in old writings to give it a name, and to call it the English *geometrical* mile, meaning, we suppose, that principally used in mathematical writings; but he does not give the least hint that any other mile, except this geometrical mile, and the statute mile, was ever in existence."

There was, however, a larger mile in use previous to the statute mile of Elizabeth, which is called the *computed* mile. Of this mile 3953 are equal to 5020 measured miles; or 100 computed miles give 127 measured miles.* The computed mile, by this estimate, is equal to 6705½ feet. The comparison is made from "a selection of the roads to which most importance was attached," out of a great number of roads measured by Ogilby in *statute* miles, and estimated in the other case in *computed* miles. D'Anville also says that the *common* or *computed* mile before Ogilby published his work (in 1675) was about a quarter longer than the statute mile. It was equal, therefore, to about 2200 yards, or 6600 feet; numbers sufficiently near to show that they belong to the Irish mile of 2240 yards, or 6720 feet.

If we subtract one-twelfth from the Welsh mile, it leaves the present English mile.

If we add two-twelfths to the Welsh mile, it produces the Irish mile.

* See Penny Cyclopædia, p. 211.

But the *computed* mile was not the Irish mile of 6720 feet, nor was it the Welsh mile of 5760 feet.

The *computed* mile is the *geographical* mile of 6000 Greek feet, or 6060 English.

This is placed beyond all doubt by the evidence of the maps in Bishop Gibson's edition of Camden's Britannia. In one of those maps, " the new Map of the North part of Scotland, by And. Johnston," there are three different scales of miles delineated : One is called " English measured miles," another " English computed miles," and the third " Scottish miles." The scale is in length exactly *four* inches, and in this length the number of English *measured* miles is stated at 70, the number of English *computed* miles at 60, and the number of *Scottish* miles at 50. The *computed* miles are exactly equal to the degrees of latitude marked on the sides of the map, each of which occupies exactly four inches. The English *measured* miles are, without fractions, roughly taken at 70 in the degree. The *Scottish* miles, taken at 50 in the degree, are exactly equal to 75 Roman miles : each contains 1½ Roman miles, or a French league, and is equal to 7273 English feet.

In the English county maps of this work, by Robert Morden, there is also a scale given of three different miles ; *small, middle,* and *great.* The middle is the *computed* mile, in most instances being equal to the miles in the *degrees* on the side of each map ; but in eight maps the computed or geographical mile is the shortest of the three, and, in a few cases, it is the longest of the three. In the two maps for North and South Wales, the scale of 17 " English *measured* miles," is as nearly equal to 15 "English *computed* miles," as it could be made on so small a scale.

# INTERIOR OF THE GREAT PYRAMID.

## CHAPTER XI.

*General Description of the Interior of the Great Pyramid, by George Sandys — More exact Description of the Interior, by John Greaves.*

### 91.

THE earliest of modern travellers, whose description of the interior of the Great Pyramid is worth recording, is George Sandys. He commenced his journey in 1610; and, having arrived in Egypt, prefaced his account with the following observations:—

"Full west of the city [of Cairo], close upon the desert, aloft on a rocky level adjoining to the valley, stand those three Pyramids, the barbarous monuments of prodigality and vain-glory so universally celebrated. . . . The greatest of the three, and chief of the world's seven wonders, being square at the bottom, is supposed to take up 8 acres of ground, every square being 300 single paces in length; the square at the top consisting of three stones only, yet large enough for three score to stand upon, ascended by 255 steps, each step above three feet high, and of a breadth proportionable. Yet this hath been too great a morsel for Time to devour, having stood, as may be probably conjectured, about 3200 years, and now rather old than ruinous : yet the north side is most worn, by reason of the humidity of the northern wind, which is here the moistest. The top at length we ascended with many pauses, and with much difficulty, from whence, with delighted eyes, we beheld that sovereign of streams and most excellent of countries: southward, and near hand, the mummies; afar off, divers huge Pyramids, each of which, were this away, might supply the repute of a wonder. During a great part of the day it casteth no shadow on the earth, but is at once illuminated on all sides. . . .

" Descending again on the east side below, from each corner equally distant, we approached the entrance, seeming heretofore to have been closed up, or so intended, both by the place itself, as appeareth by the following picture, and conveyances within. Into this our janissaries discharged their harquebusses, lest some should have skulked within to have done us a mischief; and guarded the mouth whilst we entered, for fear of the wild Arabs.

" To take the better footing, we put off our shoes and most of our apparel; foretold of the heat within, not inferior to a stove. Our guide, a Moor, went foremost; every one of us with our lights in our hands. A most dreadful passage, and no less cumbersome, not above a yard in breadth, and four feet in height — each stone containing that measure. So that always stooping, and sometimes creeping, by reason of the rubbish, we descended (not by stairs, but as down the steep of a hill) one hundred feet: where the place for a little circuit enlarged; and the fearful descent continued, which, they say, none ever durst attempt any further. Save that a Bassa of Cairo, curious to search into the secrets hereof, caused divers condemned persons to undertake the performance, well stored with lights and

other provision; and that some of them ascended again
well nigh thirty miles off in the deserts : a fable devised
only to beget wonder. But others have written, that
at the bottom there is a spacious pit, 86 cubits deep,
filled at the overflow by concealed conduits; in the
midst a little island, and on that a tomb containing
the body of Cheops, a king of Egypt, and the builder
of this Pyramid. For since, I have been told by one
out of his own experience, that in the uttermost depth
there is a large square place (though without water)
into which he was led by another entry opening to the
south, known but unto few (that now open being shut
by some order), and entered at this place where we
feared to descend. A turning on the right hand leadeth
into a little room, which, by reason of the noisome
savour and uneasy passage, we refused to enter.

" Clambering over the mouth of the aforesaid dun-
geon, we ascended as upon the bow of an arch, the
way no larger than the former, about 120 feet. Here
we passed through a long entry, which led directly
forward; so low that it took even from us that uneasy
benefit of stooping, which brought us into a little room
with a compact roof, more long than broad, of polished
marble, whose grave-like smell, half full of rubbish,
forced our quick return. Climbing also over this entrance, we ascended as before, about 120 feet higher.
This entry was of an exceeding height, yet no broader
from side to side than a man may fathom; benched on
each side, and closed above with admirable architecture; the marble so great, and so cunningly joined, as
it had been hewn through the living rock.

" At the top we entered into a goodly chamber, 20
foot wide, and 40 in length; the roof of a marvellous
height; and the stones so great that eight floor it, eight

roof it, eight flag the ends, and sixteen the sides, all of
well-wrought Theban marble. Athwart the room, at
the upper end, there standeth a tomb, uncovered,
empty, and all of one stone; breast high, 7 feet in
length, not 4 in breadth, and sounding like a bell. In
this, no doubt, lay the body of the builder: they
erecting such costly monuments, not only out of a vain
ostentation, but being of opinion, that after the disso-
lution of the flesh, the soul should survive, and when
36,000 years were expired, again be joined unto the
self-same body, restored unto his former condition;
gathered in their conceits from astronomical demon-
strations. Against one end of the tomb, and close to
the wall, there openeth a pit, with a long and narrow
mouth, which leadeth into an under chamber. In the
walls on each side of the upper room, there are two
holes, one opposite to another, their ends not discernible, nor big enough to be crept into; sooty within,
and made, as they say, by a flame of fire which darted
through it. This is all that this huge mass containeth
within his darksome entrails; all, at least, to be discovered."*

Considering the early period at which Sandys wrote,
and the exciting nature of the circumstances under
which he made his exploration, there is more literal
truth in his description than might have been expected.
His remarks, however, are chiefly valuable, as showing
how much we owe to the clear head, firm nerves, and
sound judgment of his immediate successor, John
Greaves.

---

* Sandys' Relation, &c., folio, 1632, p. 127—131.

## 92.

Almost all the information which we possess concerning the interior of the Great Pyramid, important as it is to the inquirer into the origin of measures of capacity and weight, is derived from the "Pyramidographia" of John Greaves, whose observations have been corroborated by the recent researches of Colonel Howard Vyse and Mr. Perring. The interior of the Pyramid is described by Greaves in the following terms, with the omission only of such parts of his account as are purely speculative.

" On the north side, ascending 38 feet upon an artificial bank of earth, there is a square and narrow passage leading into the Pyramid, through the mouth of which (being equidistant from the two sides of the Pyramid) we enter, as it were, down the steep of a hill, declining with an angle of 26 degrees. The breadth of this entrance is exactly 3 feet, and 463 parts of 1000 of the English foot; the length of it beginning from the first declivity, which is some 10 palms without, to the utmost extremity of the neck or streight within, where it contracts itself almost 9 feet continued, with scarce half the depth it had at the first entrance (though it keep still the same breadth), is 92 feet and a half. The structure of it hath been the labour of an exquisite hand, as appears by the smoothness and evenness of the work, and by the close knitting of the joints; a property long since observed and commended by Diodorus,* to have run through the fabric of the whole body of this Pyramid.

" Having passed with tapers in our hands this narrow streight, though with some difficulty (for at the

* Diod. Sic., l. i.

farther end of it we must serpent-like creep upon our
bellies), we land in a place somewhat larger, and of a
pretty height, but lying incomposed; having been dug
away either by the curiosity or avarice of some, in
hope to discover a hidden treasure; or rather by the
command of *Almamon*, the deservedly renowned caliph
of Babylon. By whomsoever it were, it is not worth
the inquiry; nor doth the place merit describing, but
that I was unwilling to pretermit anything, being only
an habitation for bats, and those so ugly, and of so
large a size, exceeding a foot in length, that I have
not elsewhere seen the like. The length of this obscure
and broken place containeth 89 feet; the breadth and
height is various, and not worth consideration. On
the left hand of this, adjoining to that narrow entrance
through which we passed, we climb up a steep and
massy stone, 8 or 9 feet in height, where we immediately enter upon the lower end of the first gallery.
The pavement of this rises with a gentle acclivity, consisting of smooth and polished marble, and, where not
smeared with dust and filth, appearing of a white and
alabaster colour. . . . By my observation with a line,
this gallery contained in length 110 feet.

" At the end of this begins the second gallery, a
very stately piece of work, and not inferior, either in
respect of the curiosity of art, or richness of materials,
to the most sumptuous and magnificent buildings. It
is divided from the former by a wall, through which
stooping, we passed in a square hole, much about the
same bigness as that by which we entered into the
Pyramid, but of no considerable length. This narrow
passage lieth level, not rising with an acclivity, as doth
the pavement below, and roof above, of both these
galleries. At the end of it, on the right hand, is the

well mentioned by *Pliny*, the which is circular and not
square, as the Arabian writers describe: the diameter
of it exceeds 3 feet; the sides are lined with white
marble; and the descent into it is by fastening the
hands and feet into little open spaces cut in the sides
within, opposite and answerable to one another, in a
perpendicular. In *Pliny's* calculation it is 86 cubits in
depth.

" Leaving the well and going on straight upon a
level the distance of 15 feet, we entered another square
passage, opening against the former, and of the same
bigness. The stones are very massy, and exquisitely
joined. This leadeth (running in length upon a level
110 feet) into an arched vault, or little chamber, which,
by reason it was of a grave-like smell, and half full
of rubbish, occasioned my lesser stay. This chamber
stands east and west: the length of it is less than 20
feet, the breadth about 17, and the height less than 15.
The walls are entire and plastered over with lime ; the
roof is covered with large smooth stones, not lying
flat, but shelving, and meeting above in a kind of arch,
or rather an angle. On the east side of this room, in
the middle of it, there seems to have been a passage
leading to some other place.

" Returning back the same way we came, as soon as
we are out of this narrow and square passage, we climb
over it, and going straight on, in the trace of the
second gallery, upon a shelving pavement (like that of
the first) rising with an angle of 26 degrees, we at
length come to another partition. The length of the
gallery, from the well below to this partition above, is
154 feet. . . . . . This gallery or corridor, or
whatsoever else I may call it, is built of white and
polished marble, the which is very evenly cut in

spacious squares or tables. Of such materials as is the
pavement such is the roof, and such are the side-walls
that flank it; the coagmentation or knitting of the
joints is so close, that they are scarce discernible by a
curious eye; and that which adds a grace to the whole
structure, though it makes the passage the more slip-
pery and difficult, is the acclivity and rising of the
ascent. The height of this gallery is 26 feet, the
breadth is 6 feet, and 870 parts of a foot divided into
1000; of which 3 feet and 435 of 1000 parts of a
foot are to be allowed for the way in the midst, which
is set and bounded on both sides with two banks (like
benches) of sleek and polished stone : each of these hath
1 foot 717 of 1000 parts of a foot in breadth, and as
much in depth. Upon the top of these benches, near
the angle, where they close and join with the wall, are
little spaces cut in right-angled parallel figures, set on
each side opposite to one another; intended, no question, for some other end than ornament. In the casting
and ranging of the marbles in both the side walls, there
is one piece of architecture, in my judgment, very
graceful, and that is, that all the courses or ranges,
which are but seven (so great are those stones), do set
and flag over one another about 3 inches; the bottom
of the uppermost course oversetting the higher part of
the second, and the lower part of this overflagging the
top of the third, and so in order the rest, as they
descend.

"Having passed this gallery, we enter another
square hole, of the same dimensions with the former,
which brings us into two *anticamerette,* as the Italians
would call them, or *anti-closets* (give me leave in so
unusual a structure, to frame some unusual terms)
lined with a rich and speckled kind of *Thebaic* marble.

The first of these hath dimensions almost equal to the second. The second is thus proportioned: the area is level, the figure of it is oblong, the one side containing 7 feet, the other $3\frac{1}{2}$, the height is 10 feet. On the east and west sides, within $2\frac{1}{2}$ feet of the top, which is somewhat larger than the bottom, are three cavities or little seats, in the manner here described—

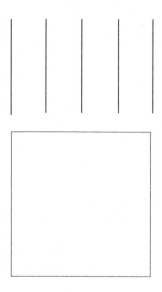

"This inner *anti-closet* is separated from the former by a stone of a red speckled marble, which hangs in two mortises (like the leaf of a sluice) between two walls, more than 3 feet above the pavement, and wanting 2 of the roof. Out of this closet we enter another square hole, over which are 5 lines, cut parallel and perpendicular in this manner—

" Besides these I have not observed any other sculptures or engravings in the whole Pyramid.  This square passage is of the same wideness and dimensions as the rest, and is in length near 9 feet (being all of *Thebaic* marble, most exquisitely cut), which lands us at the north end of a very sumptuous and well proportioned room.  The distance from the end of the second gallery to this entry, running upon the same level, is 24 feet."*  The room here mentioned is called the King's Chamber.

* Pyramidographia, p. 85—93.

## CHAPTER XII.

*The King's Chamber, and the Monument within it, described —
The Air-channels described — Col. Howard Vyse's Account of
the Air-channels — Why the Chamber was built, and the
Monument placed in it.*

### 93.

G REAVES continues his description of the King's
    Chamber as follows : — " This rich and spacious
Chamber, in which art may seem to have contended
with nature, the curious work being not inferior to the
rich materials, stands, as it were, in the heart and centre
of the Pyramid, equi-distant from all the sides, and
almost in the midst between the basis and the top.
The floor, the sides, the roof of it, are all made of vast
and exquisite tables of *Thebaic* marble, which, if they
were not veiled and obscured by the steam of tapers,
would appear glistering and shining.    From the top of
it descending to the bottom, there are but six ranges
of stone, all which, being respectively sized to an equal
height, very gracefully in one and the same altitude
run round the room.    The stones which cover this
place are of a strange and stupendous length, like so
many huge beams lying flat, and traversing the room,
and withal supporting that infinite mass and weight
of the Pyramid above.    Of these there are nine which
cover the roof; two of them are less by half in breadth
than the rest; the one at the east end, the other at

the west. The length of this chamber on the south side, most accurately taken at the joint or line where the first and second row of stones meet, is 34 English feet and 380 parts of the foot divided into 1000. The breadth of the west side, at the joint or line where the first and second row of stones meet, is 17 feet, and 190 parts of the foot divided into 1000. The height is 19 feet and a half.

" Within this glorious room (for so I may justly call it) as within some consecrated Oratory, stands the *Monument* of *Cheops* or *Chemmis*, of one piece of marble, hollow within, and uncovered at the top, and sounding like a bell; which I mention, not as any rarity, either in nature or in art (for I have observed the like sound in other tombs of marble cut hollow like this), but because I find modern authors to take notice of it as a wonder. . . . This monument, in respect to the nature and quality of the stone, is the same with which the whole room is lined, as by the breaking of a little fragment of it I plainly discovered, being a speckled kind of marble, with black, and white, and red spots, as it were equally mixed, which some writers call *Thebaic* marble.

" The figure of this tomb without is like an altar, or, more nearly to express it, like two cubes finely set together, and hollowed within : it is cut smooth and plain, without any sculpture or engraving, or any relevy or imbossment. The exterior superficies of it contains in length 7 feet 3½ inches; in depth it is 3 feet 3¾ inches, and it is the same in breadth. The hollow part within is in length, on the west side, 6 feet and 488 parts of the English foot, divided into 1000 parts; in breadth at the north end, 2 feet and 218 parts of the foot divided into 1000 parts. The

depth is 2 feet and 860 of 1000 parts of the English
foot. A narrow space, yet large enough to contain
a most potent and dreadful monarch, being dead, to
whom living, all *Egypt* was too streight and narrow a
circuit. . . .

"It may justly be questioned, how this Monument
of Cheops could be brought hither, seeing it is an
impossibility, that by those narrow passages before
described, it should have entered. Wherefore we must
imagine, that by some *machina* it was raised and conveyed up without, before this oratory or chamber was
finished, and the roof closed. The position of it is
thus : It stands exactly in the meridian, north and
south, and is, as it were, equi-distant from all sides of
the chamber, except the east, from whence it is doubly
remoter than from the west. Under it, I found a little
hollow space to have been dug away, and a large stone in
the pavement removed, at the angle next adjoining to it,
which Sandys erroneously imagines to be a passage into
some other compartment ; dug away, no doubt, by the
avarice of some who might not improbably conjecture
an hidden treasure to be reposited there. . . .

"The ingenious reader will excuse my curiosity, if,
before I conclude my description of this Pyramid, I
pretermit not anything within, of how light a consequence soever. This made me take notice of two inlets
or spaces, in the south and north sides of this chamber, just opposite to one another; that on the north
side was in breadth 700 of 1000 parts of the English
foot, in depth 400 of 1000 parts, evenly cut, and running in a straight line 6 feet and farther into the
thickness of the wall—that on the south is larger,
and somewhat round, not so long as the former, and
by the blackness within it, seems to have been a

receptacle for the burning of lamps. . . . And thus have I finished my description of all the inner parts of this Pyramid; where I could neither borrow light to conduct me, from the ancients, nor receive any manuduction from the uncertain informations of modern travellers, in those dark and hidden paths " (p. 101).

### 94.

The wise and careful observer, from whose work we have made these large extracts, had a feeling of the future value of his calculations, which seems to have been almost prophetic. He does not tell us what expectations he entertained; but since they led him to take every precaution to ensure the most minute accuracy in all his measurements, he must have made them with a view to some such issue as that on which we are now bringing them to bear. He has left nothing unnoticed; he has omitted no remark which could in any way tend to elucidate the purpose for which the Pyramid was built. As if he had supposed it to have been intended to serve as a standard of measure, he has anticipated every question which could have been put by any one whose object was to prove the case which we are endeavouring to support. It is very interesting to see that even the two inlets or spaces on the south and north sides of the chamber were as fully investigated and described by him as was possible at that time; and most satisfactory it is to find, that though our ingenious antiquary could assign no cause for them, their use as air channels has been completely established by Colonel Howard Vyse, in the following extract from his Journal, May 12, 1837.

" Mr. Hill proceeded with his operations at the southern *Air-channel,* and about 7 feet from the surface

of the Pyramid, he found within it a large stone, which
he was afraid would get fixed farther down.  He therefore removed it with the utmost caution, which was
fortunate for Mr. Perring, who was employed in the
King's Chamber, and having contrived to force his
head and shoulders at that very moment into the lower
part of the channel, would probably have been killed,
had the stone in question fallen through it.  Upon the
removal of this block the channel was completely open;
an immediate rush of air took place; and we had the
satisfaction of finding that the ventilation of the King's
Chamber was perfectly restored, and that the air
within it was cool and fresh.  The channel above the
stone was clean; but below, it was much blackened
with fires made from time to time in the lower part,
to discover its direction.  It was nearly or quite horizontal through the wall of the King's Chamber, and
afterwards ascended in one continued line to the opening
on the outer side of the Pyramid; but as the King's
Chamber is to the southward of the centre of the
Pyramid, and as the openings of both the air-channels
are at the same height, the line of the southern is considerably shorter and more inclined than that of the
northern.  The length of the southern air-channel is
174 feet 3 inches, and that of the northern 233 feet.
Had not the upper part of the latter channel been
forced, and that of the southern filled up with the
above-mentioned stone, both of them would, in all
probability, have remained open; and the ventilation of
this wonderful structure would have continued as perfect
as when it was first built. — It is to be remarked, that
as the apartment is to the eastward, the ventilation by
the air-channels, which are in the centre, is oblique.

"These channels had probably always excited particular attention; indeed, we are informed by Greaves, that the lower part of the southern had been formerly forced, and was found black with smoke in 1638. They are noticed by various travellers, and have given rise to many fanciful conjectures by Mr. Maillet and others; it is therefore surprising that their direction was so long unknown. It is, however, satisfactorily proved by these operations, that they were intended to ventilate the King's Chamber, and that they have no communication with any other apartment; and, consequently, it might be inferred, that no chambers or passages exist in the Pyramid, besides those already discovered.

"The excavation in search of a southern entrance was therefore given up, which had been carried to a considerable depth without finding the least indication of a passage, either by an inclination in the courses of the stones, or by any other circumstance. The great magnitude of the building, compared with the smallness of the chambers and passages, and also the position of the entrance to the eastward in the northern front, induced a conjecture that an entrance to the westward in the southern front might conduct to passages and apartments constructed in the great space between the three chambers entered from the north. But this does not appear to be the case; and it is to be believed, that *the King's Chamber is the principal apartment, and the security of the Sarcophagus within it the great object for which the Pyramid was erected.*"

This conclusion leaves the reader in complete possession of all the information that can be given on the subject. A drawing accompanies this account, taken from Col. Vyse's work, to which the reader's attention is requested. It is essentially the same as that which Greaves had introduced, with the exception of the *air channels.* Their existence shews the care which had been taken by the founders to render this magnificent chamber as well ventilated, to the end of time, as it was when it was constructed.

### 95.

What could be the reason that this Chamber, containing the King's Monument, should have had so much pains bestowed on it? and that an apartment, with no other furniture in it than an empty porphyry coffer, should have been ventilated as perfectly as if it were intended for the abode of a human being? By the prudent foresight and exact measurements of Greaves, we are enabled to give such an answer to this question as carries with it, at least, a great air of probability.

It is not likely that the chamber was designed for the reception of a dead body, for ventilation was in that respect unnecessary; and, as Greaves remarks, " Diodorus hath left, above 1600 years since, a memorable passage concerning *Chemmis* the builder of this Pyramid, and *Cephren* the founder of the next adjoining. Although (saith he) these kings intended them for their sepulchres, yet it happened that neither of them were buried there. For the people being exasperated against them by reason of the toilsomeness of these works, and for their cruelty and oppression, threatened to tear in pieces their dead bodies, and with ignominy to throw them out of their sepulchres, wherefore, both of them dying commanded their friends to bury them in an obscure place."*

It is not likely, however, that this story should be true; for there is no reason to suppose that the King's

* Greaves, by Birch, vol. i. p. 128.

Chamber could have been intended for a sepulchre, or that any rational beings had constructed it for such a purpose. Yet no living creature could have provided himself with such a domicile, or lived in it for any length of time, if so absurd a thought had entered his head. The only conclusion to which we can come is, that the coffer called the King's Monument was itself the object for which all this care and foresight were taken. That this coffer was, for some purpose or other, designed to be kept safe in its cell, incapable of being removed, if it were discovered, and made as secure from injury in the lapse of ages, as porphyry, in a well-ventilated room, might reasonably be supposed to be, when the material of which it was formed was so perfectly homogeneous as to emit a sound like a bell, on being struck. But let us observe further, what solicitude was shewn concerning its position. "It stands exactly in the meridian north and south, and is, as it were, equi-distant from all sides of the chamber, except the east, from whence it is doubly remoter than from the west." All these circumstances intimate, very plainly, that its position was determined by some persons of highly intelligent minds, who foresaw well what they were about, and carried into execution precisely what they intended.

A further proof of design is found in the position which this monument occupies, not only in the King's Chamber, but in the Pyramid itself. It was placed on the floor of the chamber, before its wondrous ceiling was put over it. The level of the *floor* was found by Col. Vyse and Mr. Perring to be 138 feet 9 inches *above the base of the Pyramid*.* Now, 80 royal cubits of

* Vol. ii. App. p. 111.

20·736 inches are equal to 137 feet 6 inches. But this is not all. " The base of the Great Pyramid was found to be above high Nile (in 1837) 138 feet 9 inches,"* which is also equal to 80 royal cubits of 20·736 inches, or 137 feet 6 inches. This measure of the cubit, we need scarcely observe, is the same as that which Sir Isaac Newton considered to be the veritable cubit of Memphis — the half of that which is now discovered to be the cubit of Karnak — and the double of that *span* which is called the foot of Pliny.

The depth of the well in the Great Pyramid has always been an object of interest, from its having been mentioned by Pliny, who says that it was 86 cubits deep, and that the water of the Nile flowed into it. On this subject, Mr. Long, in a work entitled " The British Museum," observes :—" As to the meaning of the word *depth*, it must be the depth from the base of the Pyramid that is meant, if the junction of the well with the water is admitted as a probable fact. The French make the whole depth of the pit 207·75 feet, of which about 145·43 feet will be in the solid rock (the well being about 62 feet above the base of the Pyramid). Now, as the base of the Pyramid is about 164 feet above the low-water mark of the Nile, and 138 feet above the mean level of the high floods of the river, it is clear, if the French measurements are correct, that the level of the bottom of the well is between the present levels of high and low water in the Nile." Supposing the cubits of Pliny were the royal cubits of 20·736 inches, the measure of 86 cubits would be equal to 148½ feet, which makes the well to descend 10 feet below high-water mark, and still to be 16 feet above the

* Vyse, vol. ii. App. p. 105.

lowest level.  Col. Coutelle's measure of the depth of
the well, 207·75 English feet, is remarkable as being
clearly 120 cubits of 20·736 inches, or royal cubits.

When the *Pyramid Coffer*, as we may call it, was
located on the floor of the King's Chamber, at the
height of 80 cubits (137 feet 6 inches) above the base
of the Great Pyramid, and twice that height, or 160
cubits (275 feet) above the mean level of the high
floods of the Nile, it was also placed at a certain corresponding distance below another remarkable limit
of the Great Pyramid, viz., a ridge-roof composed of
eleven slabs of calcareous stone, each 12 feet 3 inches
long.  The height of this roof above the floor of the
King's Chamber was 69 feet 3 inches, or exactly 40
cubits of 20·736 inches.  The intermediate space between this angular roof and the flat roof of the King's
Chamber was occupied by five low chambers, called
chambers of construction, distinguished by certain
names, as Davison's, Wellington's, Nelson's, Lady
Arbuthnot's and Col. Campbell's chambers.  There had
not been any doorway or entrance into any of these
chambers.  They were merely vacuities, or cavities
formed to take off the weight of the building from the
King's Chamber.  "In the ceilings alone was any
exactness of construction preserved.  These were beautifully polished, and had the finest joints, in order, most
probably, to prevent the slightest accumulation of dust
or rubbish.  In all other respects the masonry in these
apartments  became less perfect as they ascended."*

Had an elephant of gold been found in the centre
of the King's Chamber, we should have probably
thought that the value of the casket was proportionate

* Vyse, vol. i. p. 106.

to that of the gem within. But when the only treasure it contained was found to be a *porphyry coffer*, the question naturally arises, What could be the reason why so much pains should have been taken for its preservation? From what has been stated with regard to other parts of the Great Pyramid, we are naturally inclined to think that *measures of capacity* must have had some connexion with the Coffer, in the estimation of those men who built the Pyramid and placed that vessel in the centre.

## Chapter XIII.

*The Pyramid Coffer the Standard of all Measures of Capacity.*
*Estimate of its Contents in Cubic Inches — The Pyramid Cof-*
*fer the Standard of Hebrew Measures of Capacity.  Table of*
*Hebrew Measures of Capacity according to the Pyramid Coffer—*
*Hebrew Measures established by Bishop Cumberland — Bishop*
*Cumberland's Hebrew Measures of Length and Capacity com-*
*pared with those of the Great Pyramid and Pyramid Coffer.*

### 96.

THOUGH many persons, at different times, have
endeavoured to obtain some standard for a *mea-*
*sure of length* from the Great Pyramid, and the French
savans even imagined that they had discovered such a
standard in the *exterior* length of the Coffer called the
*King's Monument;* no one appears to have thought
that the *interior* of that vessel might have been intended to serve as a standard of *measures of capacity.*
Yet the extraordinary exactness with which Greaves
made a measure of its contents, might lead us to infer
that he had some idea of its value in that respect.   To
him alone we are indebted, in early times, and to Col.
Vyse and Mr. Perring in the present day, for the subjoined particulars.

*Estimates of the Capacity of the Coffer.*

| (1)   By Greaves. | (2)   By Vyse and Perring. |
|---|---|
| Cubic Inches. | Cubic Inches. |
| Length. . . 77·856 | Length . . . . 78·0 |
| Width . . . 26·616 | Width . . . . 26·5 |
| Depth . . . 34·320 | Depth . . . . 34·5 |

From the measurement of Greaves, the cubic contents of the coffer are found to be 71,118·429 cubic inches. From that of Vyse and Perring, the contents are 71,311·5 cubic inches.

It is reasonable to presume, that if the Pyramid Coffer were intended to form a standard of measure for all vessels of capacity, its contents would form the cube of some measure of length employed in the construction of the Great Pyramid. There is one measure of length made use of, which is remarkably well defined, and is the largest measure of that age of which we have any knowledge; it was much used by the builders of the Pyramids, and for many centuries afterwards by their successors, and is even recorded as having been one of the measures of the world before the flood. This measure is the *Karnak Cubit*, which measure is twice the length of the *Royal Cubit*, or cubit of Memphis. We have seen its length very exactly determined in the former part of this work, without our having any expectation at that time that it would be a measure to which we should again find it necessary to refer. Taking it, as it was there shewn, to be equal to 41·472 English inches, the number of cubic inches in the cube of that measure is 71,328·8. Greaves's estimate of the contents falls short of this cube only 210 cubic inches: and that of Vyse and Perring only 16½ cubic inches, an increase of *one-tenth of an inch in the depth*, would make Greaves's measure equal to 71,325·650 cubic inches.

This agreement between the theoretic contents obtained from the cube of the Karnak cubit and the actual contents of the Pyramid Coffer, is so extraordinary as to force us to conclude that the number of cubic inches in the cube of the Karnak cubit is the

true content of the Pyramid Coffer. But what wonderful
evidence have we here of the accuracy with which the
Coffer was made, and the care with which Greaves
measured it ! The *porphyry* Coffer, and the *larch* Cubit,
are irresistible proofs of an identity of measure existing
from 3,000 to 4,000 years ago.

### 97.

If any people were likely to adopt the cube of the
*Karnak cubit* as the standard of their measures of capacity, it would be the *Hebrew nation,* since they made
great use of that cubit as a measure of length in the
earliest ages, and must have been acquainted with it at
the time of their sojourn in Egypt. Taking this for
granted, and endeavouring to proportion their measures
to this standard, we find little difficulty in assigning to
each of the Hebrew vessels of capacity its proper
content, with reference to the Pyramid Coffer.

*Table of Hebrew Measures of Capacity, according to the
Pyramid Coffer.*

|  |  | Cubic Inches. |
|---|---|---|
| 1 Log |  | = 24·8 |
| 4 Logs | = 1 Cab | = 99·1 |
| 3 Cabs | = 1 Hin | = 297·2 |
| 2 Hins | = 1 Seah | = 594·4 |
| 3 Seahs | = 1 Bath, or Epha | = 1,783·2 |
| 5 Baths or Ephas | = 1 Lethekh | = 8,916·0 |
| 2 Lethekhs | = 1 Chomer | = 17,832·2 |
| 4 Chomers, or 120 Seahs | = 1 Coffer | = 71,328·8 |

We will assume, then, that these numbers are correct
numbers, solely on the supposition that the Pyramid
Coffer was the standard to which they were intended
to be conformed. Let us now bring them to another
kind of test, wholly different from this.

### 98.

Among the many works which have been written in our own country, on the subject of ancient weights and measures, none is entitled to more respectful mention than "An Essay towards the Recovery of the Jewish Measures and Weights," written in 1685, by Dr. Richard Cumberland, Bishop of Peterborough. This work contains the original of those "Tables of Scripture Measures and Weights" which are found at the end of our *Bibles*. It was written with the view of supplying that information, and well deserves the high credit it has obtained.

Unfortunately, the foundation which Bishop Cumberland took for the basis of his calculations was not so sound as he supposed it to be. He imagined there was but one early Jewish cubit; and he thought the cubit which Mr. John Greaves had found and measured in Cairo was that ancient cubit. "I saw reason to believe," he says, "that the Egyptian cubit had been preserved there, from the utmost antiquity of the Pyramids unto this day." He judged accordingly, "that if we could recover one old eastern standard cubit, of a known number of hand-breadths, we should be able to determine all their measures of length by that standard. Such I conceive and think (he adds) I have proved the Egyptian *derah*, or cubit, still kept at Cairo, to be, whose length is evidently 6 palms. And this Mr. John Greaves, Astronomy professor at Oxford, in his Book of the Roman Foot, hath given us accurately adjusted to the thousandth part of an English standard foot."* The measure of this *derah*, or cubit, which Greaves found in use at Cairo, is 21·888 English inches.

* Essay, etc., p.7.

The cubit of Karnak is equal to two royal cubits, or cubits of Memphis, and one royal cubit is equal to 20·736 English inches. There is, consequently, a difference of about 1 inch, or one-twentieth part, between Bishop Cumberland's standard cubit and that of the Pyramid Coffer; a difference large enough to affect the value of all this learned man's calculations. The disparity is made greater by the change which has since taken place in the size of our own English measures of capacity. But the good sense, sound judgment, and learning exercised by this excellent man in his undertaking, enabled him to work his way so skilfully through the difficulties which beset his path, as to render his book a most agreeable one to read, though not altogether a safe authority to rely on.

His work is dedicated—" To the Honourable Samuel Pepys, Secretary to the Admiralty, and President of the Royal Society," the well-known author of the "Diary." In his dedication, the Bishop speaks so pleasantly of his task, and of the manner in which he had tried to execute it, that we are tempted to subjoin a few passages, as a model for our own work.

"The subject of it is not any quarrelsome interest, or distinguishing tenet of a party of men, but the peaceable doctrine of *measures and weights,* which, in their general nature, are the common concern of all mankind, as being the necessary instruments of just dealing and fair commerce between all nations. For I may, without arrogancy, affirm, that not only the principles and method of this discourse do give light to that general doctrine, but also that the particular measures and weights therein stated, have an universal influence thereupon. Because these being the next ancient and sacred examples of that kind, and the rules of that righteousness whereof Noah, the father of all men now living, was a preacher, it is highly probable that all nations did derive, as their pedigree from him, so *their measures and weights from the imitation of his* (although length of time, neglect, and corrupt customs have made great alterations), which I have briefly proved by the example of those used by the most learned nations, the Greeks and Romans.

" But whatever the success of my labours may be as to the subject or matter of this tract, I am secure that the calm manner of my writing it will be very agreeable to the known candour and serenity of your temper. For I have industriously avoided all appearance of contention against any man that may herein differ from me, so far as not to name the known diversities and opinions of men about this matter ; and have employed all my diligence to prove mine own assertions, either by arguments peculiar to them, or by shewing the approach of others of the best reputation to agreement with me.

" By this means, I have contracted my thoughts into so small a book, that it may seem incongruous to present it to a man of such great worth as you are, for which I shall offer no other apology than this — that if in this little room mine undertaking be not well performed, the shorter follies are, the better ; and if it be, I know you will not think the worse of a book, because in a few sheets it determines many and great difficulties."

It will be interesting now to compare Bishop Cumberland's estimate of the Jewish measures with those which we have obtained from the standard of the Pyramid Coffer; as without some such test our estimate may be thought of little value.

## 99.

*Bishop Cumberland's Hebrew Measures of Length and Capacity compared with those of the Great Pyramid and Pyramid Coffer.*

### I. MEASURES OF LENGTH.

|  | Dr. Cumberland. Linear inches. | Pyramid. Lin. inches. |
|---|---|---|
| The Jews' Cubit in English inches . . | 21·888 | 20·736 |
| *Hence are deduced* | | |
| 1. Its parts, or less measures. | | |
| Zereth, the span, ½ cubit . . . | 10·944 | 10·368 |
| A Palm, hand's breadth, $^1/_6$th . . | 3·648 | 3·456 |
| A Digit, finger's breadth, $^1/_{24}$th . . | ·912 | ·864 |
| The East used also a span of a cubit . | 7·296 | 6·912 |
| 2. Aggregate Numbers of Cubits. | | |
|  | Eng. feet. | Eng. feet. |
| Orgyia, a fathom, 4 cubits . . . | 7·296 | 6·921 |
| Ezekiel's Reed, 6 cubits . . . | 10·944 | 10·368 |
| The Arabian Canna, or pole, 8 cubits . | 14·592 | 13·824 |

### II. MEASURES OF CAPACITY.

|  | Dr. Cumberland. Cubic inches. | Pyramid Coffer. Cubic inches. |
|---|---|---|
| Epha, or Bath . . . . . . | 1,747·7 | 1,783·2 |
| Corus, or Chomer (10 ephas) . . | 17,477·0 | 17,832·2 |
| Seah (third of epha) . . . . | 582·5 | 594·4 |
| Hin (sixth of epha) . . . . | 291·25 | 297·2 |
| Homer (tenth of epha) . . . . | 174·77 | 178·3 |
| Cab (eighteenth of epha) . . . | 97·03 | 99·1 |
| Log (seventy-second of epha) . . | 24·25 | 24·8 |

The Table to the left of the perpendicular line, is taken from Dr. Cumberland's Essay. The Column to the right of it contains our estimate of *length*, obtained from the *royal cubit*, or cubit of Memphis; and of *capacity*, obtained from the cube of the *cubit of Karnak*. Our measures of *capacity* exceed those of Dr. Cumberland only 2 *per cent.*

## CHAPTER XIV.

*The Pyramid Coffer the Measure of the Laver in the Scriptures—
The Pyramid Coffer the Measure of the Molten Sea in the
Scriptures.*

### 100.

THE shape of the vessel in the Great Pyramid, which
we have called the Pyramid Coffer, resembles that
of a *hot bath*, though, from the material of which it is
made (*porphyry*), and the place in which it is located,
we may presume that it was not intended to be used
for that purpose, or to contain hot water at any time.
If a vessel of this kind were designed to be used as a
*caldron*, it would probably be made of brass, copper, or
iron ; and such a vessel was in use, as a caldron, among
the Hebrews. This we learn from the following passage, in 1 Sam. ii. 12—14 : "Now the sons of Eli were
sons of Belial ; they knew not the Lord. And the
priest's custom with the people was, that when any
man offered sacrifice, the priest's servant came, while
the flesh was in seething, with a flesh-hook of three
teeth in his hand ; and he struck it into the pan, or
kettle, or *caldron*, or pot ; all that the flesh-hook brought
up, the priest took for himself. So they did in Shiloh
unto all the Israelites that came thither." The word
for this particular vessel in the Hebrew language is
*Kiyowr*, a *laver*. To establish its connexion with the
word *caldron*, we may adduce the following passage in

2 Chron. iv. 14 : " He made also bases, and *lavers* made
he upon the bases." Here the word rendered by *lavers*
in the text, is rendered in the margin by *caldrons*. Like
all the other vessels and instruments made by Hiram
for the house of the Lord, these *lavers* or *caldrons* were
of bright brass. That these *lavers* were in the shape of
the Pyramid Coffer, may be inferred from this use of
the term ; but we have further proof of it in the following passage, 1 Kings vii. 38 : " Then made he ten
lavers of brass : one laver contained forty baths; and
every laver was four cubits, and upon every one of the
ten bases one laver." The Pyramid Coffer, as we have
seen, contained 40 baths, and each bath 1783·2 cubic
inches = 71,328·8 cubic inches, so that the laver and
coffer were of the same capacity. Every laver, it is
said, was 4 cubits ; and each cubit, as we have seen,
was 20·736 inches. The length of each laver, therefore, was 82·944 inches ; and as the Pyramid Coffer
was in length, in the inside, 77·856 inches, this length
would allow 2½ inches at each end for the thickness of
the brass of which the vessel was made. The length of
the Pyramid Coffer being 87½ inches, each end of the
porphyry vessel would be 5 inches thick. From these
particulars we may conclude with great probability,
that the shape of the *laver* was like that of the Pyramid
Coffer, or a *hot bath*, though it was commonly filled, as
we may suppose, with cold water.

The *laver* is first mentioned in Exodus xxx. : " Thou
shalt also make a laver of brass, and his foot also of
brass, to wash withal; and thou shalt put it between
the Tabernacle of the congregation and the Altar, and
thou shalt put water therein. For Aaron and his sons
shall wash their hands and their feet thereat." The
*foot*, as it is called, was a stand on which the laver was

set. When the lavers were cast for the service of Solomon's Temple, 500 years after, they were of the same capacity, the same length, and the same shape as this : " One laver contained forty baths, and every laver was four cubits." The chief difference was in the *stand* on which they were set. The *bases*, as they are now called, were 4 cubits in length, 4 cubits in breadth, and 3 cubits in height; that is, 7 feet 3½ inches long, the same in breadth, and 5 feet 2 inches in height. Every base had four brazen wheels, like chariot-wheels; and the height of each wheel was a cubit and a half, or half the height of the *stand* on which the laver was placed. Ten lavers were set upon ten of these bases, and five of them were put on the right shoulder of the House, and five on the left. The water was probably let down from the laver by means of " undersetters," as they are called, which were cast and contained in the base itself, one at each corner. " And in the top of the base there was a round compass of half a cubit high," or 10·368 inches, through which we may suppose the water was drawn down from the lavers into the " undersetters," for " the washing of such things as they offered for the burnt-offering" (1 Kings vii. 27).

By comparing this description with the form and size of the Pyramid Coffer, we may obtain a tolerably clear idea of the laver and its base. As the stand was square on which the laver was placed, there was on each side of it one cubit (20·736 inches), unoccupied by the laver. Such part of this as was not required for the men to stand on, in order to fill or clean the lavers, was ornamented by Hiram's skill; "For on the plates of the ledges thereof, and on the borders thereof he graved cherubims, lions, and palm-trees, according to the proportion [or *nakedness*, as it is in the

margin] of every one, and additions round about,"
(1 Kings vii. 36). Hiram appears to have been allowed
to embellish the castings, so long as he did not interfere with the original design of the work, or the proportions allotted to it.

### 101.

The Pyramid Coffer was also a measure of the *Molten
Sea* mentioned in Scripture.—The following is the description given of the molten sea in the 7th chapter of
the 1st Book of Kings : "And he made a molten sea,
ten cubits from the one brim to the other : it was round
all about, and his height was five cubits : and a line of
thirty cubits did compass it round about. And under
the brim of it round about there were knops compassing it, ten in a cubit, compassing the sea round
about : the knops were cast in two rows, when it was
cast. It stood upon twelve oxen, three looking toward
the north, and three looking toward the west, and three
looking toward the south, and three looking toward
the east : and the sea was set above upon them, and all
their hinder parts were inward. And it was a hand-
breadth thick, and the brim thereof was wrought like
the brim of a cup, with flowers of lilies : it contained
two thousand baths." In the parallel passage in the
2nd Book of Chronicles, 4th chapter, we are told, "it
received and held 3000 baths."

The chief difficulty we have to encounter here, is how
to understand the very different account which is given
in *Kings* and *Chronicles* of the contents of the Molten
Sea. From the experience we have had in other passages of these two books, where they differ, we should
suppose that the intention was to apprize us that these
3000 baths were made of a measure two-thirds less

than that which is given as forming 2000 baths, both
measures being equally called a bath.

Each of the lavers contained 40 baths, and the ten
lavers in the whole contained 400 baths; but the Molten
Sea contained 2000 baths, or five times as much water
as the whole of the lavers put together. Its size,
therefore, must have been considerable, as its name,
indeed, implies. A measure of 10 cubits, from the one
brim to the other, in royal cubits, is equal to 207·36
inches, or 17 feet 2·8 inches. Bishop Cumberland, assuming the cubits to be equal to 218·88 inches, makes
the diameter 18 feet 2·4 inches. He then reasons concerning it as follows :—

" Its height is 5 cubits ; its diameter, called breadth,
is 10 ; its figure is affirmed to be round ; but it is not
determined in the Scripture whether this round figure
were an hemisphere or a cylinder, equally wide at the
bottom and the top, or a decurted cone, that was wider
at the bottom than the top, where its wideness is
expressed ; or whether some other irregular figure of a
protuberant belly. Yet it is ordinarily represented to
us in cuts as an hemisphere."

The Bishop, soon after, proceeds to treat it as if the
figure were cylindrical. " Let us suppose the figure of
this sea to be cylindrical, because I shall soon shew this
to be more likely than that of a hemisphere. The diameter of the base of this cylinder being 10 cubits, must,
according to our determination of the cubit, be in inch
measure 218·88 ; and its height, 5 cubits, is in inches,
109·44. To find the solidity or content of this cylinder,
we must first find the area of its base by this analogy
taught by *Archimedes* : as 14 is to 11, so is the sqnare
of its diameter, viz., 47908·4544, to the area of its
base, 37642·1357. Then we must multiply the area by

the height; the product of which multiplication is the cylinder's content, viz., 4,119,579·44. Lastly, this divided by the solid inches of the epha, 1747, will quote 2358·08, the number of ephas contained in that cylinder. Hence it appears that it will contain above 2000 ephas or baths, which is the number expressed in the Book of Kings."

Pursuing the same course as this which Bishop Cumberland has taken to prove his case, and supposing the figure of a cylinder to be chosen as the one most likely to be in accordance with the scriptural account, but making all our calculations according to the royal cubit of 20·736 inches, we find the cylinder's content to be in cubic inches 3,503,868·3598. Dividing this number by the cubic inches of our epha, viz., 1783·2, we find that 1965 baths or·ephas are contained in the Molten Sea. This number is only 35 baths less than the required number of 2000. As 40 baths are contained in one laver, our measure is thus brought within less than one laver of the proper quantity. A very slight curvature outwardly of the brim of the vessel, adding to the depth 1 inch, would allow space for these 35 baths, and that such a curvature was made, we think may be gathered from this further description of the Molten Sea:—" It was a hand-breadth thick, and the brim thereof was wrought like the brim of a cup, with flowers of lilies; it contained 2000 baths." This is the account in the 7th chapter of Kings: in the 4th chapter of the 2nd of Chronicles, it is said, " The thickness of it was an hand-breadth, and the brim of it like the work of the brim of a cup, with flowers of lilies; and it received and held 3000 baths." The brim of a cup, commencing just above the cylinder's edge, would provide space for the 35 baths, and the farther rim of flowers would give a form of elegance to the figure which the rigid outline of a cylinder seems to require.

To account for the difference in the statements, as to the number of baths in the Molten Sea, Bishop Cumberland thinks " Grotius hath well suggested that, in the first place, ordinarily, when it was not filled up it had 2000 baths of water in it; but, secondarily, upon extraordinary occasions, when more was requisite, as at the great festivals, it could and did hold that greater number of baths."

But if, on those extraordinary occasions, when the number of animals sacrificed was so greatly increased, the number of 400 baths (contained in the whole 10 lavers) was found sufficient for the washing of all such things as they offered for the burnt offering, is it likely that the 2000 baths contained in the Molten Sea, which was only " for the priests to wash in," would be so inadequate for that purpose, as to require on those occasions the addition of half as many more baths? This supposition cannot reasonably be entertained. We must therefore fall back on the other means of accounting for the higher number, which we have found useful on former occasions of a similar kind, and enquire whether the 3000 baths may not be understood as having reference to a measure of the same name, but less magnitude, than the usual bath.

The proper bath of 1783·2 cubic inches contained *three* seahs of 594·4 cubic inches each. A measure of *two* seahs would be equal to 1188·8 cubic inches, of which measure the Molten Sea would contain 3000. If we could find that a measure of this capacity had been at any time in use amongst the Hebrews, as a *bath* or *epha*, it would obviate the difficulty at once. Bishop Cumberland does not enable us to prove that there was ever such a measure as this of two seahs, called by the name of an epha or bath, but he states some facts which render it not unlikely to have been the case.

"Epha," he says, "is the sixth part of the cube of the Egyptian cubit, which cube is called an *ardub*." He gives as his authority "the express affirmation of the Arabian accountants and mathematicians, *Alsephadi*, and *Ebn Chalecan*, printed in *Dr. Wallis's* Arithmetic, and received from *Dr. Pocock*. Only there," he adds, "the epha is by an usual commutation of the quiescent letters, and of the labial *p* into *b*, called *oeba*, or as Dr. Wallis expresseth it, *waiba*."* Bishop Cumberland then assumes that his former cubit, of 21·888 inches, produced the cube which was the content of the *ardub*, in solid inches. But we have seen that this cubit is not to be relied on as an authority for the Hebrew measure ; and we have had proof that another Egyptian cubit, that of 41·472 inches, did indeed produce a cube which is equal in content to the cubic inches of the Pyramid Coffer. Let us, therefore, try whether this cubit may not be the one intended by the Arabian authorities. Dividing the product 71,328·8 by *six*, the number of *waibahs* said to be in the *ardub*, we obtain 11·888 cubic inches for the quotient, which is exactly the number required for that *waibah* or *epha*, of which 3000 are contained in the Molten Sea.

In a postscript, Dr. Cumberland adds to his other authorities that of the chief Arabian lexicographer, the Author of the Dictionary called *Kamus*, who expressly affirms *ardub* to be a *great Egyptian measure* containing *six waibahs*. Now the Pyramid Coffer may

* Essay, p. 65.

deserve to be called "a *great* Egyptian measure," but that name could hardly be applied to a vessel, of not more than *one seventh* the size of the coffer. On all these accounts, therefore, we conclude that the *waibah* of 1188·8 cubic inches was probably the *epha* of the Book of Chronicles, 3000 of which were contained in the Molten Sea.

One thing, however, is certain, the Molten Sea contained 2000 baths of 1783·2 cubic inches. Its size, therefore, cannot be doubted. Whether it possessed the shape assigned to it by Bishop Cumberland, or whether it had some other form, imparting to it a greater degree of elegance, as the Talmudists supposed, is a question of inferior interest. But if it were a cylinder, twice as wide as it was deep, relieved round the brim with "flowers of lilies," and set on the backs of oxen, half as high as the sea was deep, which is about their natural height, it would not present an inelegant appearance.

## Chapter XV.

*The Pyramid Coffer the Standard of Grecian Measures of Capa-*
*city.  Table of Grecian Measures of Capacity according to*
*the Pyramid Coffer — The Pyramid Coffer the Standard of*
*Roman Measures of Capacity.  Table of Roman Measures*
*of Capacity, according to the Pyramid Coffer — Grecian and*
*Roman Measures of Capacity according to the Pyramid Coffer,*
*compared with those established by Dr. Hussey — The Pyramid*
*Coffer identical with the English Chaldron — The Pyramid*
*Coffer the Standard for the Weight of the Troy Pound.  The*
*Troy Pound; Avoirdupois Pound; Merchant's Pound.*

### 102.

THE earliest measures of capacity, next to the Hebrew,
are the *Grecian,* of which the linear foot is equal
to 1·01 of the English, or 12·12 English inches.  The
cube of this foot is contained 40 times in the volume
of the Pyramid Coffer.  This cube agrees, therefore,
with the contents of the laver in Solomon's Temple;
and hence the Grecian measures of capacity may be
presumed to have had their origin in the number of
cubic inches contained in the Pyramid Coffer.  We
have before noticed the very early connexion of the
Grecian foot with the Pyramid measure, in the remarkable fact that the circumference of the Earth as it was
ascertained by the founders of the Pyramid, is expressed
by the numbers 129,600,000 in the "Table of Constants," which numbers are those of the Grecian foot,

equal to 1·01 of the English. This connexion of the Grecian measures of capacity with the measure of the Pyramid Coffer, is a further proof that the Grecian measures were all derived from those of the Great Pyramid. The cube of 12·12 inches is equal to 1780·36 cubic inches, which number multiplied by 40 is equal to 71,214·4 cubic inches. The contents of the Pyramid Coffer, by the cube of the Karnak cubit, is 71,328·8; and by the measure of Greaves, 71,118·4. — The Grecian measure of the Pyramid Coffer exceeds that of Greaves by nearly 3 pints, and falls short of that of the Karnak cubit by a little more than 3 pints.

*Table of Grecian Measures of Capacity, according to the Pyramid Coffer.*

| | | | | Cubic Inches. | Nearest English Measures. |
|---|---|---|---|---|---|
| 1 *Cochlearion* | . . . . . = | | | ·288 | |
| 10 *Cochlearia* | = 1 *Cyathus* | = | | 2·88 | |
| 1½ *Cyathi* | = 1 *Oxybaphon* | = | | 4·34 . . | ⅛ Gill. |
| 4 *Oxybapha* | = 1 *Cotyla* | = | | 17·38 . . | ½ Pint. |
| 2 *Cotylæ* | = 1 *Xestes* | = | | 34·77 . . | 1 Pint. |
| 2 *Xesteis* | = 1 *Choenix* | = | | 69·54 . . | 1 Quart. |
| 4 *Chœnices* | = 1 *Hemiecton* | = | | 278·18 . . | 1 Gallon. |
| 2 *Hemiecta* | = 1 *Hecteus* | = | | 556·36 . . | 1 Peck. |
| 6 *Hecteis* | = 1 *Medimnus* | = | | 3,338·16 . . | 6 Pecks. |
| | | | | | |
| 6 *Xesteis* | = 1 *Chous* | = | | 208·62 . . | 6 Pints. |
| 8 *Choes* | = 1 *Ceramion* | = | | 1,668·96 . . | 6 Gallons. |
| 12 *Choes* | = 1 *Metretes** | = | | 2,503·44 . . | 9 Gallons. |
| 60 *Hecteis* | =10 *Medimni* | = | | 33,338·00 . . | 60 Pecks. |

\* Or *Amphoreus.*

In order to bring up these measures to the content of the Pyramid Coffer we must supply the following links : —

|  |  |  | Cubic Inches. | Nearest English Measures. |
|---|---|---|---|---|
| 8 *Hecteis* | = . . . . . | = | 4,450·9 | . . 8 Pecks. |
| 16 „ | = . . . . . | = | 8,901·8 | . . 2 Bushels. |
| 32 „ | = . . . . . | = 17,803·6 | . . 1 Quarter. |
| 64 „ | = . . . . . | = 35,607·2 | . . 1 Coomb. |
| 128 „ | = 1 Coffer | . . = 71,214·4 | . . 1 Chaldron. |

### 103.

*Roman* measures of capacity are closely connected with the Greek, and in general are esteemed the same. The *earlier Roman foot* has been proved, in the former part of this work, to be equal to ·972 of the English foot, or 11·664 English inches. Taking it as equal to 11·66 inches, the cube consists of 1585 cubic inches, which cube is contained 45 times in the capacity of the Pyramid Coffer. The product of this number is 71·325 cubic inches, or the same as the Pyramid measure.

*Table of Roman Measures of Capacity, according to the Pyramid Coffer.*

|  |  |  | Cubic Inches. | Nearest English Measures. |
|---|---|---|---|---|
| 1 Ligula | = . . . . . . | = | ·72 |  |
| 4 Ligulæ | = 1 Cyathus | = | 2·90 | . . ¼ Gill. |
| 1½Cyathi | = 1 Acetabulum | = | 4·35 | . . ½ Gill. |
| 2 Acetabula | = 1 Quartarius | = | 8·70 | . . 1 Gill. |
| 2 Quartarii | = 1 Hemina | = | 17·41 | . . ½ Pint. |
| 2 Heminæ | = 1 Sextarius | = | 34·83 | . . 1 Pint. |
| 8 Sextarii | = 1 Semimodius | = | 278·61 | . . 1 Gallon. |
| 2 Semimodii | = 1 Modius | = | 557·23 | . . 1 Peck. |

|  |  |  |  | Cubic Inches. | Nearest English Measures. |
|---|---|---|---|---|---|
| 6 Sextarii | = 1 Congius | = | 208·95 | . | 6 Pints. |
| 4 Congii | = 1 Urna | = | 835·82 | . . | 3 Gallons. |
| 2 Urnæ | = 1 Amphora* | = | 1,671·65 | . . | 6 Gallons. |
| 20 Amphoræ | = 1 Culeus | = | 33,432·86 | . . | 120 Gallons. |

To bring these measures up to the content of the Pyramid Coffer, we must supply the same links as are in the Greek table, ending with—

| 128 Modii | = 1 Coffer | = 71,325·0 | . . | 1 Chaldron. |
|---|---|---|---|---|

The Roman and Grecian measures of capacity being so nearly the same, the remarks which have been made in the one case will apply equally to the other.

### 104.

*Grecian and Roman Measures of Capacity, according to the Pyramid Coffer, compared with those established by Dr. Hussey, and with the nearest Imperial Measures.*

|  | Pyramid Measures. Cubic Inches. | Dr. Hussey's Measures. Cubic Inches. | Imperial Measures. Cubic Inches. |  |
|---|---|---|---|---|
| G. *Cyathus* | 2·88 ⎫ | | | |
| R. Cyathus | 2.90 ⎬ 2·1468 | .. | 2·166 | |
| G. *Oxybaphon* | 4.34 ⎫ | | | |
| R. Acetabulum | 4·35 ⎬ 4·2937 | .. | 4.332 | .. ½ Gill |
| R. Quartarius | 8·70 | 8·5874 .. | 8·665 | .. 1 Gill |
| G. *Cotyla* | 17·38 ⎫ | | | |
| R. Hemina | 17·41 ⎬ 17·175 | .. | 17·330 | .. ½ Pint |
| G. *Xestes* | 34·77 ⎫ | | | |
| R. Sextarius | 34·83 ⎬ 34.35 | .. | 34·660 | .. 1 Pint |
| G. *Choenix* | 69·54 | 68·70 .. | 69·320 | .. 1 Quart |

\* *Or* Quadrantal.

|  | Pyramid Measures. Cubic Inches. | Dr. Hussey's Measures. Cubic Inches. | Imperial Measures. Cubic Inches. |  |
|---|---|---|---|---|
| G. *Hemiecton* .. | 278·18 | 277·80 .. | 274·274 .. 1 Gallon |  |
| R. Semimodius.. | 278·61 |  |  |  |
| G. *Hecteus* .. | 556·36 | 549·60 .. | 554·548 .. 1 Peck |  |
| R. Modius .. | 557·23 |  |  |  |
| G. *Chous* .. | 208·62 | 206·10 .. | 207.960 |  |
| R. Congius .. | 208·95 |  |  |  |
| R. Urna .. | 835·82 | 824·40 .. | 831·840 |  |
| G. *Ceramion* .. | 1,668·96 | 1,648·80 .. | 1,663·680 |  |
| R. Amphora .. | 1,671·65 |  |  |  |
| G. *Metretes* .. | 2,503·44 | 2,473·51 .. | 2,495·466 |  |
| R. Culeus .. | 33,432·86 | 32,976·00 .. | 33,172·880 |  |
| G. 128 *Hecteis* .. | 71,214·40 | 70,348·80 .. | 70,982·144 | 1 Chal-dron |
| R. 128 Modii .. | 71,325·00 |  |  |  |

The difference in the contents of the *Pyramid Coffer*, and of 128 *Hecteis* or Modii, as estimated by Dr. Hussey, is equal to one part in 73, or 14 English quarts in the chaldron.

The measures in the preceding Table display an extraordinary degree of affinity with each other, if we consider the very different sources from which they are derived. Those in the first column are founded on the contents of the Pyramid Coffer, with which standard, the cube of the Grecian foot, and that of the earlier Roman, are in close connexion. The *later* Roman measures would also approach very nearly to the contents of the Pyramid Coffer, if they were carried out. The foot of 11·636 inches, gives a cube of 1577 inches, which is contained 45 times in the Coffer, when taken as equal to 70,965 cubic inches. The Modius of this measure is equal to 554·4 cubic inches.

The estimates in the second column are based on calculations of a different kind, made by Dr. Hussey,

from the best authorities he could meet with; and,
considering how opposite his plan of proceeding was
from ours, it is remarkable that the results should so
nearly correspond. He makes no distinction between
the Grecian and Roman measures.—The third column
has nothing in common with the two others. It is
founded on a recent determination of the contents of
the English pint measure by the English legislature;
yet it holds a middle place between the measures
obtained from the Pyramid Coffer, and those of which
Dr. Hussey approved. The only way in which we
can account for the harmony of these several numbers,
is that which has been already stated : viz., that they
have all of them had their origin, at various periods of
the world's history, from that most ancient *porphyry
Coffer*, which was *preserved in the King's Chamber of
the Great Pyramid.*

105.

This Vessel, being thus constructed by the founders
of the Great Pyramid and preserved in the King's
Chamber, was recognised by the Hebrew nation as the
standard of all their measures of capacity, or it could
not have happened that the contents of the Pyramid
Coffer would have been equal to *four chomers* of wheat.
The Pyramid Coffer must also have furnished the
standard of all measures of capacity to the earliest
Greek nations as well as the Hebrew, or we should not
have found their foot measure of such a length, that
its cube would contain a space equal to one-tenth the
capacity of the Hebrew chomer; and that *forty* of these
cubes when filled with wheat, would be equal in content to the Pyramid Coffer. From the same cause, also,
it happened, that the Pyramid Coffer contained 128
*hecteis* of wheat, a measure made use of by the Greeks

at a later period. The Romans had respect to the same standard, and hence they made their vessels of capacity for wheat of such a size, that 128 *modii* were equal to the contents in wheat of the Pyramid Coffer.

But no nation, ancient or modern, is so remarkable for having preserved a close agreement with the Pyramid Coffer as our own. First, our *peck* of wheat, like the *hecteus* and modius, is contained 128 times in that Coffer; secondly, 32 of our *bushels* of wheat, or 4 of our *quarters* of wheat, would fill a vessel of that same capacity if we had one still in use; but, thirdly, though a vessel of this capacity is not in existence with us at present, we must have had such a measure in earlier times, since we daily make reference to it; for, when we say 8 bushels of wheat are a *quarter*, we affirm it to be the *fourth part* of some entire measure, which is exactly equal in capacity to the Pyramid Coffer.

This measure was our *chaldron*, in Latin *caldarium*, a *hot bath*; and though our measure was never used as a *bath*, we cannot wonder that such a name was given to the vessel, if it resembled, as it probably did, the *Pyramid Coffer*; for that is made exactly in the form of a *hot bath*. But no other nation, as far as we can ascertain, has ever made use of such a *measure of capacity* besides the English, and given it a *name* so exactly corresponding with that which would be a true description of the Pyramid Coffer. The *laver* of the Scriptures represents the same vessel in size and shape, but it was not used as a *measure of capacity*. The Roman *labrum*, which is the same word as *laver*, was applied to a *bath* in which a person may recline or bathe; as, also, to a *wine-vat*,* but not to a measure of capacity: and,

* *Spumat plenis vindemia labris :*" " the vintage foams in the full vats."—VIRG. GEORG. ii. 6.

probably, in no other country than our own, is the
word *chaldron*, which means a *hot bath* (as the word
*caldron* means an *iron or copper vessel containing hot
water*), retained as the proper term for a *measure of
capacity*, precisely equal to that of the *Pyramid Coffer*.
By these several minute and singular coincidences, the
English nation appears to be more closely identified
with the people who founded the Great Pyramid, than
many of those nations of antiquity, who were apparently
brought into closer contact with Egypt in the earliest
ages.

### 106.

Measures of capacity are the source of measures of
weight. We are able to ascertain what number of *Troy
pounds* are contained in the *Pyramid Coffer*, by taking
the number of Troy pounds in a cubic foot of water,
which, according to the " Table of Constants," is
75·7374000, and multiplying this number by 41·278
the number of cubic feet contained in the Pyramid
Coffer. The quotient is 3126·2884, or 3126 pounds
Troy. There can be no great mistake in this number,
because there has been no dispute at any time as to the
number of Troy grains in the Troy pound; and there
can be none as to the number of pounds in the cubical
contents of the coffer. The above number of 41·278
is also the cube of a palm of the Karnak cubit, which,
in combination with the cube of the English foot
(1728 cubic inches), either as multiplier or multipli-
cand, produces the precise number of cubic inches contained in the coffer, viz., 71,328. In 3128 pounds of
of 5760 grains, there are exactly 18,005,760 grains Troy,
an excess of 1 pound Troy.

H

### Table of the Troy Pound.

Grains.

| | | | | | | | |
|---|---|---|---|---|---|---|---|
| 24 | = | 1 | pennyweight. | | | | |
| 480 | = | 20 | „ | = 1 ounce. | | | |
| 5760 | = | 240 | „ | = 12 | „ | = 1 pound. |

The *pennyweight* is also declared to be equal to 32 *wheat corns of a middling size,* by the old laws of England.

As the Pyramid Coffer contains 18,005,760 Troy grains, or 18,000,000 grains (omitting 5760 grains, equal to 1 pound), so it contains 3125 pounds Troy of 5760 grains. But this is the weight of water. If the coffer were filled with wheat, the weight would be only 2500 pounds, or one-fifth less. Accordingly, 10 pounds Troy of water would occupy the space of 8 pounds Troy of wheat. The coffer was probably intended for a corn measure in the first instance, but it was also found that the same vessel which would hold 2500 pounds of wheat would hold 3125 pounds of water or wine. Hence, any vessel of capacity which would hold 10 pounds of 5760 grains was considered to hold 8 pounds of 7200 grains. This was the original, in all probability, of our *Avoirdupois pound.*

The name of *Avoirdupois* does not appear to have been given to any kind of weight in England earlier than the 9th year of Edward III. It is again mentioned in the 24th year of Henry VIII., when a statute directs "that beef, pork, mutton and veal shall be sold by weight called *Averdupois;*" whence we may infer, that butchers' meat had previously been sold by Troy weight. If there was an older weight which expressed the relation that water was supposed to bear to wheat, when both occupied the same space, viz., that of 5 to 4, or 7200 grains to 5760 grains, no other peculiar name for it has come down to our times.

But there was, from the earliest ages, a different pound from the Troy pound made use of, by which the *merchant* bought his goods; and his profit was obtained by selling them again at the same price in a less pound. This pound was called the *Merchant's Pound*. Its ounce was the same as the Troy ounce of 480 grains, but, instead of 12, it contained 15 ounces. Fleta says, *Quindecim unciæ faciunt libram mercatoriam,* " 15 ounces make the merchants' pound." It was equal, therefore, to 7200 grains Troy; but its object was not to represent the comparative weight of wine and wheat, or water and wheat, but to give an advantage equal to 20 per cent., or *one-fifth* to the merchant, or wholesale buyer, in making his purchases. He *sold* his goods at the *same price per pound* at which he *bought* them, the increment of *three* ounces in *fifteen*, or 20 per cent., being his profit. Further advantages were also given him; as when 112 pounds and 120 pounds were in some cases reckoned to the 100 pounds, on his taking a large quantity. Thus the *Merchants' pound* was a sort of *rough wholesale* pound, in which small amounts were disregarded, these being designed to be given to the merchant; and hence it was that the *Avoirdupois pound,* when it was established, took no cognizance of any weight below a scruple. In goods not weighed, but *counted,* a *larger number* was allowed the merchant at the retail price of the smaller number.

CHAPTER XVI.

*The Pyramid Coffer the Standard of English Measures under Henry III. — Tables of Wine, Corn, and Ale Measures under Henry III. — Alteration of English Measures under Henry VII. — Tables of Corn, Wine, and Ale Measures under Henry VII. — Imperial Measures established in the Reign of George IV. — Tables of Imperial Corn, Wine, and Ale Measures.*

107.

THE following extracts contain the earliest notice of the English measures of capacity for *wine, ale,* and *corn,* which is to be found in our statute books. It commences with Henry III., but is of much greater antiquity.

The 25th chapter of the Great Charter of the 9th of Henry III. (1225) declares, that " *one measure of wine* shall be throughout our realm, and *one measure of ale,* and *one measure of corn*; that is to say, the quarter of London; and one breadth of dyed cloth, that is to say, 2 yards within the lists; and it shall be of weights as it is of measures." A statute of the 51st Henry III. (1266), ordains that " an English *penny,* called a *sterling,* round and without any clipping, shall weigh 32 wheat corns in the midst of the ear, and 20 pence do make an ounce, and 12 ounces do make a pound, and 8 pounds do make a gallon of wine, and 8 gallons of wine do make a London bushel, which is the 8th part of a quarter."

By the first of these statutes, it is declared that only

*one measure* shall be used throughout the realm, for the measure of wine, ale, and corn; and only *one weight* shall be used throughout the realm. By the second, it is ordained that this weight shall be the *troy pound*, because it is said that the penny of this weight shall weigh 32 wheat corns in the midst of the ear, and that 20 pennies do make an ounce, and 12 ounces a pound; which declarations are true only of the Troy pound, and are strictly descriptive of it at the present day. The penny at first was a penny *weight*, or 24 grains Troy.

A "Sterling" (says an old Scots writer) is "ane kind of *weicht* conteining 32 cornes or graines of wheat. The Sterling penny is swa called, because it weyes sa mony graines, as I have sindry times proven by experience."* The grains, he says, should be "without tayles." That the penny-weight is equal to 32 wheat corns is capable of proof at any time. Forty years ago the writer of these pages found it true, and again, within the present year, he has verified it.

When the silver *penny*, which was anciently called a *Sterling*, was made the weight of 22½ grains Troy, there was a possibility that this ordinance might be misunderstood, and that the silver *penny* might be confounded by some with the penny *weight*; but the possible chance of error was soon removed, by the further diminution of the *weight* of the silver *penny*, viz., from 22½ to 22 grains Troy in 1300, to 20¼ grains in 1344, to 20 grains in 1346, to 18 grains in 1351, to 15 grains in 1412, to 12 grains in 1464, to 10½ grains in 1527, to 10 grains in 1543, to 8 grains in 1552, and to 7¾ grains in 1601, after which period, the penny having been reduced to *one third* its original weight, ceased to be issued as a silver coin.

We have evidence, therefore, that 24 grains made

* Skene, *De Verborum Significatione.*

the *penny weight* before the *silver penny* of Henry III.
could have been coined. This weight is preserved in
the *standard* of our silver money, which was composed
of fine silver and alloy as follows : —

> 11 ounces 2 dwts. fine Silver, to 18 dwts. Alloy,

| × 20 dwts. | × 24 grains. |
|---|---|
| 222 | 432   „ |
| × 24 grains. | |
| 5328 | |
| 432 alloy. | |

5760 grains = 1 pound Troy.

Silver of this fineness is called the *old standard of England*, in an ordinance of the year 1300, 28th of Edward I.

Let us now observe what the statute of the 51st of
Henry III says of the *measure* of the gallon of wine,
viz., that it is equal to 8 pounds Troy. It does not
define it further. If the wine were sold in bottles,
a *pound weight of wine* (putting an empty bottle of the
like kind in the opposite scale) would be a *pint of wine*.
If it were sold in any kind of vessel, such as a barrel,
hogshead, butt, or tun, which vessels would contain,
respectively, a certain number of gallons of wine, the
knowledge that each gallon ought to weigh 8 Troy
pounds, would enable the buyer to discover with ease
whether he had got his proper quantity, without the
necessity of *measuring* the contents. Wine, being a
foreign commodity, would always be imported in some
kind of casks or bottles, and hence a measure of *weight*,
and not of quantity would be its proper test.

With corn and ale, the rule would be the opposite.
Here *quantity* would be a better test than weight.
With ale, quantity would be the sole test. With corn,

the buyer might combine both quantity and weight, as he appears to have done, having by this means a double check on the honesty of the vendor. It is perhaps, desirable with regard to wheat, that the measure should again be tested by a reference to *weight* as well as to *quantity*.

The statute next declares that 8 gallons of wine do make a London bushel. Here is a transition made from weight to quantity, on account of the different nature of the two articles, wine and wheat. A vessel to contain as much wheat as would be equal in weight to 8 gallons of wine, must be *one-fourth larger* to make the requisite counterpoise. The bushel, therefore, must hold 64 pounds Troy of wheat; and to do that, it must be capable of holding 80 pounds Troy of water. But there is to be only *one measure* for wheat and for ale, the consequence of which must be that 8 gallons of ale will be found to weigh one-fourth more than 8 gallons of wine, since this quantity of ale will fill a measure one-fourth larger than that which would contain 8 gallons of wine. Ale, being an article of home production, is more conveniently sold by measure than by weight, and does not require the double check that wheat does, its quality not being capable of estimation by weight.

The provisions of these statutes of the 9th and 51st of Henry III. are very simple, and concisely expressed; but they were perfectly effectual unto the purpose for which, "by the consent of the whole realm of England, the measure of the king was made." A vast deal of ingenuity has since been employed to make obscure what common sense had made so plain; but the nation is now endeavouring to return to more correct principles; and by a recent act of the legislature a great improvement has been effected.

## 108.

*Table of the Weights of the various Wine Measures of Henry* III.

|  |  |  |  | In Troy Pounds. |
|---|---|---|---|---|
| 1 Pint . . . . . = | | | | 1 |
| 2 Pints | = | 1 Quart | = | 2 |
| 4 Quarts | = | 1 Gallon | = | 8 |
| 63 Gallons | = | 1 Hogshead | = | 504 |
| 84 Gallons | = | 1 Tertian | = | 672 |
| 126 Gallons | = | 1 Pipe or Butt | = | 1,008 |
| 252 Gallons | = | 1 Tun | = | 2,016 |

*Table of the Capacity of the various Corn and Ale Measures of Henry* III.

| CORN MEASURES OF HENRY III. | | | In Cubic Inches. | The same Measures in Cubic Inches, compared with the Pyramid Coffer. | |
|---|---|---|---|---|---|
| | | | | By the Karnak Cubit. | By Greaves' Measure. |
| 1 Pint . . . . | = | | 35·0 | 34·8 | 34·725 |
| 2 Pints | = 1 Quart | = | 70·0 | 69·6 | 69·450 |
| 4 Quarts | = 1 Gallon | = | 280·0 | 278·6 | 277·800 |
| 2 Gallons | = 1 Peck | = | 560·0 | 557.2 | 555·600 |
| 4 Pecks | = 1 Bushel | = | 2,240·0 | 2,229·0 | 2,222·450 |
| 8 Bushels | = 1 Quarter | = | 17,920·0 | 17,832·2 | 17,779·600 |
| 4 Quarters | = 1 Chaldron | = | 71,680·0 | 71,328·8 | 71,118·400 |

| ALE MEASURES OF HENRY III. | | | In Cubic Inches. | The same Measures in Cubic Inches, compared with the Pyramid Coffer. | |
|---|---|---|---|---|---|
| | | | | By the Karnak Cubit. | By Greaves' Measure. |
| 1 Pint . . . . | = | | 35·0 | 34·8 | 34·725 |
| 2 Pints | = 1 Quart | = | 70·0 | 69·6 | 69·450 |
| 4 Quarts | = 1 Gallon | = | 280·0 | 278·6 | 277·800 |
| 8 Gallons | = 1 Firkin | = | 2,240·0 | 2,229·0 | 2,222·450 |
| 4 Firkins | = 1 Barrel | = | 8,960·0 | 8,916·1 | 8,889·800 |
| 4 Barrels | = 1 Hogshead | = | 35,840·0 | 35,664·4 | 35,559·200 |
| 8 Barrels | = 2 Hogsheads | = | 71,680·0 | 71,328·8 | 71,118·400 |

By a statute of the 2nd year of Henry VI. (1424), a tun of wine is declared to contain 252 gallons, a pipe 126 gallons, a tertian 84 gallons, and a hogshead 63 gallons.  But at a subsequent period, the vessel which is here called a *tertian* was called a *puncheon,* and the name of *tertian* or *tierce* was given to a vessel containing the third part of a *pipe* or butt, viz. 42 gallons.

In all other respects, the standard remained in use which had been established in the reign of Henry III., according to the preceding Tables.  There was only one measure of weight and one measure of capacity acknowledged throughout the realm.  The weight was 8 pounds Troy for the gallon of wine.  The measure also contained 8 pounds Troy of wheat ; but the same measure of capacity contained 10 pounds Troy of ale. The corn bushel contained 64 pounds Troy, the bushel being heaped to make up that weight, if in any case the measure of capacity fell short of it.  For two centuries this rule had been observed, without any attempt being made to depart from it ; and certainly it was well calculated to give satisfaction to the whole kingdom.

### 109.

In the 15th century, a change took place in the standards of weight and capacity, which had been preserved from the earliest times, and had been confirmed by the statutes of Henry III. and Henry VI.  It was a change which the people did not call for ; and for what purpose it was made no one seems to have known or cared, nor has it ever been explained.  The cause of it was an ordinance of the 11th year of Henry VII. (1433), which appointed " 8 bushels *rased and stricken* to the quarter of corn."* Another statute of the following year ordered, " that the measure of a bushel contain 8 gallons of wheat, and that every gallon contain 8 pounds of wheat of Troy weight, and every pound 12 ounces of Troy weight, and every ounce 20 sterlings, and every sterling be of the weight of 32 corns of wheat, that grew in the midst of the ear of wheat, according to the old laws of the land." The *sterling* here mentioned is of course the *pennyweight*, for the silver penny of that time weighed only 15 grains Troy. The pound is the Troy pound.

The actual innovation was made by the substitution of the 8 bushels *rased and stricken* for the bushels which had not been before so treated. By this enactment, the ordinance of the following year was controlled, which provided, " that the measure of a bushel contain 8 gallons of wheat, and that every gallon contain 8 pounds of wheat of Troy weight:" for if the *measure* was thus *stricken,* the *weight* must have been subordinated to the *measure,* whereas, before that time, the *measure* was governed by the *weight.*

By means of the expressions " *rased and stricken,*" we are introduced to a new measure of capacity, called a *strike.* " To *rase,*" says Johnson, " is to *skim,* to *strike on the surface ;*" and as applied to the bushel of wheat, it would take away all that portion of corn which constituted the *heaped* measure. A *strike,* therefore, by reducing the measure of corn to the level of the brim of the bushel, might be expected to make some considerable change in the weight of the bushel. By the following Tables it will be seen, that the strike of wheat contained only 62 pounds Troy, while the old bushel

* Statutes at large.

contained 64 pounds; that is, the strike constituted a measure less by one *thirty-second* part than the previous bushel; for if we reduce the cubic inches in the gallon (280·0) in that proportion, the measure will contain only 272·0 cubic inches; and the Winchester gallon in the following Table contains only 272·08 inches.

## 110.

*Table of Winchester Corn Measures under Henry* VII.

| | | | | In Cubic Inches. |
|---|---|---|---|---|
| 1 Gill | | . . . . . | = | 8·5 |
| 4 Gills | = | 1 Pint | = | 34·01 |
| 2 Pints | = | 1 Quart | = | 68·02 |
| 4 Quarts | = | 1 Gallon | = | 272·08 |
| 2 Gallons | = | 1 Peck | = | 544·16 |
| 4 Pecks | = | 1 Bushel | = | 2,176·64 |
| 4 Bushels | = | 1 Coomb | = | 8,706·56 |
| 2 Coombs | = | 1 Quarter | = | 17,413·12 |
| 4 Quarters | = | 1 Chaldron | = | 69,652·48 |

*Table of Wine Measures under Henry* VII.

| | | | | In Cubic Inches. |
|---|---|---|---|---|
| 1 Gill | | . . . . . . | = | 7·219 |
| 4 Gills | = | 1 Pint | = | 28·875 |
| 2 Pints | = | 1 Quart | = | 57·750 |
| 4 Quarts | = | 1 Gallon | = | 231·000 |
| 42 Gallons | = | 1 Tierce | = | 9,702·000 |
| 63 Gallons | = | 1 Hogshead | = | 14,553·000 |
| 84 Gallons | = | 1 Puncheon | = | 19,404·000 |
| 126 Gallons | = | 1 Pipe or Butt | = | 29,106·000 |
| 252 Gallons | = | 1 Tun | = | 58,212·000 |

*Table of Ale Measures under Henry* VII.

|  |  |  |  |  |  | In Cubic Inches. |
|---|---|---|---|---|---|---|
| 1 | Gill |  | . . . . . | = | 8·75 |
| 4 | Gills | = | 1 Pint | = | 35·01 |
| 2 | Pints | = | 1 Quart | = | 70·02 |
| 4 | Quarts | = | 1 Gallon | = | 280·08 |
| 8 | Gallons | = | 1 Firkin | = | 2,240·64 |
| 2 | Firkins | = | 1 Kilderkin | = | 4,481·28 |
| 2 | Kilderkins | = | 1 Barrel | = | 8,962·56 |
| 1½ | Barrels | = | 1 Hogshead | = | 13,443·84 |
| 2 | Barrels | = | 1 Puncheon | = | 17,925·12 |
| 3 | Barrels | = | 1 Butt | = | 26,887·68 |
| 2 | Butts | = | 1 Tun | = | 53,775·36 |
| 8 | Barrels | = | 4 Puncheons | = | 71,700·48 |

From these Tables it will be seen, that while the Winchester *corn* gallon was reduced in contents one *thirty-second*, the *wine* gallon of the same system was increased in capacity just as much, or one part in *thirty-one*. The proper gallon for wine ought to have been equal only to 224 cubic inches, but it was increased to 231. Yet, strange to say, this contradiction between theory and practice excited no notice; and when, in 1688, the Commissioners of Excise memorialised the Lords of the Treasury, stating that the true standard wine gallon ought to contain, and did contain, only 224 cubical inches, whereas the statute measure was 231, Sir Thomas Powis, the Attorney-General, replied, that "he did not know how 231 cubical inches came to be taken up; but he did not think it safe to depart from the usage." The question which was then raised, on account of the excise and customs' duties, was not set at rest till an act passed in the fifth year of Queen Anne, confirming the statute.

The ale measures in the above table underwent no alteration; nor was the bushel for other articles (as coals) reduced to the size of the Winchester corn bushel.

### 111.

In consequence of the great diversity of the several measures of capacity under the preceding system,—the wine measure differing from the ale measure, and the corn measure differing from both,—a Select Committee on Weights and Measures was appointed, in the first year of the reign of George IV., to investigate the subject. In their report, dated May, 1821, they say — " Your Committee are, on the whole, induced to believe that the *gallon of England was originally identical for all uses*; and that the variations have arisen, in some cases, from *accident*, and in others, from *fraud*." They then recommend " that the pint be considered as equal in bulk to 20 ounces of distilled water, at the temperature of 62°, the cubic inch weighing 252·456 grains in air, at the mean height of the barometer;" under which circumstances, "the imperial gallon will contain 277·276 cubic inches, weighing exactly 10 pounds *avoirdupois*." Founded on this report, an act was passed in the 5th of George IV., by which a uniform system of weights and measures was established, under the denomination of IMPERIAL WEIGHTS and MEASURES ; and their use was enforced under severe penalties.

This system has for its basis, or primary unit, the *imperial gallon*, which contains 277·274 cubic inches. It is declared by the statute, that such imperial standard gallon shall be the only standard measure of capacity for wine, beer, and all sorts of liquids, and for such dry goods as are measured like liquids and not heaped ; and that from this all other measures shall be derived.

When heaped measure is used, it is declared that the bushel shall contain 80 pounds avoirdupois, being made cylindrical, and having a diameter not less than double its depth; that the goods measured shall be heaped in the form of a cone, the height of which shall be at least three-fourths of the depth of the measure; and that the outside of the bushel shall be the extremity of the base of the cone. Three such bushels shall be a sack, and 12 sacks a chaldron. The contents of the imperial heaped bushel amount to 2,815·4887 cubic inches.

The avoirdupois pound here mentioned is the avoirdupois pound of 7000 grains, of which pounds 144 are equal to 175 Troy pounds. The difference between the two pounds is supposed to represent the relative weights of water and wheat. Accordingly, the imperial gallon, which contains 277·274 cubic inches, and holds 10 avoirdupois pounds of water, wine, or ale, will hold but 8 avoirdupois pounds, or 10 Troy pounds of wheat.

## 112.

*Table of Imperial Corn Measures (George IV.), compared with those of the Pyramid Coffer by Greaves's Measure* *

|  |  |  | Imperial. Cubic Inches. | Greaves's Measure. Cubic Inches. |
|---|---|---|---|---|
| 1 Gill | . . . . . . | | 8·665 | 8·681 |
| 4 Gills | = | 1 Pint | 34·659 | 34·725 |
| 2 Pints | = | 1 Quart | 69·319 | 69·450 |
| 4 Quarts | = | 1 Gallon | 277·274 | 277·800 |
| 2 Gallons | = | 1 Peck | 554·548 | 555·600 |
| 4 Pecks | = | 1 Bushel | 2,218·192 | 2,222·450 |
| 4 Bushels | = | 1 Coomb | 8,872·768 | 8,889·800 |
| 2 Coombs | = | 1 Quarter | 17,745·536 | 17,779·600 |
| 4 Quarters | = | 1 Chaldron | 70,982·144 | 71,118·400 |

* The measure of the Pyramid Coffer, according to the Karnak cubit, is 71,328 cubic inches for the chaldron, and 69·66 cubic inches for the *quart*.

*Table of Imperial Wine Vessels (George* IV.).

|  | Contents iu Cubic Inches. | Contents in Imperial Gallons. |
|---|---|---|
| 1 Tierce . . . | 9,702 | 34·99066 |
| 1 Hogshead . . | 14,553 | 52·48599 |
| 1 Puncheon . . | 19,404 | 69·98132 |
| 1 Pipe or Butt . . | 29,106 | 104·97198 |
| 1 Tun . . . | 58,212 | 209·94396 |

*Table of Imperial Ale Vessels (George* IV.).

|  |  |  | Contents in Cubic Inches. | Contents in Imperial Gallons. |
|---|---|---|---|---|
| 8 Gallons | = | 1 Firkin | 2,218·192 | 8 |
| 2 Firkins | = | 1 Kilderkin | 4,436·384 | 16 |
| 2 Kilderkins | = | 1 Barrel | 8,872·768 | 32 |
| 1½ Barrels | = | 1 Hogshead | 13,309·152 | 48 |
| 2 Hogsheads | = | 1 Butt | 26,618·304 | 96 |
| 2 Butts | = | 1 Tun | 53,236·608 | 192 |
| 8 Barrels | = | 1 Pyramid Coffer | 70,982·144 | 256 |

The imperial gallon, in comparison with the Winchester *corn* gallon of 272·08 cubic inches, adds to it *one part in thirty-one.* The same gallon, in comparison with the corresponding *wine* gallon of 231 cubic inches, adds to it *one part in five;* and the same gallon, in comparison with the corresponding *ale* gallon of 282 cubic inches, reduces it *one part in sixty.*

But, in comparison with the gallon for corn and ale, previous to the statute of Henry VII., the imperial gallon reduces it not quite *one part in a hundred.*

The difference between the contents of the *imperial chaldron* and the contents of the *Pyramid Coffer,* as measured by Greaves, is only 136·256 cubic inches, rather less than four imperial pints. In comparison with the Pyramid Coffer, according to the Karnak cubit, the difference is 346·656 cubic inches, or 10 pints.

Thus the old corn measure, which had been departed from for nearly three centuries and a half, was restored *very nearly*; and, as if we were conscious that we had infringed a standard of great antiquity, which had been long preserved, we returned to that measure (within *one hundredth part*) which had been adopted originally from the coffer in the Great Pyramid. But it is to be regretted that the ancient Troy pound was superseded by what is called the avoirdupois pound, which is of recent date in its present form, and which was, at first, nothing more than an *accommodation pound*, dependent on the Troy pound, and established only for merchants' use.

## Chapter XVII.

*English Weights derived from English Measures — Table of the Weight of Imperial Measures — Hebrew Weights derived from Hebrew Measures — Tables of the Weight of Hebrew Measures — Difference in Hebrew Weights before and after the Captivity.*

### 113.

IN the course of this inquiry into the origin of measures of capacity and weight, we have taken occasion to remark that measures of capacity were founded on measures of length, and that measures of weight were founded on measures of capacity. Even in our own age and country, the same principles have been acted upon. From the measure of an inch in length a hollow vessel is now constructed, containing a cubic inch of space; and in the capacity of this vessel, when it is filled with distilled water, at the temperature of 62° Fahrenheit, is found the weight of 252·458 grains Troy. By this weight we regulate all our pounds and ounces. The founders of the Great Pyramid acted on the same principle, but with greater wisdom, when they constructed a large vessel in the shape of an oblong double cube, whose contents should be equal to the cubic inches of space contained in a cube of their *largest* (not as we have done, their *smallest*) measure of length; which space, when it was filled with wheat, they declared to be equal to 2500 pounds in weight, each pound being equal to 5760 grains Troy.

By using so small a vessel as one containing a cubic inch of space, we are forced to be very minute and exact in our proceedings; and few persons, therefore, are competent to construct for themselves, or to verify, our measures of capacity and weight. We are compelled to make use of distilled water, at a certain temperature, on account of this great need of exactness. The ancients made use of rain water, which served their purpose equally well, though from its change of temperature, at different seasons and in different places, there might be a little variation. The consequence of this refinement is, that our modern measures are not quite equal to those of an earlier day, even when they profess to resemble them. Greaves says — " The proportion the rain water hath to fountain water is as 1,000,000 to 1,007,522 ; and the proportion that it hath to water *distilled* is as 1,000,000 to 997,065, as it hath been observed by *Snellius*." *   In 1685, the weight of a cubic foot of spring water was found, by an experiment made at Oxford, to be precisely 1000 ounces avoirdupois. In the "Table of Constants," it is declared, on the other hand, that the weight of a cubic foot of distilled water, at the temperature of 62° Fahrenheit, is only 997·1369 ounces, thereby verifying Greaves's remark.

Whether the Pyramid Coffer was intended to be a measure of capacity for *wine* as well as wheat may be doubted. Judging from our own practice in the earliest times, we should infer that its founders were not likely to consider it a measure for wine, but that they would make the test of the *weight* of wine by the Troy pound supply the place of a measure, as we did in the reign of Henry III., and as probably other nations did in former

* Of the Denarius, p. 299, note.

times. It was as easy and as natural for the most ancient people in the world, to determine by the *weight* of the Troy pound the quantity of wine contained in their leathern bottles, as it was for us to ascertain by the same test the quantity contained in our glass bottles. In general we may conclude, that all commodities which are usually conveyed in bottles, casks, chests, or baskets, and which cannot be unpacked and subjected to measure without liability to waste in *quantity* or injury in *quality*, are more properly tested as to quantity by *weight* than by measure, making allowance for the *tare*; and as wine is peculiarly exposed to loss or detriment from being measured, it must in all ages have been more likely to be subjected to the test of *weight* than that of measure.

*Table of the Weights of the Imperial Measures of George* IV.

|  |  | Cubic Inches. | Troy Pounds. Wheat. | Avoirdupois Pounds. Wine. | Wheat. |
|---|---|---|---|---|---|
| Pint | = | 34·659 | 1¼ | 1¼ | 1 |
| Quart | = | 69·319 | 2½ | 2½ | 2 |
| Gallon | = | 277·274 | 10 | 10 | 8 |
| Peck | = | 554·548 | 20 | 20 | 16 |
| Bushel | = | 2,218·192 | 80 | 80 | 64 |
| Coomb | = | 8,872·768 | 320 | 320 | 256 |
| Quarter | = | 17,745·536 | 640 | 640 | 512 |
| Chaldron | = | 70,982·144 | 2,560 | 2,560 | 2,048 |

From the above Table, it would be difficult to discover what advantage we have gained by substituting the Avoirdupois pound for the Troy pound.

## 114.

In theory, it might be expected that *Hebrew weights* would be derived from *Hebrew measures of capacity* : let us now see whether this was practically the case. We find that Dr. Hussey commences his chapter on Hebrew weights by remarking: " Hitherto, while we have been engaged with the Greeks and the Romans, the difficulty has been to choose between the results calculated from different data, and to decide which was most probable where several were plausible: but, in the case of the Hebrews, we labour under *a want of data altogether.* There is no certain method of obtaining an absolute value of any one element, from which a system of values may be calculated, for the period before the captivity of the Jews. No weights, coins, or measures of that age exist; and we must have recourse tò probable inference or conjecture for determining the value of all."*

Under these circumstances, the possibility of an appeal to a standard established more than a thousand years before the Jews were carried into captivity becomes a matter of immense importance, and brings at once to an issue the claims we have advanced on behalf of that ancient standard. If it should enable us further to follow up the discoveries we have made of the cubical contents of the Hebrew measures of capacity, by shew-ing that these contents are in accordance with certain measures of weight also, the value of our standard will be doubly confirmed, and every degree of certainty will be introduced into a discussion which has not hitherto possessed a single fact on which any reliance could be placed.

### 115.

The following statement will, after the acknowledg-ment made by Dr. Hussey, be read with equal pleasure

* Essay on Ancient Weights, &c., chap. xi.

and surprise. The cubical contents of the severa
measures are copied from the Table of Hebrew Measures of Capacity given in our former article. The
value in Troy grains of each measure is calculated from
the weight of the same in relation to a cubic inch of
distilled water.*

*Table of the Contents and Weights of Hebrew Measures
of Capacity.*

| | | Contents in Cubic Inches. | | Weight in Troy Grains. | |
|---|---|---|---|---|---|
| 1 Log | = | 24·8 | . | 6,250 | . | (6,260·9) |
| 1 Cab | = | 99·1 | . | 25,000 | . | (25,043) |
| 1 Hin | = | 297·2 | . | 75,000 | . | (75,130) |
| 1 Seah | = | 594·4 | . | 150,000 | . | (150,261) |
| 1 Bath or Epha | = | 1,783·2 | . | 450,000 | . | (450,784) |
| 1 Lethekh | = | 8,916·0 | . | 2,250,000 | . | (2,253,924) |
| 1 Chomer | = | 17,832·2 | . | 4,500,000 | . | (4,507,848) |
| 120 Seahs or 4 Chomers | = | 71,328·8 | . | 18,000,000 | . | (18,031,392) |

The Bath or Epha, according to this Table, contains
1,000 ounces of 450 grains Troy. " The epha or bath,"
says Dr. Cumberland, " contains just 1,000 ounces avoirdupois, or 2,000 shekels weight of pure rain-water." The
avoirdupois ounce, however, contains only 437·5 grains.
But by Dr. Cumberland's calculation of the contents of
the epha, which he makes equal to 1,747 cubic inches
(though he admits that it ought not to exceed 1,728
inches) his ounce is raised to 440 grains (p. 69). His
principle, notwithstanding, is correct, when he says,

* Estimated in distilled water at 252·458 grains Troy to the
cubic inch, the log is equal to 6,260·9 grains, and the 4 chomers
are equal to 18,031,392 grains. There are 2,500 pounds of 7,200
grains in 18,000,000, which is no doubt the correct number.

" that the ancients determined their vessels of capacity by weight of water. So the Roman *congius* held just 10 pounds of water, and that of rain; as Dioscorides hath noted : their amphora 80 such pounds, their sextary 20 ounces. And 't is certain (says the bishop), that the reckoning of weights by round numbers of shekels, or their *double*, which are *ounces*, is most ancient."

The shekel of the Sanctuary was an ounce; and by our standard of the Pyramid Coffer it was an ounce of 450 grains. The half-shekel was called a *beka* (Exod. xxxviii. 26), and this weighed 225 grains. The fourth part of the shekel is mentioned in 1 Sam. ix. 18; its weight would be 11·25 grains. There was also a weight called a *gerah*, 20 of which were equal to the shekel of the Sanctuary; its weight, therefore, was 22½ grains.

These weights were, after the captivity, reduced one-half, and the shekel was then called the *profane* or *common shekel*. It weighed, according to our standard, 225 grains, and the rest of the measures were reduced in proportion.

### Table of Hebrew Weights before the Captivity.

Grains
| | | | | | | |
|---|---|---|---|---|---|---|
| 22½ = | 1 Gerah | | | | | |
| 112·5 = | 5 | „ | = 1 Reba (or one-fourth) | | | |
| 225· = | 10 | „ | = 2 | „ | = 1 Beka (or one-half) | |
| 450 = | 20 | „ | = 4 | „ | = 2 | „ = 1 Shekel |
| 1,350,000 . . . . . . . 3,000 „ = 1 Kikkar or Talent | | | | | | |

### Table of Hebrew Weights after the Captivity.

| Grains. | | By Dr. Hussey's Estimate. |
|---|---|---|
| 11·25 = 1 Gerah . . . . . | | 10·94 |
| 56·25 = 5 „ = 1 Reba . . . . | | 54·71 |
| 112·5 = . . . 2 „ = 1 Beka . . | | 109·43 |
| 225·0 = . . . . . 2 „ = 1 Shekel | | 218·86 |
| 675,000· = 3,000 Shekels = 1 Kikkar. . . | | 656,580·00 |

" It has always been a common opinion," says Dr.
Hussey, " that there was more than one standard of
weight for the shekel. The universal tradition among the
Jewish writers is, that there were two standards, that of
the *sanctuary* and the *royal*, or, as it is called in opposition
to the former, the *profane*; and that the former of these
was just *double* the latter." Accordingly, he concludes
" that the Hebrews, before the captivity, had more than
one standard of weight;" but, at the same time, he
observes, " that the proportion between the standard
shekel of the sanctuary and any other is uncertain.
That commonly assigned, namely, 2 to 1, rests on no
certain authority. It is probable enough; for some
countries in that part of the world are said to have had
similar systems, bearing that ratio to each other, as Tyre
and Alexandria; and two such are described as having
been used in Egypt alone; but it wants proof" (p. 183).
Having made these statements, Dr. Hussey gives " a
Table of Hebrew Weights *before the Captivity*, according
to the Standard of the Sanctuary," which table contains his estimate, as it is embodied in our *second* table.
Thus Dr. Hussey appears to have thought the shekel of
218·86 grains was the shekel of the sanctuary. He then
concludes with these words : — " There are no satisfactory means of calculating the value of any other
standard, since different proportions are assigned, each
with some degree of probability; and, therefore, we
must be content to confess, that in all the expressions
of weight or value, where other shekels are used than
those of the sanctuary, we can only conjecture their
real value." The result is, that the estimates which he
has given above, as those only on which reliance can be
placed for the weight of the shekel of the sanctuary

*before the captivity*, are those which belong to the period *after the captivity*.

By the evidence of the contents of the Pyramid Coffer, all these errors and doubts are removed. It is satisfactorily established, 1. That the epha, or bath, contained 1000 ounces (not of 437·5 grains, as Dr. Cumberland supposed, but) of 450 grains; the old Hebrew ounce, if we may so call it, since it is the weight it had in the time of Solomon.

2. That 500 years before this, the shekel of the sanctuary weighed 450 grains, even in the time of Moses, when the atonement-money of the children of Israel was fixed at half a shekel, which all were to pay. "The rich shall not give more, and the poor shall not give less than half a shekel, when they give an offering unto the Lord, to make an atonement for your souls" (Exod. xxx. 15).

3. That, earlier still, the 400 shekels of silver weighed each an ounce (of 450 grains), when Abraham, 350 years before the time of Moses, "weighed to Ephron the silver which he had named in the audience of the sons of Heth, silver current with the merchant, for the field of Ephron, which was in Machpelah, which was before Mamre, the field, and the cave which was therein, and all the trees that were in the field, that were in all the borders round about." The value of that weight of silver (silver being then considered in general worth one-tenth its weight in gold), at 8s. per ounce, was £160 in our money. It may be inferred that Abraham brought this silver out of Egypt about sixty years before, when he returned from that country " very rich in cattle, in silver, and in gold."

4. The weight of the shekel of the sanctuary being

equal to 450 grains, corroborates the opinion of those
Jews who state that the gerah, before the captivity, was
the weight of 32 grains of barley. "Basnage," says
Dr. Hussey, "computed the shekel to weigh 262·4
grains (Troy); this was from the Jewish tradition of
the weight of the gerah in grains of barley. Basnage
then ascertained the weight of that number of grains
of barley in France, and thence inferred the weight of
the shekel. It is really surprising," Dr. Hussey continues, "that any one can seriously have recourse to so
deceitful an experiment, as weighing a few small seeds
in one country, in order to calculate from them a
system of weights used in a different country." Yet,
if Dr. Hussey had weighed these small seeds, as they
are found in England, which any one could have supplied him with, he would have come nearer the weight
of the shekel of the sanctuary than when he reckoned
it at 218·86 grains Troy. We have had 32 grains of
barley, of English growth, weighed this year, taking
those of middling size only, and they are equal to 22
grains Troy. The weight of the gerah was 22½ grains.
It may be deemed a remarkable coincidence; but the
nearness of this weight to its supposed original would
have shown Dr. Hussey that his weight of 10·94 grains
Troy for the gerah, which he allows to be purely con-
jectural, as being founded on "some coins of an age
later than the captivity," was much less worthy of
regard than that of this barley standard.

Nor is it unreasonable, that by the weight of a few
small seeds grown in one country, a system of weights
should be calculated for the use of a different country.
Founded on this natural standard are the Cologne
weights, which are used throughout all Germany in
weighing gold and silver: 32 *Es*, equal to our wheat

corns, make an *Englisch,* which is our pennyweight; and the ounce is identical with our old tower ounce, each consisting of 450 grains Troy.*

The shekel, as a certain *weight* of silver, was equal to an ounce of 450 grains, in which form, or as a half-ounce, or beka, it was employed by the Hebrews in the time of Moses. Afterwards, the gerah, as Maimonides† informs us, weighed only 16 grains of barley, and the shekel was only half its former weight. Later still, among the Greeks and Romans, the shekel represented only the fourth part of an ounce. "Apud Græcos et Latinos, *Sicel* est quarta pars unciæ, et stateris medietas, drachmas appendens duas: apud Hebræos vero est unciæ pondus." "Siclus, apud Hebræos moneta notissima; uncia apud Hebræos: apud Latinos quarta pars unciæ." ‡

As a certain *weight* of silver, and not as a coin, the shekel was used by the early Hebrews: as a coin only, it passed current for a less weight, and ultimately for a quarter of an ounce. Now, as some have thought, that coin had its origin as an *instrument of taxation,* the Jews, whose payments to the Sanctuary were made by weight, were probably unacquainted with the shekel as a *coin* till after the captivity, because they were previously free from taxation by the state.

Another weight is sometimes mentioned as being in use among the Jews, the *maneh.* It was the same as the *mina* of the Greeks and Romans, and represented a hundred silver coins, each of a certain weight. We find the *maneh* mentioned in 1 Kings x. 16, where it is

* Clarke's Connexion of Roman, Saxon, and English Coins, 4to., p. 24.

† On Valuations, cap. i. sec. 4.

‡ Du Cange, vol. vii. p. 478.

said : " King Solomon made 200 targets of beaten gold :
600 [shekels] of gold went to one target. And he made
300 shields of beaten gold : 3 pound [maneh] of gold
went to one shield." In the corresponding passage
from 2 Chron. ix. 16, we are told, that 300 [shekels] of
gold went to one shield. Thus a maneh, or pound, was
equal in weight to 100 of some coins, which are called
shekels by our translators ; but perhaps they were not
properly so called, since the name is not inserted in the
Hebrew text. Whatever they were, they are more like
the profane shekel in weight than the shekel of the
sanctuary.

We meet with some further information concerning
the maneh and its weight in Ezekiel xlv. 12. The
prophet is foretelling, in terms taken from the history
of his people, the future glories of the church ; and
having said, " Ye shall have just balances, and a just
epha, and a just bath," he adds, " and the shekel shall
be twenty gerahs : twenty shekels, five and twenty
shekels, fifteen shekels, shall be your maneh." When,
in this place, he tells the people that the shekel shall
be 20 gerahs, he means, perhaps, that it shall be
restored to its original weight of an ounce ; but when
he further informs them that 60 shekels shall be their
*maneh*, he apparently intends to make known to them
that 60 of those shekels would in weight be equal to
100 of such silver coins (called, probably, shekels also)
as they were then accustomed to reckon in their *maneh*.
Now, as 60 shekels of 450 grains are equal to 100 silver
coins of 270 grains each, we may learn incidentally
from this allusion to their chief current money, what
its weight and value then was. The coin was a *tetradrachm*, weighing about 270 grains. Of these coins, we
have the following account given us in the treatise of

Mr. John Greaves on the Denarius : " Weighing many *Attick tetradrachmes*, with the image of *Pallas* on the fore part, and of the *noctua* [owl] on the reverse, I find the best of these to be 268 grains; that is, each particular drachme 67 grains." * To this may be subjoined the testimony of Bishop Hooper, by which the Attick tetradrachm is connected with the Jewish shekel : " It is positively affirmed by *Philo* in Claudius's time, that the shekel of the Hebrews was equal to the tetradrachm of the Athenians. Josephus likewise explains the shekel by four Attick drachmas. Neither is he to be surmised, though living under Domitian, to have reckoned by a lighter drachma than Philo." † The Septuagint interpreters are added as an authority, whose " translation was certainly made above 200 years before our Saviour, and when the drachma of Athens may be rated at 65 grains at least. Neither is it necessary to think that they reckoned by the common current didrachm of their time ; but rather likely, that they respected the standard given not long before by *Alexander*, which may be justly rated at 67 grains, if not higher than 68·4, as it was suspected by me upon another occasion."† The tetradrachms, or shekels, which were alluded to by Ezekiel as constituting the *maneh* of his time, were of an age two centuries and a half anterior to the reign of Alexander, and, therefore, less likely to be diminished in weight than those of a later period here referred to.

But if we assume that the shekel which Ezekiel said should be 20 gerahs meant the profane and not the sacred shekel, its weight, in that case, would be 225 grains, and the silver coin, of which 100 made the

* Greaves's Works, p. 262.
† Dr. Hooper's Inquiry, pp. 190 & 192.

maneh, would weigh only 135 grains. This was a *didrachm*. The Attic drachma weighed about 66·5 grains, according to Dr. Hussey, who says, " It may be concluded, that the legal weight of Solon's currency was 66·5 grains, which continued in use till Athens lost her independence" (p. 22). In many of the early coins quoted by Dr. Hussey, the weight of the tetradrachm was not less than 270 grains, and the drachma, therefore, was 67·5 grains, belonging to a system of weight of which the ounce would be equal to 450 grains, and the pound to 7200 grains.

## Chapter XVIII.

*Grecian Weights derived from Grecian Measures — Table of the
Weight of Grecian Measures — Roman Weights derived from
Roman Measures — Table of the Weight of Roman Measures —
Various Weights of the Congius according to different Authori-
ties — Exact Weight of the Roman Pound — Table of the
Roman Commercial and Monetary Pound.*

### 116.

WE have seen, when we were regarding the Pyramid
Coffer as a standard of Grecian measures of
capacity, that the cube of the Grecian foot of 12·12
inches English contained 1780·36 cubic inches; and
that this number multiplied by 40 is equal to 71,214·4
cubic inches, about three pints less than the contents of
the Coffer, according to the measure of the Karnak
cubit. This cube of the Grecian foot contains 1000
ounces of 450 Troy grains in weight, 16 ounces forming
the Grecian pound (in distilled water, the ounce would
be equal to 449·466 grains).

*Table of the Weights of Grecian Measures of Capacity.*

| | Contents in Cubic Inches. | | | Weight in Troy Grains. | | | Weight in Mensural Ounces. |
|---|---|---|---|---|---|---|---|
| Cyathus · | 2·88 | . | . | 549·3 | . | . | 1¼ |
| Oxybaphon . | 4·34 | . | . | 1,098·6 | . | . | 2½ |
| Cotyla . | 17·38 | . | . | 4,394·5 | . | . | 10 |
| Xestes . | 34·77 | . | . | 8,789·0 | . | . | 20 |
| Choenix . | 69·54 | . | . | 17,578·0 | . | . | 40 |
| Chous . | 208·62 | . | . | 52,734·0 | . | . | 120 |
| Hemiecton . | 278·18 | . | . | 70,312·5 | . | . | 160 |
| Hecteus . | 556·36 | . | . | 140,625·0 | . | . | 320 |
| Ceramion . | 1,668·96 | . | . | 421,872·0 | . | . | 960 |
| Metretes . | 2,503·44 | . | . | 632,808·0 | . | . | 1,440 |
| Medimnus . | 3,338·16 | . | . | 842,745·0 | . | . | 1,920 |
| 128 Hecteis | 71,214·40 | . | . | 18,000,000·0 | . | . | 40,960 |

Unlike the Table of Hebrew Measures and Weights, in which the ounce of 450 grains has a recognized place, that ounce, though contained 40 times in the Grecian measure of the Pyramid Coffer, has no *mensurable status* here.

### 117.

It has been seen that the Roman measures of capacity were founded on a foot of ·972 or 11·664 inches; but that there was also a smaller measure founded on the foot of ·9697 or 11·636 inches. Of the larger foot, 45 cubic feet are equal to 71,325 cubic inches. Of the smaller foot, 45 cubes are equal to 70,965 cubic inches. We subjoin the weights belonging to the larger measure, according to the number of ·18,000,000 Troy grains in the Pyramid Coffer, inserting the number of mensural ounces, according to the best authorities, opposite each measure.

*Table of the Weights of Roman Measures of Capacity.*

|  | Cubic Inches. | | Troy Grains. | | Mensural Ounces. |
|---|---|---|---|---|---|
| Cyathus . | 2·90 | . . | 549·3 | . . | 1¼ |
| Acetabulum | 4·35 | . . | 1,098·6 | . . | 2½ |
| Quartarius . | 8·70 | . . | 2,197·2 | . . | 5 |
| Hemina . | 17·41 | . . | 4,394·5 | . . | 10 |
| Sextarius . | 34·83 | . . | 8,789·0 | . . | 20 |
| Congius . | 208·95 | . . | 52,734·0 | . . | 120 |
| Semimodius | 278·61 | . . | 70,312·5 | . . | 160 |
| Modius . | 557·23 | . . | 140,625·0 | . . | 320 |
| Urna . | 835·82 | . . | 210,936·0 | . . | 480 |
| Amphora . | 1,671·65 | . . | 421,872·0 | . . | 960 |
| Culeus . | 33,432·86 | . . | 8,437,440·0 | . . | 19,200 |
| 128 Modii . | 71,325·00 | . . | 18,000,000·0 | . . | 40,960 |

In this, as in the preceding Table, the 10 mensural ounces are represented by the weight of 4,394·5 grains

Troy, according to which the pound would be equal to 5273·4 grains Troy.

The Romans made a distinction between *mensural* ounces and *ponderal* ounces; between ounces relative to a certain measure, and ounces independent of measure: the former being invariable in measure, but variable in weight, corresponding to the distinction we make between cubic inches of space, according as the same are filled with wheat or wine. G. Agricola says: " Sextarius vero Romanus comprehendit libram et bessem, id est, uncias viginti: μετρικὰς intelligo, quas, verbum è verbo exprimentes, mensurales dicemus, ut σταθμικὰς ponderales. Atque libræ quidem, et unciæ mensurales, cuique mensuræ fixæ semper et immobiles manent, cum ponderales pro rerum, quas metimur, varietate sæpius mutentur. Hinc autem non difficulter et intelligere et colligere possumus numerum librarum vel unciarum, quarum unaquæque mensura est capax. Ut igitur à sextario quasi initio quodam et fundamento incipientes, per majores ipso mensuras ad culei usque perveniamus capacitatem; quia is, ut jam dixi, uncias viginti, congius capit libras decem. Urna, quadraginta. Amphora, octoginta. Culeus, mille et sexcentas."*

The sextarius contained, as Agricola says, 20 mensural ounces, which *measure* would always remain fixed and immoveable, though the weight contained might be variable, depending on the quality of the things which it comprised. With this understanding as to weight, the scale is well preserved. The sextarius, as a measure, contains 20 ounces; the congius, 10 pounds, or 120 ounces; the urna, 40 pounds, or 480 ounces; the amphora, 80 pounds, or 960 ounces; the culeus, 1600 pounds, or 19,200 ounces.

* Agricola, lib. i. p. 4. Edit. 1550.

Two of the measures in the Table (but these are not mentioned by Agricola) do not fall in so readily with the pound of 12 ounces as with that of 16 ounces, and, for that reason, they were probably omitted by him. The *modius* of wheat (for instance) contains 20 pounds of 16 ounces, or 320 ounces ; and the *semimodius,* 10 of these pounds, or 160 ounces. The pound of 16 ounces is a Greek pound. The 128 modii in the Pyramid Coffer weigh collectively 256 pounds of 16 ounces.

In the greater part of the Grecian Table, especially in the larger measures, the pound of 16 ounces must have been used. The *xestes,* of 20 ounces, is $1\frac{1}{4}$ pounds; the *choenix,* of 40 ounces, $2\frac{1}{2}$ pounds ; the *hemiecton,* of 160 ounces, 10 pounds ; the *hecteus,* of 320 ounces, 20 pounds ; the *ceramion,* of 960 ounces, 60 pounds ; the *metretes,* of 1440 ounces, 90 pounds ; the *medimnus,* of 1920 ounces, 120 pounds ; the 128 *hecteis* contained in the Pyramid Coffer weigh 256 pounds. All these are pounds of 16 ounces each.

## 118.

The reader may be curious to know how far the measures derived from the Pyramid Coffer coincide with those obtained from other sources : " The last and best way to discover the true weight of the Roman pound," says Greaves, " is by the *congius Romanus,* whereof, by a special Providence, as *Pætus* and *Villalpandus* have well observed, the original standard of Vespasian is still extant at Rome. This, as the superscription upon it (X P) demonstrates, contains the weight of 10 Roman pounds, and is equal (by the joint confession of all authors treating this argument) to 6 sextarii."* Greaves then produces " two observations

* Greaves, p. 297.

of the congius with fountain-water, made by two very eminent and able men, Villalpandus and Gassendus, the one at *Rome*, with the Roman weights, from the original *congius* itself; the other at *Aix*, with the Paris weights, from a model or copy of that at Rome, procured by *Peireskius*."* The measure of *Villalpandus* gives 52,560 English grains; that of *Gassendus*, 52,800 English grains. Auzout, about 1680, obtained from the congius, by weighing it full of water, only 51,463·2 Troy grains; but Dr. Hase, who recognized it at Dresden in 1824, to which city it had been removed before 1721, had it filled with water, and carefully weighed, and the weight of the water was found to be equal to 52,037·69 Troy grains.†

Greaves made an attempt to take the measure of this congius when he was at Rome in 1637; but "all that I could do," he says, "was to fill the capacity with *milium* [*millet*] well cleansed, and to compare it with the English measures taken from the standard. It contained of our measures for wine, three quarts, one pint, and one-eighth part of a pint: of our corn or dry measures, three quarts and about one-sixth part of a pint." The wine pint then in use contained 28·875 cubic inches, and the corn pint 34·01 cubic inches. But the *millet* in the wine pint gave a very different estimate from the millet in the corn pint, and one of the measures must have been wrong. The contents of the congius from the wine pint was 205·7 cubic inches, and from the corn pint 209·7 cubic inches. By the former the weight of the pound would be 5194·7, by the latter 5294·7 Troy grains.

* Greaves's Works, pp. 303, 304.
† Hussey's Essay, p. 126.

*Various Weights ascribed to the Ounce and Pound of the
Congius by different Authorities.*

|   |   | Ounce. | Pound. |
|---|---|---|---|
| 1 | By Villalpandus . . . | 438 Gr... | 5,256 Gr. |
| 2 | By Gassendus . . . . | 440 „ .. | 5,280 „ |
| 3 | By Greaves, from the Wine Pint | 441 „ .. | 5,294 „ |
| 4 | By Greaves, from the Corn Pint | 433 „ .. | 5,196 „ |
| 5 | By Auzout . . . . | 429 „ .. | 5,146 „ |
| 6 | By Dr. Hase . . . . | 433½„ .. | 5,203 „ |

In our Tables of Grecian and Roman Measures of
Capacity obtained from the Pyramid Coffer, the weight
of the congius is found to be 52,734 grains for the 10
pounds; or 439·5 for the ounce, and 5273 for the
pound; which measure approaches nearest to that of
Gassendus, and that of Greaves from the wine pint.

" The ancient *weights* in themselves," says Dr. Hussey,
" are too unequal and inconsistent with each other to
give any certain result." He speaks thus of the old
metallic weights; but of these he regards more favour-
ably the two obtained from Herculaneum, " the only
two large specimens which are perfect; those of 50
and 100 Roman pounds. Of these, the former, weighing 256,564 English grains, gives a pound of 5131·28
grains: the other, weighing 518,364, gives a pound of
5183·64 grains, which, it will be seen, is but 21 grains
less than the result of the congius [according to
Dr. Hase]; and so small a difference in the two calculations is not of much importance, when we find much
greater between the Roman weights themselves. If,
therefore, all the other specimens be set aside, and we
take the liberty to confine the calculation to these two,
or rather this one, the larger of the two, without taking
the others, which give different values, into the account
at all, we may consider the result as so nearly agreeing

with that, which will be given as the most probable
value of the pound, as to strengthen the general conclusion in fixing upon that as the standard."* Acting
on this principle, Dr. Hussey adopts Dr. Hase's weight
of the congius, adding to it " only about one quarter of
a grain for the sake of making it up to the whole
number of 5204 grains," as the most correct of any of
the series.

We shall have gained, however, but little advantage
from all these investigations, if they bring us at last to
no greater certainty than this, as to the value of the
Roman ounce and pound. It is desirable that some
other means should be devised, to obtain a more exact
knowledge on the subject, if any such can be discovered.
Why should we not attempt to find out the weight of
the Roman ounce or pound by analogy from the
Grecian.? We can prove the measure of the Roman
*foot* by its relation to the Grecian, and why not that of
the *ounce* by the same process? Having ascertained
the length of the Roman foot to be 11·636 inches, we
have only to add one twenty-fourth part to this number;
and we know that if our estimate of the Roman foot
be correct, it will result in giving us the Grecian foot:
now 11·636 inches, with the addition of ·484 inches, is
equal to 12·12 inches — the Grecian foot. Why, then,
reversing the operation, may we not from the Grecian
ounce of the Pyramid Coffer of 450 grains deduct one
twenty-fifth part, and equally obtain the Roman ounce?
The result will be as follows :—From 450 grains deduct
18, and it leaves 432 for the weight of the Roman
ounce. Twelve of these ounces will give us 5184
grains for the Roman pound. If Dr. Hussey was
delighted to find how near Dr. Hase's measure of the

* Essay, p. 122.

congius came to that of the larger and more perfect of
the Herculaneum weights, exceeding it by only 21
grains, how much more reason have we to feel satisfied
with the confirmation which that same weight gives to
our estimate of the Roman pound? That weight of
5183·64 grains falls short only *one-third of a grain in
one pound* from our measure.

*Table of Roman Pounds, Commercial and Monetary.*

| Troy Grains. Commercial. | | Monetary. | | | | |
|---|---|---|---|---|---|---|
| 432 | = | 450 | = | Uncia | | |
| 864 | = | 900 | = | 2 | = | Sextans |
| 1,296 | = | 1,350 | = | 3 | = | Quadrans |
| 1,728 | = | 1,800 | = | 4 | = | Triens |
| 2,160 | = | 2,250 | = | 5 | = | Quincunx |
| 2,592 | = | 2,700 | = | 6 | = | Semis |
| 3,024 | = | 3,150 | = | 7 | = | Septunx |
| 3,456 | = | 3,600 | = | 8 | = | Bes, or Bessis |
| 3,888 | = | 4,050 | = | 9 | = | Dodrans |
| 4,320 | = | 4,500 | = | 10 | = | Dextans |
| 4,752 | = | 4,950 | = | 11 | = | Deunx |
| 5,184 | = | 5,400 | = | 12 | = | Libra |
| 6,912 | = | 7,200 | = | 16 | = | „ (*English avoirdupois and merchants' pound*= 7000 and 7200 grains). |

The Roman *commercial* ounce consisted of 432 grains, and the
pound of 5184 grains.

The Roman *monetary* ounce consisted of 450 grains, and the
pound of 5400 grains.

## CHAPTER XIX.

*English and French Systems of Metrology compared, from the Statement of John Quincy Adams — Names, taken from the Human Body, applied to Measures of Length, not as a Standard, but for Convenience only.*

### 119.

IT is generally thought that the natural standard of the English system of measure is the length of the human foot, divided by the barleycorn; while that of the French system is an aliquot part of the circumference of the earth decimally divided. " Considered as a whole," says Mr. Adams, " the established weights and measures of England are but the ruins of a system, the decays of which have been often repaired with materials adapted neither to the proportion, nor to the principles of the original construction. The metrology of France is a new and complicated machine, formed upon principles of mathematical precision, the adaptation of which to the uses for which it was devised is yet problematical, and abiding, with questionable success, the test of experiment."* But this statement, made by an impartial observer of the two systems, is now shown to be incorrect in one respect. The English system has, for its foundation, all the scientific accuracy attributed to the French, with the further recommendation, that it has stood the test of actual experiment for about

* Quincy Adams's Report, p. 71.

4000 years; and though it has been repaired from time to time by those who were ignorant of the principles on which it was constructed, their work has always been executed in such a manner, that it has not caused the machine to lose its original scientific cha-- racter. Adding to our yard measure *one-eleventh* part of its length, we can produce a *meter*, which is as true a representative of an aliquot portion of the earth's circumference as is the French *mètre*. The only difference is, that our English meter is derived from a measure made in lat. 30°, and the French is formed from one supposed to be made in lat. 45°. The utility and accuracy of both is in either case the same.

" To the English system," says Mr. Adams, " belong two different units of weight and two corresponding measures of capacity, the natural standard of which is the difference between the specific gravities of *wheat* and *wine*. To the French system there is only one unit of weight and one measure of capacity, the natural standard of which is the specific gravity of water.

" The French system has the advantage of unity in the weight and the measure, but has no common test of both: its measure gives the weight of water only. The English system has the inconvenience of two weights and two measures; but each measure is, at the same time, a weight. Thus the gallon of wheat and the gallon of wine, though of different dimensions, balance each other. A gallon of wheat and a gallon of wine, each weigh eight pounds avoirdupois." Mr. Adams drew up this report in 1821, before the reform had taken place in our English measures under George IV. The imperial gallon is now of the same capacity both for wine and wheat; it is the weights alone which differ. The gallon of wheat now weighs

eight pounds avoirdupois, while the gallon of wine
weighs ten of the same pounds; but the gallon of
wheat still weighs ten Troy pounds. Thus the same
opportunity is yet afforded us, which Mr. Adams so
much valued, of testing the measure of wine or wheat
by the weight, and the weight by the measure, as was
found under the old system, if we choose to avail ourselves of it.

" The *litre,* in the French system," observes Mr.
Adams, " is a measure for all grains and all liquids;
but its capacity gives a weight only for distilled water.
As a measure of corn, of wine, or of oil, it gives the
space which they occupy, but not their weight. Now,
as the weight of these articles is quite as important in
the estimate of their quantities as the space which they
fill, a system which has two standard units for measures
of capacity, but of which each measure gives the same
weight of the respective articles, is quite as uniform as
that which, of any given article, requires two instruments to show its quantity — one to measure the space
it fills, and another for its weight. In the difference
between the specific gravities of corn and wine, nature
has also dictated two standard measures of capacity,
each of them equiponderant to the same weight.

" This diversity existing in nature, the Troy and
Avoirdupois weights, and the corn and wine measures
of the English system are founded upon it. In England, it has existed as long as any recorded existence of
man upon the island; but the system did not originate
there, neither was Charlemagne the author of it. The
weights and measures of Greece and Rome were
founded upon it. The Romans had the *mina* and the
*libra,* the nummulary pound of 12 ounces, and the
commercial pound of 16. The avoirdupois pound came

through the Romans from the Greeks, and through
them, in all probability, from Egypt. Of this there is
internal evidence in the weights themselves, and in the
remarkable coincidence between the cubic foot and the
1000 ounces avoirdupois, and between the ounce avoirdupois and the Jewish shekel; and if the shekel of
Abraham was the same as that of his descendants, the
avoirdupois ounce may, like the cubit, have originated
before the flood.

"The result of these reflections is, that the uniformity of nature for ascertaining the quantities of all
substances, both by gravity and by occupied space, is
a uniformity of *proportion*, and not of *identity*; that
instead of one weight and one measure, it requires two
units of each, *proportioned* to each other; and that the
original English system of metrology, possessing two
such weights and two such measures, is better adapted
to the only uniformity applicable to the subject, recognised by nature, than the new French system, which,
possessing only one weight and one measure of capacity,
identifies weight and measure only by the single article
of distilled water; the English uniformity being relative
to the *things* weighed and measured, and the French only
to the *instruments* used for weight and mensuration."

With regard to the decimal principle, it is the opinion
of Mr. Adams that it can be " applied, only with many
qualifications, to any general system of metrology;
that its natural application is only to *numbers*; and that
*time, space, gravity,* and *extension* inflexibly reject its
sway" (p. 84). He thinks it "doubtful whether the
advantage to be obtained by any attempt to apply decimal arithmetic to weights and measures, would ever
compensate for the increase of diversity which is the
unavoidable consequence of change. Decimal arith-

metic is a contrivance of man (he observes) for computing numbers, and not a property of *time*, *space*, or *matter*. Nature has no partialites for the number *ten*: and the attempt to shackle her freedom with it will for ever prove abortive" (p. 85).

When Mr. Adams recorded these conclusions in his Report on Weights and Measures, addressed to the Senate of the United States, he entertained the opinion that the English system of metrology was founded on the natural standards of the human body; and he thought that, with all its disadvantages, it had one great advantage over all others, in this respect, that "the habits of every individual inure him to the comparison of the definite portion of his person with the existing standard measures to which he is accustomed. There are few English men or women but could give a yard, foot, or inch measure, from their own arms, hands, or fingers, with great accuracy. But they could not give the *mètre* or *decimètre*, although they should know their dimensions as well as those of the yard or foot" (p. 75). This observation is worthy of notice, as are all those which we have quoted from this philosophic writer.

There are two reasons why these popular names, derived from the human body, should be retained for our measures of length, even when we acknowledge that our measures were derived at first from a perfectly scientific standard, founded on the measure of the earth : the one is, that these *names* enable us to *describe* the several measures by apposite terms, which every one to whom we address ourselves can easily understand; the other, that guided by the terms thus made use of, most persons, on an emergency, are able to *extemporise* for themselves the measures alluded to, in the absence of more authentic models. A *digit* (a finger's breadth), an *inch* (a thumb), a *nail* (from the tip to the middle joint of the longest finger), a *palm* (the breadth of the four fingers), a *hand* (clasped with the thumb uppermost), a *span* (the thumb and fingers expanded to their greatest extent), a *foot* (of man), a *cubit* (from the elbow to the end of the longest finger), a *yard* (the girth of a man's body), a *step* (made when each foot advances alternately), a *pace* (two steps), a *fathom* (the width to which a man's arms and hands can be extended), are all of them measures, though not originally derived from, yet very fairly described by, those parts of the body to which these names refer. We could not explain our meaning to each other without their aid; nor could we make any reasonable attempt to supply the absence of the exact measure at all times, and in every place, without having recourse to the natural measure, indicated by the name, and supplied by every man in his own person. Of universal occurrence, and equally correct application, is the weight of 32 grains of wheat, of middling size, as the representative of the pennyweight, equal to 24 Troy grains, from which the Troy ounce and the pound may be raised.

## CHAPTER XX.

*Etymological Illustrations — Character of Mr. John Greaves, by
Dr. Hooper and Dr. Pocock. — Reason of the Shape of the
Pyramid Coffer. — Table of the Royal Cubit, etc.*

### 120.

THE *name* of the *Troy* pound suggests no idea to an
English reader. Its etymology has never been
satisfactorily ascertained. Some have ascribed it to
*Troyes,* a city of France, where anciently a great fair
was held; some have referred it to Troy, in Asia Minor.
In the last Report of the Commissioners on Weights
and Measures, it is supposed to be derived from *Troy
novant,* a name given by a few monkish historians to
*London,* in connexion with the fabulous legend of
*Brute.** But these are conjectures merely, without any
substantial foundation. The *name* is probably a descriptive term, and it may have had some connexion
with the *Pyramid Coffer.* Had we found such a phrase
as the *chaldron pound* made use of by our earliest
writers, we should have had no doubt that it had reference to the form of the vessel contained in the Great
Pyramid.

* "The Troy weight appeared to us to be the ancient weight
of this kingdom, having, as we have reason to suppose, existed
in the same state from the time of St. Edward the Confessor;
and there are reasons, moreover, to believe that the word *Troy*
has no reference to any town in France, but rather to the
monkish name given to London of *Troy novant,* founded on the
legend of Brute."—*Evidence of Davies Gilbert, Esq., M.P.*

But there is a word in our own language which is applicable to this vessel as a descriptive term, and not very dissimilar in sound from *Troy*. The word *trough*, which is pronounced *troh* in the West of England, may have been the original of the word *Troy* in the case before us. It truly represents such a vessel as the *caldarium*, or *laver*, or *chaldron*; and every Englishman would, without hesitation, call a vessel made in the form of two cubes set together, hollowed out of one block of stone or marble, a *trough*. The learned Jacob Bryant, in his " Analysis of Antient Mythology," published in 1774—6, speaks of this vessel as a *trough* in the following passage:—" It is indeed said, that a stone coffin is still to be seen in the centre room of the Chief Pyramid; and its shape and dimensions have been accurately taken. It is easy to give a name, and to assign a use, to anything which comes under our inspection; but the truth is not determined by our surmises. There is not an instance, I believe, upon record, of any Egyptian being entombed in this manner. The whole practice of the country seems to have been entirely different. I make no doubt but this *stone trough* was a reservoir for water, which, by means of the well, they drew from the Nile."*

The Anglo-Saxon word is "ᚦᚱᚩᚷ, ᚦᚱᚩh, or ᚦᚱᚩch, *a trough, tub, a small boat*" (*Bosworth's Anglo-Saxon Dictionary*). The Anglo-Saxon ᚷ is in general pronounced like *y* at the end of words: as Dæᚷ, *day*; Weᚷ, *weigh* or *wey*; Boᚷ or Boh, *an arm, a shoot, a branch, a bough*: whence probably we have our word *boy*. The Latin *Trua*, and the English *Troy*, may have had the same origin. Thus, when we speak of *Troy weight* we mean *Trough weight*, as being derived from a vessel of capacity made in the

* Bryant's Works, 8vo., 1807, vol. v. p. 198.

form of a *trough*, probably the original form of our *chaldron*.

Descriptive terms in some other language will often preserve a record of things or events, which belong to a people and a language no longer met with in the country where those terms are used. The ancient name of *Memphis* has given way to the Greek name *Metra-henny*, which, as being composed of μετρεω, *to measure*, and ἔνος or ἔνος, *the year*, was undoubtedly intended to commemorate the fact, that in this place had been made or recorded a *measure of the year*. The village of Metrahenny, about 10 miles south of the Great Pyramid, marks the site of the great city of Memphis, once the rival of Thebes in magnitude and splendour. "High mounds," says Hamilton, "enclose a square of 800 yards from north to south, and 400 from east to west. The entrance in the centre of each side is still visible. The two principal ones faced the desert and the river. We entered by the last, and were immediately much gratified by the sight of thirty or forty large blocks of very fine red granite lying on the ground, evidently forming parts of some colossal statues, the chief ornaments of the temple." The Greek name must have been given to this place at a very early period, since it refers clearly to one of the purposes for which it now appears the Pyramids of Gizeh were built : but whether it was bestowed earlier or later than the name of *Memphis* we cannot tell. All we know is, that when it was conferred, the memory of the earth's circumference having been measured near that place had not entirely passed away. But who could now recognise a reason for its meaning, apart from the discoveries which have been made in these pages?

Greaves observes of *Matarea*, that it is " a place some

five miles from Cairo, north-east of it, as I remember,
and about a mile from *Nilus*, where, besides the *Aguglia*
(a great obelisk, or *needle*), there are other huge stones,
that have served for some great works" (vol. ii. p. 528).
*Matarieh* (as it is sometimes spelt), or *Matarea*, is celebrated for its spring of fresh-water, which made the
Arabs call it *Ain-Schems*, "the fountain of the sun."
The ruins which attracted Greaves's notice are those of
*Heliopolis*, or *On* (the city of the Sun), one of the most
famed of Egyptian cities. They are described as being
in the form of a rectangle, and about three miles in
circuit. The city of Heliopolis was deserted even in
Strabo's time: two of its famous obelisks had been
carried to Rome, and the rest were considerably
damaged. But what we desire to notice is the meaning
of the name *Matarea*. It is evidently the same as the
Greek word μεταρροια, *a change of stream*. Now this
name *Metarrœa* most clearly alludes to the branching
off of the Nile at this place in two different directions,
one branch leading to Rosetta, the other to Damietta.
The division of the stream forms the great *Delta* — the
land of Goshen. At what period the name *Metarrœa*
was given to it we know not; but as it is descriptive of
a work of nature older than any of those works of art
which are commemorated by the name of *Heliopolis*, or
*On*, we may imagine its origin was quite as early.

"The ancients derived Πυραμις (*a Pyramid*) sometimes
from πῦρ (*fire*), because of its pointed shape: sometimes from πυρός (*wheat*), as if the *Pyramids* had been
*granaries*! No doubt the word, as well as the thing, is
Egyptian." So say Scott and Liddell; but there is
reason to suppose that the name Πυραμις may have
had reference to πυρός, *wheat*, if we reflect that the
Pyramid Coffer (the *caldarium*, or *trough*) in the Great

Pyramid was a *measure of capacity for wheat.* Hence the
Pyramid itself may have been called a *wheat measure,*
long after the word by which the fact is commemorated
had ceased to have any propriety of application in the
estimation of the people who made use of it.

The oldest names are the simplest; and they are
almost always descriptive of some natural quality in
the object. Few persons are aware, when they utter
our word *mud,* that they use a word which is the same
in meaning, and quite as old, as the Greek word *chaos*;
but so it is. *Mud* was a word employed by the Phœnicians to represent that intermingled condition of earth
and water before the Creation, which the Greeks called
*chaos*; which mixture of earth and water on a small
scale we still call *mud,* whatever be the cause to which
it is owing. The Phœnician chronicler, *Sanchoniatho,*
in his " *Cosmogony,*" supposes, " that the beginning of
the UNIVERSE was dark and condensed windy Air, or a
breeze of dark air, and a Chaos, turbid and indistinct
like Erebus; and that these things were infinite, and
for a long time had no bound : but when (they say) the
WIND became enamoured of ITS OWN PRINCIPLES, and a
mixture took place, the EMBRACE was called Desire;
and this was the beginning of the creation of all things.
But this (wind) knew not ITS OWN PRODUCTION. And
from this EMBRACE of the WIND was produced Môt,
Μωτ, which some call *mud,* ιλυν; others, the putre-
faction of a watery mixture; and from this was produced all the seed of the creation, and the generation
of the UNIVERSE." *

* Την των όλων αρκην ύποτιθεται Αερα ζοφωδη και πνευματωδη, η
πνοην αερος ζοφωδους, και Χαος θολερον, ερεβωδες. ταυτα δε ειναι
απειρα, και δια πολυν αιωνα μη εχειν περας. ότε δε (φησιν) ηρασθη
το πνευμα των ιδιων αρχων, και εγενετο συγκρασις, ή πλοκη εκεινη

"Sanchoniatho," says Mr. Cory, "is considered to
be the most ancient writer of the heathen world. In
what age he wrote is uncertain; but his history was
composed in the Phœnician language, and its materials
were collected from the archives of the Phœnician
cities. It was translated into Greek by Philo Byblius;
and for the preservation of these fragments we are indebted to the care of Eusebius."

Among these "Ancient Fragments" Mr. Cory has
given the "Old Egyptian Chronicle" preserved by Syn-
cellus. It commences as follows: "Among the Egyptians there is a certain tablet called the Old Chronicle,
containing 30 dynasties in 113 descents, during the
long period of 36,525 years." As these are of course
fabulous years, we must look for some other solution of
this mystical number; and the most obvious one is to
consider it as representing the number of days in a
year. According to the "Table of Constants," the
sidereal revolution of the earth, in mean solar days, is
365·25636, and the tropical revolution, in the same, is
365·24224. The coincidence of this mystical number
of the old Egyptian Chronicle with the mean solar
days in the sidereal year, is a remarkable confirmation
of our opinion, that the name of *Metrahenny* was given
to the site of the city of Memphis, from its having
been the place where *a measure of the year* was once
made or recorded, which measure was 365·25 days.

Since the English language can reckon among its

---

εκληθη Ποθος. αυτη δε αρχη κτισεως άπαντων. αυτο δε ουκ εγινωσκε
την αυτου κτισιν, και εκ της αυτου συμπλοκης του πνευματος εγενετο
Μωτ. τουτο τινες φασιν ιλυν. οιδε υδατωδους μιξεως σηψιν. και
εκ ταυτης εγενετο πασα σπορα κτισεως, και γενεσις των ολων.—
Cory's Ancient Fragments, p. 3, 1828 (printed without accents).

K

primitive words one of the commonest import (*mud*), which was also employed by the people of the most ancient nation in the world in the same sense, it would not be surprising that another English word should be found in common use which was descriptive of the vessel of content in the Great Pyramid, and which is still applicable to all vessels of that shape. We believe, therefore, that we are correct in affirming that *Troy weight* originally meant *Trough weight*. The proportion of weight which water held to wheat was sufficiently indicated by Troy weight alone; the Trough holding 2500 pounds of wheat, and 3125 pounds of water, or *one-fourth* more of water, both being Troy pounds of 5760 Troy grains.

### 121.

We have now completed that part of our inquiry which is founded on the *Interior of the Great Pyramid*. Nothing has been forced. The development has taken place with hardly any effort on the writer's part. He has followed especially the footsteps of the earliest of modern discoverers, JOHN GREAVES, Savilian Professor of Astronomy in the University of Oxford, of whom Dr. Hooper, Bishop of Bath and Wells, speaks in the following terms :—

" It is a great pity, for many reasons, that the accurate judgment and exquisite learning, with which he was furnished, met with those unhappy times in which an honest man was not only discouraged, but disabled, from·the prosecution of such studies. And the reader will regret this the more when he takes the honest and knowing Dr. Pocock's character of him, as he gives it, *de Moribus Arabum*, p. 158. ' The most learned,' says he, ' and my most loving friend, John

Greaves, than whom none ever devoted himself, and his
studies, and his expenses, with a more entire affection
to the public advantage of learning.' This elogy of
him," continues Dr. Hooper, " I could not forbear pro-
nouncing, in gratitude for the information I have received from him; and with a wish that these conjectures
from them I am now offering had been prevented by
his solid conclusions.  For I cannot but flatter myself
that he had some such design in his view, concerning
the Jewish measures, as that at which I am now aim-
ing."*  Mr. Greaves died in 1652, at the age of fifty
years.

Such was the testimony of these distinguished men
to the ability, learning, and judgment of Mr. Greaves.
How much greater reason has the writer of the present
book to acknowledge his obligations to the Author of
the *Pyramidographia*, without whose aid he could not
have produced that chain of argument which, he trusts,
will be found to have supported his opinions.

### 122.

While this sheet was in type, and ready to be struck
off, it occurred to the writer that he had not yet succeeded in discovering on what principle the Pyramid
Coffer was formed, to be of the measures assigned to it;
and that he had not noticed the alleged deficiency in
the foot-rule, which Greaves took with him when he left
England.

With respect to the latter circumstance, Raper, who,
about a century later than Greaves, measured the more
important parts of the public buildings in Rome, inferred from a comparison of his own measures with

---

* Dr. Hooper's Inquiry, p. 216.

those of Greaves, that the foot-rule of the latter must have been about 2 parts in 1000 shorter than the proper standard.* This correction is adopted by Dr. Hussey.†

But the question of greatest interest is, On what principle was the Pyramid Coffer constructed, to be of its admitted *length, depth,* and *breadth?* Is there any *common measure,* any *even number* of some acknowledged division of the Cubit, or Foot, of that period which would accord with these measures as they are represented by Greaves, or by Colonel Howard Vyse and Mr. Perring? We readily perceive that one such acknowledged measure is presented in the *depth,* which is estimated by Greaves at 34·320, and by Vyse and Perring at 34·50, English inches. These numbers are evidently those of the Royal Cubit, 10 *palms* of which are equal to 34·56 inches; but the same measure appeared to be unable to explain the length and breadth.

Further consideration, however, shows us, that what could not be explained by the *palm,* may be accounted for by the *digit.* Four digits make a palm of 3·456 inches, in which case each digit is equal to ·864 parts of the English inch. From this measure we obtain a satisfactory solution of every difficulty. The *length* is equal to 90 *digits,* or 77·760 inches (which by Greaves's foot-rule is 77·856 inches, and by his reduced measure of ·002 in the foot, is 77·70 inches). The *depth* is equal to 40 *digits,* or 34·560 inches (which by Greaves's foot-rule is 34·320, and by his reduced measure is 34·260 inches). The *breadth* is equal to 30 digits, or 25·92 inches (which by Greaves's foot-rule is 26·616, and by his reduced measure is 26·56 inches). But a vessel measuring 90 royal *digits* in length, 40 in depth, and

* Philos. Trans., 1760.　　　　　† Essay, p. 227.

30 in breadth, contains only 69,657 cubic inches, and the cube of the cubit of Karnak contains 71,328 cubic inches. To admit the 1621 inches, which are wanting, one of these measures must be enlarged. If the *breadth* receive the necessary expansion, it must be increased from 25·92 inches to 26·56 inches, which is Greaves's reduced measure,—and this addition renders the contents equal to 71,376 inches, only 48 cubic inches more than the required quantity.

But why, it may be asked, was not the Coffer made at once in the shape of the cube of the Karnak cubit? From its obvious unfitness, if it were of that shape and size, to serve as a *model measure.* The framers of the standard would naturally have regard to the portability, and convenient use, of the wooden measures which were to be formed on that model, and if men of the present day would prefer the shape of a *trough* to that of a *cube* of such inconvenient dimensions, we may give the founders of the Great Pyramid credit for so much common sense as would lead them to the same conclusion. To all inhabitants of the East the *hot-bath* was a familiar object, and in the appropriation of its *form* to the purpose of a *corn measure,* we see how it happened that this *vessel* received the name of *caldarium,* a *chaldron,* a *laver.* It was that which it had possessed from the earliest times, long probably before its employment as a *corn measure* had been thought of.

As to the question, whether Greaves obtained from Guildhall a foot-measure ·002 in 1·000 shorter than it ought to have been? or whether Raper was in error when he attributed to it that deficiency? we may leave it undetermined. There can be no doubt, that the care and circumspection, with which Greaves made all his measurements, deserve our highest admiration.—

A learned and studious man, not accustomed to travel, he went alone, without either friend or servant to protect or assist him, in order to *measure* the most ancient structures in Rome, Constantinople, and Egypt, and to inspect and *weigh* the fairest and best preserved of all the oldest coins he could meet with. Amidst many real dangers, and so many imaginary ones as would have paralyzed the exertions of most men, he persevered in his purpose with a degree of coolness, minuteness, and precision, which has never been surpassed, if equalled, under the most favourable circumstances. He travelled at his own expense, published his book at his own expense, was abused for all the trouble he had taken, and not till a century afterwards was justice done to his memory, by Dr. Birch's re-publication of his works, and by Sir Isaac Newton's vindication of many of his measurements. He was sustained by a firm faith that the time would come when his labours would be appreciated; and if not, that he had performed, to the best of his ability, the task which he had undertaken.

123.

*Table of the Royal Cubit, the Foot of Pliny, and Cubit of Karnak.*

English Inches.

| | | | | |
|---|---|---|---|---|
| ·864 = | 1 Digit. | | | |
| 3·456 = | 4 = | 1 Palm. | | |
| 10·368 = | 12 = | 3 = | 1 Foot of Pliny, or Royal Span. | |
| 20·736 = | 24 = | 6 = | 2 = | 1 Royal Cubit. |
| 41·472 = | 48 = | 12 = | 4 = | 2 = 1 Cubit of Karnak. |

# THE FOUNDERS OF THE GREAT PYRAMID.

## CHAPTER XXI.

*Introductory Remarks—Probable Age of the Great Pyramid.*

### 124.

WE have now completed our description of the
*exterior* and *interior* of the Great Pyramid—a
work undertaken in the earliest ages of the world, and
still remaining without a parallel, the wonder of all
subsequent ages. We have endeavoured to explain the
purpose for which this work was constructed, and, in so
doing, have acknowledged our obligations to all those
writers who have assisted us in our enquiry. There is
scarcely one who, in the facts which he has recorded
concerning it, has not had the merit of throwing some
light on the subject. Instead of contradicting each
other, as it was imagined they had done, by those who
gave their writings a cursory or prejudiced perusal,
they have each contributed to produce a mass of evidence of the most unimpeachable character, which,
when it is collected together, astonishes us by the
extent and depth of its illustration. We know, by
their united testimony, as much of the purpose for

which the Pyramids were constructed, as we should probably have done, had one of the chambers in the Great Pyramid been found to contain, in some secret recess, a detail of the undertaking, and of the motives which led to it.

But, of one portion of this subject we are still ignorant. Seeing such undoubted proofs of the exercise of immense intellectual power, profound scientific knowledge, and great wisdom in the conception and execution of the vast design, we naturally wish to know to whom we are indebted for so grand a performance. By what body of men, and in what age of the world, could such a work have been achieved? Is it possible that at an earlier epoch than any to which the annals of human learning extend, there were persons in existence so highly civilized, so skilled in the mathematics, so profoundly wise, benevolent, and just, as to be both able and desirous to benefit mankind through all succeeding ages? Did they foresee the advantage of devising some common bond, which should for ever remind mankind that they were originally brethren, sprung from one father, of which origin the use of the same measures of length, capacity, and weight, would remain an indubitable testimony to the end of time? Was there ever a people on the face of the earth, in the very infancy of society, as well informed as ourselves? And is it true that, after the successive accumulations of stores of thought from century to century, which the arts of writing and printing have preserved from perishing, and rendered accessible to all men, we are only now recovering some ground which has been lost, instead of pioneering our way to regions which man's intellect has never before penetrated? Doubtless the men of modern times have much to boast of, to which no former age can lay claim; but it is also probable, that to some human beings in the earliest ages of society, a degree of intellectual power was given by the Creator, which raised them far above the level of those succeeding inhabitants of the earth, with whom it has been the custom of later ages to confound them.

Niebuhr says, that "As there are animals, of tribes that seem to have belonged to a period of other forms, and to have been left behind as aliens to pine away in an altered world, so the Pelasgians, in the portion of history within the reach of our monuments and legends, appear only in a state of ruin and decay: and this is what renders them so mysterious. The old traditions spoke of them as a race pursued by the heavenly powers with never-ending calamities; and the traces of their abode, which were found in very widely distant regions, gave rise to the fancy that they had roamed from land to land, in the hope of escaping from these afflictions."* But the people whose trace we are now following, are apparently of an earlier family than these Pelasgians; for they are not found in a state of ruin and decay, nor had they been as yet pursued by never-ending calamities. The wanderings of mankind had scarcely commenced when those stupendous structures were raised, which, as we conceive, were intended to bind the families of the earth together by a common system of weights and measures, before they had so far quitted each other's society as to form separate communities.

### 125.

It is commonly believed that the Pyramids of Gizeh were built about 4000 years ago—an opinion which

---

* Roman History, by Hare and Thirlwall, vol. i. p. 28.

was adverted to by Napoleon I with startling effect, in one of his most famous bulletins. About a thousand years later, other Pyramids were raised; and from the uses to which they were applied, it is probably owing that the nations of antiquity entertained so readily the belief, that those of Gizeh were designed to be the tombs of kings.

One great peculiarity which distinguishes the earliest structures from those of later ages, is the absence of all hieroglyphics. A further difference is found in the shape of the Coffer, or Sarcophagus. The chest, or coffer, in the Great Pyramid, is so shaped as to be in every part rectangular—from side to side, and from end to end; and the bottom is also cut at right angles with the sides and end, and made perfectly level. This was the case also with the coffers of the Second and Third Pyramids. None of the coffers had any hieroglyphics carved on them. Sir Gardner Wilkinson remarks: "It has always been a matter of surprise, that no hieroglyphics are met with, either in the interior or on the exterior of the Pyramids, and that, above all, the Sarcophagus should be destitute of those sacred characters, so generally found on Egyptian monuments." When we hear, therefore, that a mummy-board was found in the Third Pyramid,* inscribed with hieroglyphics, which show that it belonged to the supposed founder of the Third Pyramid, we may reasonably infer that it was not placed there at the time this Pyramid was built.

The era preceding that of the hieroglyphic period, is too indefinite in extent to allow us to fix on any probable number of years for its duration. We should,

* Vyse, ii. p. 94.

therefore, have been compelled to leave the problem of the real age of the Pyramids in some degree unsolved, had not a circumstance lately occurred which has contributed to its development. On the night of March 21, 1817, Captains Irby and Mangles saw, through the long inclined passage of the Great Pyramid, the polar star, at the period of its culmination. M. Caviglia, about the same time, made a similar observation. From this fact, that the polar star had been seen from the bottom of the inclined passage, it was somewhat hastily inferred that the polar star occupied the same position in the heavens at the time the Pyramid was built. The angle of the passage was found by Col. Vyse and Mr. Perring, to be 26° 41′: its length is 320 feet 10 inches; its height 3 feet 11 inches; and its breadth 3 feet 5½ inches. In 1839, Col. Howard Vyse communicated these particulars to Sir John Herschel, and requested his opinion whether the direction of the passage was likely to have been determined by the polar star, at the time the Pyramid was constructed. His reply is given in the following extract of a letter to Col. Howard Vyse, published by the latter in the second volume of his work, "On the Pyramids of Gizeh":—

"Four thousand years ago," says Sir John Herschel, "the present polar star, *a Ursæ Minoris*, could by no possibility have been seen at any time in the twenty-four hours, through the gallery in the Great Pyramid, on account of the precession of the equinoxes, which, at that time, would have displaced every star in the heavens, from its then apparent position on the sphere, by no less a quantity than 55° 45′ of longitude, and would have changed all the relations of the constellations to the diurnal sphere.

"The supposed date of the Pyramid, 2123 B. C.,

added to our present date, 1839, form 3962 years (say 4000), and the effect of the precession on the longitudes of the stars in that interval having been to increase them all by the above-named quantity, it will follow that the pole of the heavens, at the erection of the Pyramid, must have stood very near to the star *a Draconis*, that is, 2° 51' 15" from it to the westward, as we should now call it; *a Draconis* was therefore at that time the polar star; and, as it is comparatively insignificant, and only of the third magnitude (if so much), it can scarcely be supposed that it could have been seen in the day-time, even in the climate of Gizeh, or even from so dark a recess as the inclined entrance of the Great Pyramid. A latitude, however, of 30°, and a polar distance of the star in question of 2° 51' 15", would bring it, at its lower culmination, to an altitude of 27° 9', and therefore it would have been directly in view of an observer stationed in the descending passage, the opening of which, as seen from a point sixty-three feet within, would, by calculation, subtend an angle of 7° 7': and even from the bottom, near the sepulchral chamber, would still appear of at least 2° in breadth. In short, speaking as in ordinary parlance, the passage may be said to have been directly pointed at *a Draconis*, at its inferior culmination; at which moment its altitude above the horizon of Gizeh (lat. 30°) would have been 27° 9'—refraction being neglected, as too trifling (about 2') to affect the question.

" No other astronomical relation can be drawn from the Table containing the angles and dimensions of the passages; for although they all point within 5 degrees of the pole of the heavens, they differ too much and too irregularly, to admit of any conclusions.

" The exterior angles of the buildings are remarkably

uniform; but the angle, 52°, is not connected with any astronomical fact, and was probably adopted for architectural reasons." *

The remarks in the last two paragraphs relate to eight other Pyramids, besides the first, of all which Col. Howard Vyse had given " a Table, showing the exterior angles of the buildings, the inclinations and proportions of the inclined passages, and also the dimensions of the Sarcophagi."   Col. Vyse's conclusion as to the First Pyramid, from this letter, is expressed in the following terms:—" It would appear that the direction of the passage was determined by the star, which was polar at the time when the Pyramid was constructed, and that the exact aspect of the building was regulated by it; but for the reasons already stated, it could not have been used for celestial observation.   The coincidence of the relative position of *a Draconis* with the supposed date of the Pyramid, is, at all events, very remarkable." †

Sir John Herschel adds, in a note to his own letter: " In the Catalogue of the Astronomical Society, the magnitude of *a Draconis* is stated as intermediate between the 3rd and 4th.   It is certainly inferior to the 3rd; and, it is to be observed, that there is not any larger star near it, which could at that epoch have been preferred as a pole star."

Having reason to believe, from these remarks, that the Pyramids may have been founded 4000 years ago, or as early as 2160 years before the Christian era, let us now endeavour to ascertain by what race, or family of men, they were most probably constructed.

* Vol. ii. p. 107.      † Vol ii. p. 106.

CHAPTER XXII.

*The Founders not the Race of Ham — The Founders were*
*Shepherds.*

126.

IT is generally supposed that the founders of the
Pyramids were the Sons of Ham, if not Ham himself. This opinion has arisen probably from the fact,
to which the Scriptures bear testimony, that Ham and
his immediate descendants were the builders of the
city and tower of Babel. Nimrod, the grandson of
Ham, had, we are told, "for the beginning of his kingdom, Babel, and Erech, and Accad, and Calneh, in the
land of Shinar; out of which land he went out into
Assyria, and built Nineveh, and the city Rehoboth, and
Calah, and Resen, between Nineveh and Calah: the
same is a great city" (Gen. x. 10). It has been conjectured, that as Ham, and those who succeeded him,
built so many large cities, and also the Tower of Babel,
they were the most likely persons to have built the
Pyramids.

The dates are not unfavourable to this supposition.
The formation of the tower and city of Babel is said,
in the Hebrew chronology, to have been begun in
2247, about 100 years after the flood, and about 100
years before the time assigned for the erection of the
Pyramids, supposing that event to have taken place
4000 years ago.

But had the sons of Ham gone down into Egypt for the purpose of building the Pyramids, they would have been dwellers among their own brethren, the Mizraim, whose religious opinions and customs would not have been different from their own. How, then, could it have happened, as Herodotus relates, that, "until the reign of Rhampsinitus, there was perfect order in Egypt, and the whole country was in a flourishing condition; but when Cheops came to govern, he plunged into every kind of wickedness. For having shut up all the temples, he first forbade the offering of sacrifices, and afterwards ordered all the Egyptians to work for himself. Some of them he compelled to draw stones from the quarries in the Arabian mountain down to the Nile; others to receive the stones when transported in vessels across the river, and to draw them to what was called the Libyan mountain. They worked to the number of one hundred thousand men at a time, each party during three months." * Diodorus tells the same story, but calls the builder of the First Pyramid Chemmis. To command the Mizraim to shut up their temples, and to forego their usual sacrifices, must have been the act of a man whose religious opinions were widely different from those of the multitude, the original inhabitants of the country.

It is a further proof that these men who thus controlled the Mizraim were not of the race of Ham, that, after they had built the Pyramids, whatever might be their object in accomplishing that undertaking, they withdrew from the country immediately, as if they were of a different family, and their departure was the cause of great rejoicing among the Egyptians. They occupied

* Herod. ii.124.

the country for one hundred and six years, during all which time the temples were never opened.

After they were gone, Mycerinus, the son of Cheops, it is said, being displeased at the conduct of his father, re-opened the temples, and permitted sacrifices, and made the most just decisions of all their kings. The mummy-board which was found in the Third Pyramid, inscribed with his name in hieroglyphics, shows that he was of a different religion from that of the founders of the Great Pyramid, from whatever race they may have sprung; and would lead us to infer that he was rather a descendant from Ham, as the Mizraim were, than a son of Cheops. At some distant period, probably, his remains were entombed in the Third Pyramid.

But if the sons of Ham were not the founders of the Pyramids, neither is it likely that the sons of Japheth should have entered Egypt for the purpose of erecting these monuments. Their mission was to occupy and populate Europe, as decidedly as that of the sons of Ham was to occupy Africa. Gomer, and Magog, and Madai, and Javan, and Tubal, and Meshech, and Tiras; and the sons of Gomer, Ashkenaz, and Riphath, and Togarmah; and the sons of Javan, Elishah, and Tarshish, and Kittim, and Dodanim (as we read in the tenth chapter of Genesis), were those by whom " the isles of the Gentiles were divided in their lands; every one after his tongue, after their families, in their nations."

### 127.

Asia was the appointed portion of Shem and his descendants; but it is remarkable that no cities are mentioned as being in their occupation. They were from the beginning of their history a pastoral people, dwelling in tents; and this was the character of their

descendants for many generations. It is said, in the
ninth chapter of Genesis, ver. 27 : " God shall enlarge
Japheth, and he shall dwell in the *tents* of Shem."
Wherever Abraham went, he pitched his *tent* : and " Lot
also, which went with Abraham, had flocks, and herds,
and *tents*." Jacob, also, was " a plain man, dwelling in
*tents*." It is true, that we read also of herdsmen and
shepherds dwelling in tents among the race of Ham ;
but the great difference between the shepherds of
Africa, and those who descended from Shem, and dwelt
in Asia, was the difference of their religious belief.

Manetho, an Egyptian priest, who lived about 300
years B.C., in his account of the Shepherd Kings,* says:
" We had formerly a king whose name was Timaos.
In his time it came to pass, I know not how, that God
was displeased with us ; and there came up from the
East, in a strange manner, men of an ignoble race, who
had the confidence to invade our country, and easily
subdued it by their power, without a battle. And
when they had our rulers in their hands, they burnt
our cities, and demolished the temples of the gods, and
inflicted every kind of barbarity upon the inhabitants ;
slaying some, and reducing the wives and children of
others to a state of slavery." Manetho mentions the
names of six, who were "the first rulers among them ;
and during all the period of their dynasty, they made
war upon the Egyptians, in the hope of exterminating
the whole race. All this nation," continues Manetho,
" was styled *Hycsos*, that is, the *the Shepherd Kings ;* for
the first syllable, *Hyc*, according to the sacred dialect,
denotes *a king*, and *sos* signifies *a shepherd*, but this according to the vulgar tongue ; and of these is com-

---

\* Cory's Ancient Fragments, p.68.

pounded the term *Hycsos. Some say they were Arabians.*
This people, who were thus denominated *Shepherd Kings,*
and their descendants, retained possession of Egypt for
the space of five hundred and eleven years."

The Egyptians say, as Herodotus informs us, that
Cheops reigned 50 years, and that his brother Cephren,
who succeeded to the kingdom, reigned 56 years.
"Thus," he adds, "106 years are reckoned, during
which the Egyptians suffered all kinds of calamities; and for this length of time the temples were
closed, and never opened. From the hatred they bear
them, the Egyptians are not very willing to mention
their names, but call the Pyramids after *Philition,* a
shepherd who at that time kept his cattle in those
parts."\*

The 106 years during which the *Shepherd Kings*
occupied Egypt, added to the 400 years (or 430 years)
during which the Israelites dwelt there, constitute the
period of 511 years alluded to by Manetho. On this
subject, Bryant makes the following reflection: " From
hence we learn that there was a two-fold race of people
who sojourned in Egypt; and however their history
may be in some respects confused, yet much light may
be obtained from it upon a close examination. They
were each of them esteemed *shepherds,* as will be found
upon further inquiry. The *first shepherds* were *lords and
conquerors*: the others were *servants,* and had the very
city given them to inhabit which the first had evacuated.
These *latter* are manifestly a separate and distinct people; and though they may have some circumstances
blended and misplaced, yet, from the name of their
leader and lawgiver (Moses), it is plain that they were

---

\* Herod. ii. 128.

*Israelites.* As to the *first,* they are supposed to have been *Arabians,* and are said to have come from the East. Indeed, every nation that ever came out of *Asia* into *Egypt,* must ultimately come from the East; there being but one way into the country, which was by the *isthmus* between the two seas. If this was the sense of Manetho, it was saying nothing. It was a circumstance common to every nation that way, which visited the land of *Ham.* His meaning was, that they came from a country situated eastward in respect to that which they came to.* . . . They have been styled *Arabian shepherds,* because all the primitive Arabians were *Nomades,* or shepherds.† . . . I hope," he proceeds, " I have given a satisfactory account of the *Arabian shepherds,* who came from *Babylonia,* and settled in *Egypt.*" ‡ Archbishop Usher refers the migration of the Shepherd Kings from Arabia into Egypt, " to the year of the world 1920, according to the Hebrew computation : in the 101st year of the life of Serug, the seventh from Noah, and in the 42nd of Terah, 88 years before the birth of Abraham. But this," says Bryant, " is a degree of exactness that I do not pretend to arrive at." § If we deduct 1920 from 4004, we shall have 2084 B.C. for the period of the migration of the Shepherd Kings into Egypt, according to Archbishop Usher, which is within 40 years of the date assumed in the preceding letter, written in 1839.

---

* Bryant's Ancient Mythology, vi. 113.  † *Ibid.,* vi. 126.
  ‡ *Ibid.,* vi. 148.    § *Ibid.,* vi. 153.

CHAPTER XXIII.

*These Shepherds were an Abomination to the Egyptians — The*
*Cause existed before the Deluge.*

128.

BRYANT maintains, and very learnedly proves, that
the ancient Egyptians did not refrain from eating
sheep or oxen; they only abstained from using them for
*sacrifice.* "They shed no blood in their temples, nor
brought victims to their altars; and though Herodotus
does make mention of bloody sacrifices in his time, yet
it was not so of old. Even when he wrote, it was not
universal. . . . When Pharaoh, therefore, to prevent the
children of Israel from going three days' journey into
the wilderness, tells Moses, that they may sacrifice to
their God in *Egypt*, he is answered, 'It is not meet so
to do; for we shall sacrifice the abomination of the
Egyptians to the LORD our God. Lo, shall we sacrifice
the abomination of the Egyptians before their eyes, and
will they not stone us?'* The abomination was a
*sacrifice of blood*; which offering was so offensive to the
Egyptians, that the Israelites, during their sojournment,
do not appear to have once ventured to sacrifice after the
custom of their fathers. They seem to have been under
a prohibition from the princes of the country, as we
may infer from the repeated requests of Moses; who,

* Exod. viii. 26.

unless he went three days' journey into the wilderness, did not think it safe to offer a burnt-offering to the Lord. In respect to sacrifices, in those early times, it was usual for people of every profession to make some returns to the gods for the benefits they enjoyed. This acknowledgment was generally made out of the increase that they were particularly blest with. Among the Egyptians, it consisted originally in handfuls of corn, grass, and of the lotus, with other fruits of the earth. In process of time they added myrrh, frankincense, and cassia for the service of the altars. Such were the offerings of the ancient *Egyptians*. On the other hand, the shepherd's increase was from the fold only; and his offerings were the firstlings of the flock. This made the Egyptians dislike *shepherds*; not their occupation, for nothing was more innocent or necessary. Besides, they had flocks of their own, and consequently people to tend them. But they disliked *foreign shepherds*, on account of their different rites and customs, which hatred must have arisen from an intimate intercourse; for we do not abominate what we are little acquainted with."*

According to this view, the Egyptians did not dislike shepherds and herdsmen merely as feeders of sheep and oxen; they hated only those shepherds and herdsmen who offered up either sheep or oxen as a religious offering. This was the case, however, with all the Israelitish shepherds and herdsmen, for they were of the race of Shem; while it was not the case with any of those shepherds and herdsmen who were of the race of Ham.

Before the sacrifices of the Mosaic Law had been enjoined from Mount Sinai, as early as the arrival of

* Ant. Mythol.. vol. vi. p.174.

Jacob and his family in Egypt, it was told him by his son Joseph, that "every *shepherd* is an abomination unto the Egyptians."* Thus, it was some custom of the shepherds, before the Israelites came among them, which made *shepherds* so obnoxious to the Egyptians, that even the name of "shepherd" was regarded as a term of reproach. How happened it then, we may ask, that this custom of offering animals in sacrifice, which had obtained among the predecessors of the Israelites, was so universally considered applicable to this class of shepherds, only, that the name of *shepherd* suggested no other idea to the Egyptian, than that of one who offered up animal sacrifices as a religious offering?

It was certainly the practice of the Israelites to make such offerings before the Law was promulgated from Mount Sinai; because when Pharaoh, after the Plague of Darkness—the last plague but one—"called unto Moses, and said: Go ye, serve the LORD; only let your flocks and your herds be stayed: let your little ones also go with you. Moses said, Thou must give into our hands also *sacrifices and burnt-offerings*, that we may sacrifice unto the LORD our God. Our cattle also shall go with us; there shall not a hoof be left behind, for *thereof* must we take to serve the LORD our God; and we know not with what we must serve the Lord, until we come thither."† Thus sacrifices and burnt-offerings were common among the Israelites, after they had dwelt in the Land of Egypt upwards of 200 years; but this, it may be said, does not account for the odium attached by the Egyptians to the name of *shepherd*, as early as the time of Joseph.

* Gen. xlvi. 34.          † Exod. x. 24.

To explain the cause we must go back to the period of the *Shepherd Kings*, and show that they were shepherds of the same obnoxious class with the Israelites under Moses; being, like them, descendants of Shem, and not of Ham. The probability of this is placed beyond all doubt, if we consider what Manetho has said of them, and what Herodotus has recorded; but it will be desirable to show also, that, as shepherds, they could be of no other class (since they differed from the Egyptians) than that which made use of sheep and oxen in sacrifice.

### 129.

In Gen. iii. 21, we read, that after the Fall, "unto Adam also, and his wife, did the Lord make *coats of skins,* and clothed them." Some animals, therefore, must have been deprived of life for this purpose; and it was not done for the sake of food, since flesh was not eaten by mankind in the world before the flood. In Gen. i. 29, God says to Adam and Eve, "Behold, I have given you EVERY HERB bearing seed, which is upon the face of all the earth, and every tree in which is the fruit of a tree yielding seed; to you it shall be for MEAT." It was not till after the Deluge that God said to Noah (Gen. ix. 3), "Every MOVING THING that LIVETH shall be MEAT for you; even as the green herb have I given you all these things. But FLESH with the LIFE thereof, which is the BLOOD thereof, shall ye not eat."

We infer from this, that as some animals were slain, soon after the Fall of man, and it was not for food, their lives must have been regarded as a vicarious offering for that of man, by which offering he was to be constantly reminded, and as constantly required to make acknowledgment, of his own guilt, and of the just judgment of God upon him, when Jehovah said, "In the day that thou eatest thereof (viz., of the forbidden fruit), thou shalt surely die" (ii. 17.) Of the truth of this inference we can have no doubt, if we consider what is related in the following passage concerning Cain and Abel.

"In process of time it came to pass, that Cain brought of the fruit of the ground an offering unto the LORD; and Abel, he also brought of the firstlings of his flock, and of the fat thereof." (iv. 3). That Abel brought "of the fat thereof," is a sufficient proof that the animals were first slain. But as "Abel was a feeder of sheep, and Cain a tiller of the ground," it may perhaps be thought that each offered unto the Lord that appropriate increase of his substance, which was justly due from him (as Bryant seems to have imagined), and that no vicarious atonement by the sacrifice of the life of an animal was required to be offered by either of them. The Hebrew text, however, if rightly interpreted, forbids this supposition. Our English Version says, with sufficient accuracy, "The LORD had respect unto Abel and to his offering; but unto Cain and his offering, he had not respect. And Cain was very wroth, and his countenance fell." But when it proceeds as follows, "And the LORD said unto Cain, Why art thou wroth? and why is thy countenance fallen? If thou doest well, shalt thou not be accepted? And if thou doest not well, *sin lieth at the door*," the translation is evidently incorrect; for this last passage should be rendered, "A SIN-OFFERING LIETH AT THE DOOR." This sin-offering was, without doubt, a LAMB; and thus, immediately after Adam's transgression, that atoning sacrifice was required to be offered, which was the type of "the Lamb slain from the foundation of the world."

That the interpretation here given is correct, may be easily proved: CHATTATH, the Hebrew word for *sin*, means also a *sin-offering;* but though the two meanings are so very different, a ready and simple rule may be given, which will enable any one to determine in which of the two senses the word ought always to be taken. It is this: Whenever CHATTATH is used *relatively*, that is, in connexion with a *possessive pronoun*, it stands for *sin*; whenever it is used *absolutely*, it stands for *sin-offering*. In the five Books of Moses, it is employed 138 times: 40 in the sense of *sin* (as my *sin*, his *sin*, &c.), and 98 times as sin-offering. Five apparent exceptions occur (in Lev. ix. 7, and x. 19, thy *sin-offering*, their *sin-offering*, and in Lev. iv. 14, and xix. 22, the *sin*); but, in these five cases, the context prevents any misconception as to the true meaning.

Hence it appears, that in this case it stands for a *sin-offering*, which Cain refused to avail himself of, involving, as it did, an acknowledgment of his sinfulness in the sight of God, and his admission of the necessity of an atoning sacrifice. He rejected the appointed means of grace: and all his posterity, it is to be feared, rejected in like manner the opportunity of reconciliation with God which had thus been provided for them. Even after the Deluge, the posterity of Ham, as it seems, recoiled from the offering of any animal sacrifice for sin, and held in abhorrence those who had recourse to it. This, then, was the real cause of their dislike to the Shepherd Kings, who practised that religious rite, and proclaimed, by so doing, that they were of a different race from the Mizraim. These Asiatic Shepherds were the progenitors of Moses, who led the Children of

Israel out of Egypt, to offer sacrifices in the wilderness; and of Abraham, who offered up the ram on one of the mountains of Moriah, as a " burnt-offering in the stead of his son." (Gen. xxii. 13). Their progenitor was Shem; and they were of the same faith with Noah, who, when he came forth from the ark, " builded an altar unto the Lord, and took of every clean beast, and of every clean fowl, and offered burnt-offerings on the altar." (Gen. viii. 20). That the founders of the Pyramids were of the same race with the Children of Israel, who afterwards dwelt in Egypt, and were brought out of that land by Moses, is further shown by *Manetho*, when he says: "This people, who were thus denominated Shepherd Kings, and their descendants, retained possession of Egypt for the space of 511 years." Even the incidental notice preserved by Herodotus, that "from the hatred they bear them, the Egyptians are not very willing to mention their names, but call the Pyramids after *Philition*, a Shepherd, who at that time kept his cattle in those parts," tends to prove that the religion of the founders of the Pyramids was the same as that of Abraham, Moses, and the Children of Israel, before the Exodus.   *Philition*, here used as a proper name, is a Greek word (φιλίτιον) signifying a *love-feast*; and the meaning probably is, that the Egyptians, when they had occasion to speak of those feasts at which the animal sacrifices were offered, and of which sacrifices the people afterwards partook, preferred calling them by this name of *love-feasts* (*philitia*), rather than by one which meant a feast at which the blood of animals was offered as a religious sacrifice.

The Spartans had public meals, of which all partook, which they called συσσιτια (*sussitia*), and at which

"wheaten bread" alone was eaten, as that name indi-
cates.    No slaughtered animals were laid upon an
altar : they were public entertainments, which had no
religious character.   The *philitia* of the founders of the
Pyramids—as of the later Jews—on the contrary, were
*public feasts,* at which *animal sacrifices* were offered,
and at which *blood* was shed, which was intended to be
commemorative of the love of God in providing *an
atonement for the sins of man,* by which his soul might be
saved.    These feasts had thus the same sacred import
in the earliest times, which the *love-feasts* (αγάπαι) of
the Christians have at the present day, when the communicants meet together to partake of the Lord's
Supper; for they then commemorate the Saviour's *love*
in the sacrifice of Himself for their sakes.   Love-feasts
denote also the love which the communicants have for
each other : but the love which the Saviour showed for
all mankind gave rise to the name.   Before the Flood,
when animal food was not eaten, the sacrifice could
only be regarded as a religious rite, and not in any
sense as a *love-feast.*  Subsequently to the Deluge, when
burnt sacrifices were offered, of which all the members
of the same family or community partook, the religious
ceremony might be properly characterized as a love-
feast (*philition*), by those who did not regard it as a
religious ceremony.   "Behold Israel after the flesh :
are not all they which eat of the sacrifices, partakers of
the altar?" (1 Cor. x. 18).   The love-feasts (αγάπαι) of
the Christians, which have superseded those of the
Jews, are not attended with the sacrifice of any creature, because the types are now all fulfilled, in the one
great Sin-offering which our Lord has made of Himself,
once for all, on the Cross: and these feasts are therefore simply commemorative of His death, by which our

lives are redeemed. But, whenever we partake of the flesh of any creature which is slain for our use, we ought to remember that, at first, on account of the substitution of an animal's life for our own, our lives were spared, which lives, in return, are due to God, and ought to be devoted to His service.

## Chapter XXIV.

*The Founders of the Great Pyramid were the Race of Shem —
Scriptural Chronology with reference to the Founders.*

### 130.

THE building of the City and Tower of Babel, on a
plain, in the land of Shinar, was begun before
mankind were "scattered abroad upon the face of the
whole earth." The attempt was frustrated on account
of the presumption by which it was attended. "So
the LORD scattered them abroad from thence upon the
face of all the earth: and they left off to build the
city." (Gen. xi. 8). The Hebrew chronology places this
event in the year before Christ, 2247.

About this time, it is said, lived *Peleg*, "for in his
days was the earth *divided.*" His name in the Hebrew
language signifies *Division.* "His brother's name was
Joktan, and Joktan begat Almodad, and Sheleph, and
Hazarmaveth, and Jerah, and Hadoram, and Uzal, and
Diklah, and Obal, and Abimael, and Sheba, and Ophir,
and Havilah, and Jobab: all these were the sons of
Joktan" (x. 25). To these men of the race of Shem,
who are all mentioned so particularly, we are disposed
to ascribe the building of the Pyramids of Gizeh.

Leaving Babylonia to the occupation of the sons of
Ham who had taken possession of it, a part of the race
of Shem were, as we conceive, led by the Spirit of God

to undertake the fulfilment of the great design by which they were actuated, in a country better adapted for their undertaking than the marshy and bituminous soil of the plain of Shinar.

In no part of the world could they have found a place better suited for their purpose than Egypt. On the elevated ground near the Nile, before that river becomes divided into two branches, a natural platform, made by a limestone rock, supplied them with the greater part of the materials required for the construction of the Pyramids, on the spot where they were intended to be built. Quarries of marble and granite were of easy access across the river, for the formation of those parts of the structure which were more exposed to injury. The air of that country was remarkably free from moisture. A river of the purest and most refreshing water ran through a fertile land, on which grew all the food necessary for the support of their numerous labourers, almost without effort on the part of man, in consequence of the annual overflowing of the river. All these circumstances constituted so many and such obvious recommendations of the place, that we cannot but suppose they may have determined the choice of the founders to that particular locality in which the Pyramids are built.

They came into the country as strangers; they were not of the same race nor of the same religion with the Mizraim, who preceded them in its occupation; they did not invade it as conquerors, though, as Manetho tells us, "they easily subdued it by their power *without a battle.*" They must, therefore, have come either in such large numbers as to make opposition hopeless, or they must have been received as benefactors by the common people whom they employed; and it was only

after their departure that their memory was calum-
niated by the stories told of their oppression. They
were evidently animated by a strong desire to perform
a certain task, and when they had accomplished it they
left the country of their own accord, confiding to the
care of the original inhabitants those wonderful works
by which they had enriched and ennobled the land.
They never returned to claim any interest in the fruits
of their labours, but occupied some other country, in
which they erected no such monuments as these.

They were so far like conquerors, or tyrants as they
were called, that they were, for the time being, the
ruling power of the country. They employed the common people in realizing their magnificent conceptions,
for which they must have given them the most minute
directions; and this evident superiority of intellect may
have caused the ignorant to envy and misrepresent
them. But that they improved the condition of the
people among whom they took up their abode during
not less than 100 years, must be admitted by all who
know how greatly an inferior race is benefited by the
invasion of a superior. If any body of men were now
to come into England, and by their wisdom direct us to
construct some works of a most durable kind, and, in
return for the labour they required from the common
people, were to provide them with food and clothing for
100 years, at the end of which time that body of men
would peaceably depart, should we not have reason to
regard them as very great benefactors, instead of
tyrants? But if they professed a religious creed different from our own, though it were of a more elevated
and spiritual character, than ours, it is very likely that
we should not long continue to speak well of them.

There could have been no motive sufficient to allure

such a people as this to the banks of the Nile, according to the views which are usually taken of men's conduct. To build sepulchres of so vast a size, in which no human being was ever laid—to build them for their own sepulchres, and then to leave them as soon as they were completed, in order to go to some other country for the rest of their lives, and there to be buried in obscure graves—is too absurd a supposition to be entertained concerning any rational creatures; and that these men were wise above most others, is shown by their works. To build storehouses for corn of so vast a bulk, without leaving in them any chambers capable of holding corn, or accessible to persons bringing it, even if the chambers were large enough, is to attri-bute to the founders of the Pyramids, a degree of folly of which no people in the world were ever capable.

For one purpose alone does it seem reasonable to con-clude that any men should have undertaken so pro-digious a labour, without looking for the slightest advantage to themselves; and it is that purpose for which we have seen so much evidence adduced, as to force us to conclude that it must have been the end for which the Pyramids were formed; viz., that they might serve as a record and memorial, to the end of time, of the Measure of the Earth; and, secondly, form a Standard of measures of length, capacity, and weight, to which all nations might appeal, as to a common authority, in their dealings with each other. But to attribute to the founders so grand and liberal a design, is to affirm that they were the greatest philosophers and the greatest benefactors the world ever knew. This is a title we shall be justified in conferring upon the sons of Shem, if no other persons were in existence to whom it would be more consistent with the facts of

history to attribute it.   Let us, therefore, take a sum-
mary view of the various eminent men then living, to
see if any might better deserve this title ; and also to
discover who among them were likely to have been
the originators and directors of this profound design
and most stupendous undertaking.

### 131.

### CHRONOLOGICAL TABLE,

*According to the Hebrew Scriptures.*

A.M.      B.C.
  1 = 4004   CREATION of ADAM.
1056 = 2948   Birth of NOAH, son of Lamech.
1558 = 2446   Birth of SHEM, son of Noah.

        *\** *The recorded contemporaries of* SHEM *were —*
        JAPHETH, the eldest son of Noah.
        HAM, the other son of Noah.

1655 = 2349   The DELUGE.
1658 = 2346   Birth of ARPHAXAD, son of Shem.

        *\** *The recorded contemporaries of* ARPHAXAD *were—*
        Four other sons of Shem : ELAM, ASSHUR, LUD,
        and ARAM.
        Seven sons of Japheth : GOMER, MAGOG, MADAI,
        JAVAN, TUBAL, MESHECH, and TIRAS.
        Four sons of Ham : CUSH, MIZRAIM, PHUT, and
        CANAAN.

1683 = 2311   Birth of SALAH, son of Arphaxad.

        *\** *The recorded contemporaries of* SALAH *were—*
        Three sons of Gomer : ASHKENAZ, RIPHATH, and
        TOGARMAH.
        Four sons of Javan : ELISHAH, TARSHISH, KITTIM,
        and DODANIM.
        Four sons of Aram : UZ, HUL, GETHER, and MASH.
        Five sons of Cush : SEBA, HAVILAH, SABTAH,
        RAAMAH, and SABTECHAH.
        The grandson of Ham : NIMROD.

A.M.   B.C.

The sons of Mizraim : LUDIM, ANAMIM, LEHABIM, NAPHTUHIM, PATHRUSIM, CASLUHIM, and CAPHTORIM.

The sons of Canaan : SIDON, HETH, the JEBUSITE, AMORITE, GIRGASITE, HIVITE, ARKITE, SINITE, ARVADITE, ZEMARITE, and HAMATHITE.

1713 = 2281   Birth of EBER, son of Salah.

*₊* *The recorded contemporaries of* EBER *were—*
Two sons of Raamah : SHEBA and DEDAN.

1757 = 2247   Birth of PELEG, son of Eber.

*₊* *The recorded contemporary of* PELEG *was—*
The other son of Eber : JOKTAN.
In the days of PELEG the earth was divided.

1787 = 2217   Birth of REU, son of Peleg.

*₊* *The recorded contemporaries of* REU *were—*
Thirteen sons of Joktan : ALMODAD, SHELEPH, HAZARMAVETH, JERAH, HADORAM, UZAL, DIKLAH, OBAL, ABIMAEL, SHEBA, OPHIR, HAVILAH, JOBAB.

1819 = 2185   Birth of SERUG, son of Reu.
1849 = 2155   Birth of NAHOR, son of Serug.
1877 = 2126   Birth of TERAH, son of Nahor.
1996 = 2008   Death of PELEG, aged 239.
1997 = 2007   Death of NAHOR, aged 148.
2006 = 1998   Death of NOAH, aged 950.
2008 = 1996   Birth of ABRAHAM, son of Terah.
2026 = 1978   Death of REU, aged 239.
2049 = 1955   Death of SERUG, aged 230.
2073 = 1921   Death of TERAH, aged 205.
2091 = 1913   MELCHIZEDEK blesses Abraham.
2096 = 1908   Death of ARPHAXAD, aged 438.
2126 = 1878   Death of SALAH, aged 433.
2158 = 1846   Death of SHEM, aged 600.
2182 = 1822   Death of ABRAHAM, aged 175.
2187 = 1817   Death of EBER, aged 464.

Omitting HAM and his descendants, and leaving it doubtful whether JAPHETH and any of his family were engaged in this great undertaking, we have, for the probable founders of the Pyramids : — 1, NOAH ; 2, SHEM ; 3, ARPHAXAD and his BRETHREN, *Elam, Asshur, Lud,* and *Aram* ; 4, SALAH and his COUSINS, *Uz, Hul, Gether,* and *Mash* ; 5, EBER ; 6, PELEG and his brother JOKTAN ; 7, REU and his COUSINS, the THIRTEEN SONS OF JOKTAN ; by some of whom, if not by all, was commenced, carried on, and completed, the most magnificent, disinterested, and glorious work that was ever conceived and executed by mankind.

## Chapter XXV.

*Noah the probable originator of the Work — The Sons of Joktan the probable Builders — Dr. Townsend's opinion concerning Jobab — All the Sons of Joktan settled in Arabia Felix.*

### 132.

TO Noah we must ascribe the original idea, the presiding mind, and the benevolent purpose. He who built the Ark was, of all men, the most competent to direct the building of the Great Pyramid. He was born 600 years before the Flood, and lived 350 years after that event, dying in the year 1998 b.c. Supposing the Pyramids were commenced in 2160 b.c. (that is, 4000 years ago), they were founded 168 years before the death of Noah. We are told that Noah was a "preacher of righteousness"; and this was his title, probably, before the Flood. But nothing could more perfectly illustrate this character of a preacher of righteousness after the Flood, than that he should be the first to establish a system of *weights and measures* for the use of all mankind, based upon the Measure of the Earth.

Shem lived 600 years, and died in 1846 b.c. If the Pyramids were commenced· in 2160 b.c., they were founded 314 years before the death of Shem. As he was next in length of life to Noah, so was he probably next in rank and dignity.

Melchizedek blessed Abraham, 67 years before the

death of Shem; and some have supposed that Shem himself may have been that king of righteousness and priest of the Most High God, by a superior title to that of Aaron. But the account given of *Melchizedek*, that he was " without father, without mother, without descent, having neither beginning of days nor end of life, but made like unto the Son of God," forbids this supposition. Whoever he might be, *Melchizedek* was on the earth at the time the Pyramids were founded.

ARPHAXAD died in 1908 B.C., at the age of 438; SALAH in 1878, at the age of 433; EBER in 1817, at the age of 464. They were each, accordingly, 186, 151, and 121 years of age at the time the Pyramids were built; and they lived after that event 252, 282, and 343 years respectively. Thus these three venerable men may have been present throughout the construction of the Pyramids.

PELEG was 87 years old when the Pyramids were built, dating them from 2160 B.C.; and he lived after that event 152 years.

REU was 57 years old in 2160, and he lived after that time 182 years. As the sons of Joktan were the contemporaries of Reu, they were probably born between 2217 and 2200 B.C., which would make the youngest of them 40 years old in 2160 : and if they lived to be as old as Reu, the eldest of them would have lived 182 years, and the youngest 199 years, after the Pyramids began to be built. Allowing 100 years for the term occupied in building them, all these sons of Shem, had they been the founders, would have had ample time to complete their great undertaking.

133.

The inquiry has been often made, " Why should the

sons of *Joktan* be mentioned to the number of *thirteen* in the 10th chapter of Genesis, when of the sons of *Peleg*, the elder brother of Joktan, only *Reu* is named?" Dr. Townsend, late Prebendary of Durham, thinks the whole of the *thirteen* are enumerated on purpose to bring in the last of them, and that *Jobab* was the same as *Job*. But it would be a more complete reason for the record of all their names if it could be shewn, that these men were probably so much distinguished above their contemporaries, because they were those *Shepherd Kings* by whom the Pyramids were built. They withdrew afterwards, as we learn, into Arabia, which makes them *Arabians ;* and the eldest had a name given him which tends to confirm this view of their occupation while they were in Egypt.

Bochart says, "ALMODAD, the eldest of the thirteen sons of Joktan, appears to have given name to the *Almodæi*, a people of Arabia, who are called by the Greeks *Allumeotæ.* You will find them," he observes, "in the Tables of Ptolemy, placed almost in the centre of Arabia Felix, near the sources of the Lar, a river which flows into the Persian Gulf. In the Greek text of Ptolemy they are called *Αλλουμαιωται.*" Bochart then remarks, that ALMODAD, in the Hebrew language, signifies *The Measurer ;* and in his comment on this name, he adds, " ALMODAD is described, in the Chaldaic Paraphrase of Jonathan, as the *Inventor of Geometry*, באשלין דמשח ית ארעא *qui mensurabat terram finibus.*" Now, what name could be more properly given to the eldest of the sons of Joktan than one which describes him as having *measured the earth to its extremities,* if he were really the founder of the Pyramids? Whether the name of ALMODAD contained a meaning which gave rise to the remark of Jonathan, or whether he reported an

opinion which had descended down the stream of time
to his days in connexion with this name; in either case,
we infer from it, that one of the sons of Joktan was
pre-eminently distinguished as the *Inventor of Geometry*
and the *Measurer of the Earth*.

The name of the second son is SHELEPH. Of him it is
said, by the same paraphrast, " שלף מוי דנהרותא *aquas
eduxit è fluminibus.*" The second son of Joktan may have
been employed in *drawing waters from the rivers*; but as
history is silent as to this fact, it is one which we have
no means of ascertaining. The great canal by which
the water was drawn off from the Nile when it came
down in too great abundance, was a work very likely to
have been coeval with the building of the Pyramids;
but there is no record of its existence at so early a
period. It is commonly called Bahr Yousef, the canal
of Joseph. This implies, however, no more than that it
was a very ancient work, and is not to be considered as
proving that it was constructed by Joseph. Whether
we regard the magnitude of the conception, or the vast
importance of the undertaking, with respect to the per-
manence of the Pyramids, and the uniform supply of
food to those who were employed in building them, this
provision for drawing off the superfluous waters of the
Nile, was an object very likely to engage the attention
of the founders in the next degree to the establishment
of the Pyramids themselves.

The name of SHELEPH, says Bochart, is evidently
taken from שלף SALEPH, which word, as a verb, means
*to draw forth*. This SALEPH (or Sheleph), he adds,
" was the father of the *Salapeni*, who removed a long
way off from the rest of their brethren, almost to the
αυχενα (*straits* or *isthmus*) of Arabia, not far from the

source of the river Betius. In the Tables of Ptolemy, the *Alapeni* are put by mistake for the *Salapeni*; for, in the text of Ptolemy, they are called Σαλαπήνοι, not Ἀλαπήνοι. These two tribes of whom I have been speaking," says Bochart, " the *Allumeotæ* and the *Salapeni*, were little known to the Greeks, because they dwelt in the very heart of Arabia Felix, far away from the sea."

The third son of Joktan was called HAZARMAVETH, which name is pronounced *Hadramauth*, or *Chadramauth*, by the Arabians. The Greeks represent the name in a variety of forms: Ασαρμωθ, Σαρμωθ, and Αρμωθ; Ατερμωθ and Αδραμντα. Dionysius Periegetes calls it *Chatramis*; Strabo, *Chatramitis*; Artemidorus, *Atramolitæ*; Eratosthenes and Pliny, *Chatramolitæ*, *Chatrimmitæ*, and even *Atramitæ* or *Adramitæ*. In the opinion of Epiphanius, ASARMOTH, or HAZARMAVETH, was the *inventor of the Arabian language*, though the Arabians themselves, he says, refer it to *Joktan*. HAZARMAVETH, or *Hadramauth*, is that region of Arabia which chiefly produces those odoriferous plants, myrrh, frankincense, aloes, cassia, and cinnamon, for which the country is celebrated. Its capital was called *Sabota* by Pliny, *Sabbatha* by Arrian, and *Saubatha* by Ptolemy.

JERAH, the fourth son of Joktan, gave name to the *Jerachæans*, who are also called the *Alilæans* (Αλιλαιοι), a people living near the Red Sea, and bordering on the Cassanitæ. Their country was not only rich in corn, but abounded also with gold, which was found sometimes of the size of a walnut (something like our modern nugget).

The name of HADORAM, the fifth son of Joktan, is traced to the remotest corner of Arabia, towards the east, where he became the ancestor of the *Drimati* (quasi *Hadoramati*), a people who dwelt near the Straits of the Persian Gulf.

UZAL, the sixth son of Joktan, established himself in the south part of Arabia Felix ; his capital was *Sanaa,* a place which has been compared with Damascus for the abundance of its fruits, and the pleasantness of its fountains. The following passage from Ezekiel is supposed to have reference to *Uzal's* territory. " Dan also, and Javan, coming *from Uzal,* occupied in thy fairs ; bright iron, cassia, and calamus, were in thy market" (xxvii. 19). *Meuzel,* " from Uzal," is rendered " going to and fro" in our Version.

DIKLAH is the name of the seventh son of Joktan. *Dicla,* in the Chaldee and Syriac languages, means a *palm-tree* or *palm-grove,* and hence by the Syrians, that part of Arabia Felix where the palm chiefly abounds, was called *Dicla.* This was the country of the *Minæi,* who were famous for their traffic in frankincense and other aromatics, which they brought from the interior of the country to sell to the Syrians. The myrrh of this region is much esteemed. Besides these *Minæi,* who were descended from Shem, and dwelt in *Arabia Felix,* there was another race of the same name inhabiting. *Arabia Deserta,* who were of the stock of Ham.

OBAL, the eighth son of Joktan, passed over the Straits of Babelmandeb, in the Arabian Gulf, and took possession of the bay, called after his name the *Avalitic* Bay, on the coast of Abyssinia, in the Troglodyte Arabia. Here his descendants carried on a large trade in myrrh of the first quality, and other odorous drugs; in ivory also, and tortoiseshell, and tin, and wheat, and wine.

In ABIMAEL, the ninth son of Joktan, we recognise

the father of the *Mali* or *Malitæ*, as the name implies.
The place which was called by this name, was remarkable for its aromatic productions; it was in immediate
connexion with the country of the Minæi, or Diklah.

SHEBA, the tenth son of Joktan, gave origin to one
of the four tribes known by the name of *Sabæans*.
The first of this name was the son of Cush; the second
was the son of Raamah; the third was the son of
Joktan; and the fourth was the son of Jokshan, and
grandson of Abraham. The son of Joktan dwelt near
the Red Sea, where the name of his metropolis, *Saba*
also called *Mariaba*, long bore witness to his fame. His
people were the richest of the Arabians in gold and
silver and precious stones, and they abounded in luxuries
of the rarest kind. The queen of this country was that
queen of Sheba, the queen of the south, who came from
the uttermost parts of the earth to hear the wisdom of
Solomon. "She came to Jerusalem with a very great
train, with camels that bare spices, and very much gold
and precious stones:"—"And she gave the king an
hundred and twenty talents of gold, and of spices very
great store, and precious stones: there came no more
such abundance of spices as these which the queen of
Sheba gave to king Solomon" (1 Kings x. 2, 10).

OPHIR, the name of the eleventh son of Joktan,
signifies, in the Arabian language, *wealth*. It is supposed that there were two places of this name, one in
*India*, the other in *Arabia*; the latter was in the pro-
vince of the *Cassanitæ* or *Gasandæ*, from which name
we get the word *magazine*, a place in which *wealth* of
any kind is reposited. This country was famous for the
abundance of its gold, which was found in broad chinks
of the earth, and of great purity. From *Ophir* came
the almug-trees which the navy of Hiram brought to

Solomon, and of which he made pillars for the house of the Lord.

HAVILAH was the twelfth son of Joktan. There were two persons of this name. Havilah, the son of Cush, is mentioned in Gen. x. 7. The name of the son of Joktan, in Arabia, is preserved in that of *Chaulan*, a place about midway between *Sanaa* and *Merea*, in that part of the land of Tehama which borders on the land of Jemen, and extends to the Red Sea.

JOBAB, the thirteenth of the sons of Joktan, was the progenitor of the *Jobabitæ*, who dwelt near the Sachalitic Bay. This name, in the Arabic language, means a *desert*, and near that bay are frequent solitudes. So much is this the general character of the country, that from Materqua, which is at the head of the Sachalitic Bay, to its termination at Cova, near the Promontory Corodamus, now called Rasalgate, a distance of nearly sixty leagues, not a single town is found.

### 134.

As we have mentioned Dr. Townsend's opinion, that the patriarch Job was the last of the sons of Joktan, and that on his account the whole of the thirteen were enumerated, it may be proper to give here some account of that learned divine's theory. He thinks that :—

" The design of Moses, after he has completed the narrative of the dispersion of the third and fourth generations of the descendants of Noah, and thus related the ancestry of the chief nations of the world, undoubtedly was to continue the line of Shem to that of Abraham only. All interest in the other patriarchal families appears to have ceased; he takes no notice of any but that of Joktan. The family of Joktan were not the ancestors of the Messiah; neither were any of the sons of this patriarch so peculiarly distinguished in the subsequent history of Israel, that the enumeration of their names only might have been anticipated in this genealogy. But nothing is written in the Holy Scriptures without an object; and in the absence of any other object for which Moses deviated from his plan, and recorded the names of the sons of Joktan only, terminating the list with the name of Jobab or Job,— I conclude that his design was to tell us, that the Job who was the youngest son of Joktan, was the Job who lived in the land of Uz, though he was not born there, and who suffered and was tempted, as the book of Job has recorded. The sons of Joktan were enumerated, that the name of Job might be placed before the children of Israel as the witness to the truth of those doctrines which their patriarchal ancestors received, which Moses taught, and which the one Church of God in all ages has believed."

Dr. Townsend finds a confirmation of his opinion in the fact, that Job's *age*, according to the chronologers, places him between *Reu* and *Serug*; the former of whom died at the age of 239 years, the latter at the age of 230 years. He thinks that Job was from 240 to 280 years old when he died.

" The arguments," says Dr. Townsend, " for the later date of the existence of Job, by Mr. Faber and others, derived from the passages that his friend Eliphaz is called a Temanite, while Teman, who gave his name to the country, was of the family of Esau — that Bildad was a Shuhite, and that Shuah, who gave name to the country of Bildad, was the youngest son of Abraham by Keturah — are easily answered. As Moses, before the days of Havilah (the son of Cush, or of Joktan), and before the days of Ophir, the son of Joktan, calls the

country round about Eden by the names of these patri-
archs, before they existed; so it was that Eliphaz,
Bildad, and Zophar, also, came to visit Job from those
parts of Idumea, or Uz, which were subsequently called
by the names of Teman, Shuah, or Naamah."* Dr.
Townsend, following Wells in his Geography, makes the
land of Uz extend " from Stony Arabia, along the east
of Palestine, up to Damascus," which, Bochart says,
was " part of the land of Uz"; Damascus having been
built by Uz, the son of Aram. Leaving the whole of
Dr. Townsend's argument to the reader's judgment, we
now proceed with Bochart's observations on the sons of
Joktan.

### 135.

Moses says of the habitations of the sons of Joktan :
" Their dwelling was from Mesha, as thou goest unto
Sephar, a mount of the East" (Gen. x. 30). Here, as if
with extended finger, Moses points out that part of
Arabia (says Bochart) of which we have been speaking.
*Mesha*, or *Musa*, was a very celebrated port in the Red
Sea, to which Egyptian and Ethiopian merchants
resorted, and from which, proceeding eastwardly to the
*Sepharitæ*, they obtained in their way the frankincense
and myrrh, and other odorous productions, which were
to be had from the Arabians. If we look at Ptolemy's
Tables, we shall see in the Arabian gulf, at the 14th
degree, the name of *Musa*, a port of the Sabæans; and
almost opposite, towards the East, the people called the
Sepharitæ, whose metropolis was *Sephar*, at the base of
Mount Climax. Moses speaks of the East, not with
reference to Judæa, which would have the Sabæans on
its south — and hence our Lord calls the Queen of
Sheba the Queen of the South — but with reference to

* Townsend's Bible, vol. i. p. 133.

the city *Mesa*, or *Musa*, to the east of which were the *Sepharitæ*, and that long range of mountains which the Greeks called κλιμακα (*Klimaca*), but which Moses calls Sephar, from the name of the neighbouring metropolis. Ptolemy mentions this mountain as being the boundary of many states; viz., the *Sabæi*, the *Anchitæ*, the *Rhabanitæ*, the *Chatramitæ*, the *Sachalitæ*, the *Masoritæ*, the *Saritæ*, the *Sepharitæ*, and the *Rhathini*.

When, therefore, Moses says, that the sons of Joktan had their habitation " from Mesha, as thou goest unto Sephar, a mount of the East," it is the same as if he had said, they dwelt in *Arabia Odorata*, to which country the Egyptians and Ethiopians had recourse for all aromatic productions. The parts of the country which they knew best, because they were most frequented by them, were the port of Musa, where they landed, and the mountainous region of the Sepharitæ, where was a royal city. With one exception, that of the Obalites, all the sons of Joktan dwelt within these limits; and even the removal of the Obalites, across the narrow strait to the coast of Africa, may have been made after the time of Moses.

For the preceding observations on the settlement of the sons of Joktan in Arabia, we are indebted to Bochart, from whose works they are extracted.

Thus, by the providence of God, THE SONS OF JOKTAN, after they had accomplished the work which had been assigned to them in Egypt, returned, like the rest of the sons of Shem, into *Asia*; and there they occupied for their portion of land that highly-favoured region which obtained in early times the name of ARABIA FELIX; and which our own great poet has commemorated in no unworthy verse : —

" As when to them who sail
Beyond the Cape of Hope, and now are past
Mozambique, off at sea, north-east winds blow
Sabæan odours from the spicy shore
Of ARABY THE BLEST."

They withdrew from Egypt, and entered into Arabia,
which to this day bears witness of their occupation in
the names which they gave to the several districts of
that country. And as if this trace of the Shepherd
Kings were a fact too important to be lost sight of,
even Manetho's report of them is, " SOME SAY THAT THEY
WERE ARABIANS."

The order of the names of the thirteen sons of Joktan
is probably not that of their actual seniority. In Shem,
Ham, and Japheth, the order observed is not that of
their age, because Japheth was the eldest. Almodad
may be mentioned first, because of the importance of
his office; and Sheleph secondly, for the same reason.
All the names appear to have been descriptive terms,
applicable to each for some reason which it required
time to develop. Several of them were unlikely to
have been given till after their location in Arabia. We
may conclude, therefore, that they bore intermediately
some other title, by which they were for the time well
known, and that such titles as were merely temporary
gave way to others of more lasting consequence. But
this remark leaves in undiminished force the value we
must attach to the two earliest-mentioned names, since
they were evidently those which had been imposed, at
the commencement of the works in Egypt by the sons
of Joktan, on the two most prominent of all the
brethren.

## Chapter XXVI.

*The Earth divided in the days of Peleg — What is meant by the Earth being divided.*

### 136.

WHEN we read, at the end of the tenth chapter of Genesis, "These are the families of the sons of Noah, after their generations, in their nations, and by these were the nations *divided* in the earth after the flood," we ought to understand that the nations were separated from each other, and that the sacred historian meant to record the *separation* of the three great families of mankind into their respective portions of the earth.

When, secondly, in ver. 5 of the same chapter, it is said of the sons of Japheth, " By these were the isles of the Gentiles *divided* in their lands; every one after his tongue, after their families, in their nations," it is the *separation* of the sons of Japheth among the isles which is pointed out. But another meaning, different from these examples, must be given to the word *divided,* when we find it used in the following verse: " Unto Eber were born two sons; the name of the one was PELEG, for in his days was the earth DIVIDED; and his brother's name was Joktan." In the two former verses the Hebrew word made use of is PARAD, which means *separation;* in the latter it is PELEG, which means *division.* The English version represents both these senses by the word *division,* which obscures the true sense of the latter word in some degree.

PARAD means *that which is separated from something else,* as in the following instances: " Now Heber the Kenite, which was of the children of Hobab, the father-in-law of Moses, had severed [*separated*] himself from the Kenites" (Judges iv. 11). " *Separate* thyself, I pray thee, from me" (Gen. xiii. 9). "And they *separated* themselves the one from the other" (ver. 11). " And the LORD said unto Abram, after that Lot was *separated* from him" (ver. 14). " Saul and Jonathan were lovely and pleasant in their lives, and in their deaths they were not divided [*separated*]" (2 Sam. i. 23). " And Jacob did *separate* the lambs" (Gen. xxx. 40). " A whisperer *separateth* chief friends" (Prov. xvi. 28). " When he *separated* the sons of Adam" (Deut. xxxii. 8).

PELEG means *that which is divided in itself,* and not separated from something else. It is the word applied to the " *divisions* of Reuben" (Jud. v. 15, 16); to the " *divisions* of the families of the Levites" (2 Chron. xxxv. 5); to the *divisions* in the surface of the earth made by water-courses: " He shall be like a tree planted by the *rivers* of water " (Psa. i. 3). " There is a river, the *streams* whereof make glad the city of God " (Psa. xlvi. 4): " who hath *divided* a water-course for the overflowing of the waters? " (Job xxxviii. 25). " *Rivers* of waters run down mine eyes" (Psa. cxix. 136). " They shall be given into his hands until a time, and times, and the *dividing* of time " (Dan. vii. 25).

The families of the three sons of Noah were capable of *separation* from each other: but the Earth was not capable of separation from something else; and, there-fore, when we read, " the Earth was *divided* in the days of Peleg," we cannot infer that Moses intended to represent, by the word DIVIDED, the *dispersion* or *separation* of mankind from each other, after the failure of the attempt to build the Tower of Babel. On the contrary, we must conceive some *division* of the earth to be meant which would not destroy its unity ; such a super-ficial *division*, for instance, as streams of water make on the surface of the earth when they run over it; or a metaphysical division,—such a *division* as is made in *time*, when it is divided into its component parts.

But the earth could not be *divided* in this way, un-less we suppose the *division* was effected *geometrically*. If we conceive of it as divided into *degrees, minutes,* and *seconds*, we have then the word used in the same sense as when we read of " *a time, times,* and the *dividing of time* " in Daniel, wherein the times mentioned are understood to be composed of a certain number of *years, months,* and *days,* into which *time* is properly *divided*. When, therefore, it is recorded, that in Peleg's days *the earth was divided,* we ought to regard it, not as a declaration that in his days the earth was por-tioned out among mankind, but that in his days the entire superficies of the earth was divided into *degrees, minutes,* and *seconds,* each having a certain measure assigned to it, and the whole surface being intersected by these divisions.

There is great etymological propriety in the employ-ment of the word PELEG to represent the ideal lines by which the earth was marked out to its extremities; since the same means which were used to define the *time* occupied by the *earth* in the revolution of a day and year, serve equally well to indicate the *space* passed over by the *earth* in its daily and annual revolution (§ 86).

Admitting this meaning of the word PELEG to be correct, the present occasion furnishes us with another

criterion for determining the period when the Great
Pyramid was built. Peleg was born in 2247 B.C., and
died in 2008, aged 239 years. Reckoning backwards
4000 years from 1839, when Sir John Herschel was
consulted by Col. Howard Vyse, we are brought to the
year 2160 B.C. for the commencement of the Great
Pyramid, which is 87 years *after* the birth of Peleg, IN
WHOSE DAYS the Earth was *divided,* whatever might be
meant by that expression.

## Chapter XXVII.

*The Canal of Joseph, and the Lake Moeris, described by M. Linant de Bellefonds. M. Niebuhr's Opinion.*

### 137.

THE second of the sons of Joktan, called *Sheleph,* is represented by the Chaldaic paraphrast, Jonathan, as *one who drew off the waters from the rivers. Shaleph* means *to draw out* or *to draw off.* It is used " to *draw out*" the sword, or "to *draw off*" the shoe; and is equally applicable to the *drawing out* or *drawing off* the waters of the Nile. If the *Bahr Yousef* was the work of Sheleph, it included probably the whole range of that canal from its connexion with the Nile near *Diospolis Parva,* to its second junction with the same river at *Beni Souef* (about 250 miles). Here a lateral trench, or fosse, would carry the side stream into the river again, or would draw off, not only it, but the waters of the river itself, into the Lake Moeris, if the overflow were likely to be too great for the fertility of the land. This alternate diversion of the canal water either into the lake or into the river, at Beni Souef, is apparently alluded to by Herodotus in the following passage: "That water which is in the lake, is not native to the place, for the land is excessively dry; but it is conveyed by a trench from the Nile: six months it flows inward into the lake, and six months outward into the Nile again."*

* Herod. ii. 149.

The Lake Moeris, in the *earliest times,* was probably a
natural basin, into which the superfluous water of the
river was conducted, whenever it was in danger of
rising too high. This was so necessary to be done,
that the founders of the Pyramids could hardly have
neglected it; but all beyond this would probably be
the work of later ages.

" The Lake Moeris," says Herodotus, " is in circumference equal to 3600 stades, or 60 schœnes; equal, in
fact, to the sea-coast of Egypt. It extends lengthwise
from north to south, and in its deepest part is equal to
50 *orgyæ.*" " The water in this lake does not spring
from the soil, for these parts are excessively dry; but is
conveyed by a canal from the Nile." " The people of
the country told me, this lake discharges itself under
ground into the Syrtes of Libya, running westward
towards the interior, by the mountain above Memphis."

The representation given of this lake by Diodorus
Siculus is as follows: " Ten schœnes above the city
[Memphis] Myris digged a lake of admirable use, the
greatness of which work is incredible. For they relate
that the circumference of it contains 3600 furlongs;
and the depth of it in many places is 50 fathoms. Who
therefore may not deservedly ask, that shall consider
the greatness of the work, how many myriads of men,
and in how many years, made it? The common benefit
of it to those who inhabit Egypt, and the wisdom of the
king, no man can sufficiently commend. For since the
rising of the Nile is not always the same, and the
country is the more fruitful the more moderate the
rising is, he digged a lake to receive the superfluity of
the water; that neither by the greatness of the inundation unseasonably drowning the country, it should
occasion marshes or lakes; nor by flowing less than it

should do, for want of water, it should corrupt the fruits of the earth. He, therefore, cut a canal from the river to the lake, 80 furlongs long, and 300 feet in breadth; by which, sometimes receiving into, and sometimes diverting from, the river, he exhibited a seasonable quantity of water to the husbandman; the mouth of it being sometimes opened and sometimes shut, not without much art and great expenses." Greaves, who quotes this account, adds, from Strabo, that the Lake of Moeris was like a sea for greatness and for colour.

The Lake of Moeris, according to these accounts, was in circumference about 223 English miles, and in depth 300 feet. It was fed from the Nile by the canal at Beni Souef, which is now stated to be about 60 miles up the river from Gizeh. Diodorus says the canal was 80 stadia in length, which measure, if reckoned by the Greek stades, is equal to about 10 miles. The distance from the Pyramids of Gizeh to those of the Faioum, opposite Beni Souef, is exactly one degree, or 69 miles.

The most modern, and apparently the most exact description which has been given of the Lake of Moeris, is contained in the *Memoire sur le lac Moeris*, by M. Linant de Bellefonds, in 1845, appended to his "Journey from Naples to Jerusalem." From this it appears, that M. Linant had discovered the site of this celebrated lake; and though his measurements fall short of the extent assigned to it by Herodotus, Diodorus Siculus, and Pliny, they approach near enough to make it probable that these early estimates were not far from the truth.

M. Linant discovered the ancient dyke which had formed the outer embankment of the lake. This he traced from its connection with the Bahr Yousef to

its return to the same point. The space which it en-
closed he estimates at 405,479,000 square metres, or
4,367,008,830 English square feet. The depth of the
water was 25 feet, or, making allowance for evaporation,
not less than 23½ feet. It supplied a quantity of water
sufficient to irrigate for six months 967,948 *feddans* of
land; compared with which, the quantity irrigated at
the present time is only about 60,000 *feddans*, or *one
sixteenth* part of the original quantity.

M. Linant conceives, that " the water brought into
the Lake Moeris by the Bahr Yousef, during a high
inundation, was the twenty-eighth part of the total flow
of the Nile. Therefore it can be imagined, that, by
directing so considerable a flow of the river, it was
possible in part to prevent the damage sustained at that
period from the superabundant overflows: it is, at the
same time, clear, that it would have at present the very
same result — the same means being applied. Thus,
the Lake Moeris would fulfil the object attributed to it
by historical tradition."

" The water, being brought by the Bahr Yousef,
which has its point of junction about 46 metres, or 155
English feet, higher than the soil of the canal at Awara-
el-Maeta, entered, as it does now, through the Illahoun
bridge, and filled up the lake to the very top of the
dyke. Those ridges, or embankments, called the Pella-
wanne and Goued-Alla Dykes, retained the water on
the side of the lands of Egypt. When the lake was
full, the Illahoun bridge was closed, and the water was
allowed to flow through the Bahr Yousef, between the
Illahoun bridge and the little mountain opposite on the
east. Finally, when the water became low in the Bahr
Yousef, and it was required to have water for irrigation,

or to complete the overflows, then they reopened the reservoir at the Goued-Alla dyke, and the water ran into the Bahr Yousef up to the environs of Alexandria.

"If, after too abundant an inundation, and when there was still in the lake a large quantity of water which would not be required, it happened that it was again augmented, it was necessary, in order to preserve to the Lake Moeris its proper flow, to let the overplus escape into a lower place. It was then conveyed into the present *Lake Keiroun*, to dissipate gradually by evaporation, which quickly took place, being diffused over so large a space."

Herodotus makes the lake, in circumference, 3600 stades; and the Egyptian stade being equal to 327·27 English feet, the circumference would be 1,178,172 feet, or 223 English miles. Pliny estimates the circumference at 250 miles; which being reckoned as Roman miles of 4848 feet English, makes the circumference 1,212,000 English feet, or 230 English miles. M. Linant's measure would make the lake 485,702 English feet, or about 92 miles, in circumference, supposing its form to be square.

The lake is now so much reduced, in comparison with its former size, that its circumference is only 92 miles English, which was, in the times of Herodotus and Pliny, 223 or 230; and its depth only 25 English feet, which was originally about 300. Its disappearance is thus accounted for by M. Niebuhr: "For my part, I don't comprehend how people can search after it, if they bear in mind the purpose it served. As the Nile, each time when the waters subsided, left behind a deposit, the lake must in the end have been filled up with it, and thus it is quite natural that we can no longer find it. It had been made of a certain size to answer a definite purpose. When the water of the Nile was let into it, it did not evaporate altogether, but made its deposit on the bottom of the lake, which thus rose every year, so that, in the course of a long time, the lake vanished either altogether, or at least the greater part of it."*

* Niebuhr's Lectures on Ancient History, vol. i. p. 66.

## Chapter XXVIII.

*The Builders of the Tower of Babel were the Race of Ham —*
*Description of the Tower of Babel.*

### 138.

THE Scriptures represent the building of the City
and Tower of Babel, as having been the result of
an attempt, on the part of some of the descendants of
Noah, to establish themselves on the plain of Shinar,
lest they should be "scattered abroad on the face of the
earth." But "the LORD did there confound the language of all the earth : and from thence did the LORD
scatter them abroad upon the face of all the earth."
When their language was thus confounded, "they left
off to build the city." (Gen. xi.)

The builders of the City and Tower of Babel were
the descendants of Ham. "The sons of Ham were
Cush, and Mizraim, and Phut, and Canaan." "And
Cush begat Nimrod : he began to be a mighty one in
the earth. He was a mighty hunter before the LORD :
wherefore it is said, Even as Nimrod, the mighty
hunter before the LORD. And the beginning of his
kingdom was Babel, and Erech, and Accad and Calneh,
in the land of Shinar." (Gen. x. 8). As the building of
Babel was determined upon, in order that the people
should not be "scattered abroad upon the face of the
whole earth," it was an act directly in opposition to the

will of God. Whether the building of the Tower of
Babel preceded, or followed, or was contemporaneous
with, the building of the Pyramids, it originated in a
spirit the reverse of that which appears to have influ-
enced the minds of the founders of the Pyramids; for
they contemplated the dispersion of the people.

Bochart infers that none of that chosen race, who
were called the " Sons of God," were engaged in building the Tower of Babel; because we read, that " the
LORD came down to see the city which the SONS OF
MEN had builded." It was a rebellious act, and therefore it could not have been participated in by the SONS
OF GOD. But above all, it was an act clearly attributed,
by the Scriptures, to the descendants of Ham only.

"They left off to build the City." It does not say
the *Tower*. That was probably completed as an observatory. We have a remarkable testimony to the early
use of this Tower, as a place where astronomical observations were accustomed to be made, in a Commentary
on the writings of a heathen philosopher, which is thus
referred to by Dean Prideaux :—

" Over the whole, on the top of the Tower, was an
Observatory, by the benefit of which it was, that the
Babylonians advanced their skill in astronomy beyond
all other nations, and came to so early a perfection in
it as is related. For when Alexander took Babylon,
Callisthenes, the philosopher, who accompanied him
thither, found they had astronomical observations for
1903 years backward from that time, which carries up
the account as high as the 115th year after the Flood,
which was within fifteen years after the Tower of Babel
was built: for the Confusion of Tongues, which followed
immediately after the building of that Tower, happened
in the year in which Peleg was born, which was 101

years after the Flood; and, fourteen years after that, these observations began. This account Callisthenes sent from Babylon into Greece, to his master, Aristotle, as Simplicius, from the authority of Porphyry, delivers it unto us, in his Second Book, *De Coelo.*"

The preciseness of this date, 1903 years backward from the time that Alexander took Babylon, bears evidence of a pretension to exactness, which common report would not have laid claim to. The reference, also, to a communication from Callisthenes, when he was at Babylon, to Aristotle, fixes a date which cannot be misconceived. For though Alexander was twice at Babylon—where he died, in 323 B.C.—it is evident that, as Callisthenes died in 328 B.C., it must have been on the first appearance of Alexander at Babylon, when he entered that city as a conqueror, that Callisthenes sent his communication to Aristotle. Alexander entered Babylon on this occasion in 331 B.C., and quitted it in the spring of 330. We must take, therefore, the year 331, and add it to 1903 years, in order to ascertain "the earliest period of the Chaldean observations sent from Babylon, by Callisthenes, to Aristotle at Athens." This makes the period 2234 B.C.—a date within thirteen years of that assigned in the Hebrew Chronology of Archbishop Usher, to the birth of Peleg, and the building of the Tower of Babel.

Mr. Grote observes, in his *History of Greece*, that the earliest Chaldean astronomical observation known to the astronomer Ptolemy, both precise, and of an ascertained date to a degree sufficient for scientific use, was a lunar eclipse, of the 19th of March, 721 B.C., the 27th year of the era of Nabonassar." But he makes this remark in addition: "That the Chaldæans had been, long before this period, in the habit of observing

the heavens, there is no reason to doubt; and the
exactness of those observations cited by Ptolemy, implies (according to the judgment of Ideler) *long previous
practice.* The period of 223 lunations, after which the
moon reverts nearly to the same position in reference
to the Apsides and Nodes, and, after which, eclipses
return nearly in the same order and magnitude, appears to have been discovered by the Chaldæans. (Plin.
ii. 13). And they deduced from hence the mean daily
motions of the moon, with a degree of accuracy which
differs only by four seconds from modern lunar tables."*

Mr. Grote again speaks of the skill of the Chaldæans
in astronomy, in the following terms: "The conception
of the revolving celestial sphere, the gnomon, and the
division of the day into twelve parts, are affirmed by
Herodotus,† to have been first taught to the Greeks by
the Babylonians; and the continuous observation of
the heavens, both by the Egyptian and the Chaldæan
priests, had determined, with considerable exactness, both
the duration of the solar year, and other longer periods
of astronomical occurrence; thus impressing upon intelligent Greeks the imperfection of their own calen-
dars, and furnishing them with a basis, not only for
enlarged observations of their own, but also for the
discovery and application of those mathematical theories, whereby astronomy first became a science."

But with all this evidence in favor of the early perfection of astronomical science among the Chaldæans,
Mr. Grote thinks "there were exaggerated statements
respecting the antiquity of their astronomical observations, which cannot be traced as of definite and re-

---

* Grote's Greece, p. 388, vol. iii.            † ii. 109.

corded date higher than the era of Nabonassar, 747 B.C." He then refers in a note to the communication of Callisthenes to Aristotle as follows : "There seem to have been Chaldæan Observations, both made and re-corded, of much greater antiquity than the era of Nabonassar, though *we cannot lay much stress on the date of* 1903 *years anterior to Alexander the Great,* which is mentioned by Simplicius (ad Aristot. de Coelo, p. 123) as being the earliest period of the Chaldæan Observations sent from Babylon, by Callisthenes, to Aristotle." *

No one, of course, can now pretend to say on what evidence the information was founded, which was given to Callisthenes; and every one must be at liberty to form his own opinion concerning the trustworthiness of of that information. But it can hardly be thought to have had its origin in a lucky guess; and yet, if any kind of calculation had been resorted to, in order to bring out this result, it would negative the supposition that it had no scientific foundation. That documents, in a written character, existed at so early a date we cannot positively say; but some record of the *earliest period* of the Chaldæan Observations would probably remain to the time of Alexander, which a succession of Chaldæan priests would know how to interpret. If they possessed a copy of the *Pentateuch*, either in the Chaldaic, the Samaritan, or the Hebrew language, it would have been sufficient to enable them to fix a probable date to the building of the Tower of Babel, and, consequently, to the earliest observations of its priests; but even this information, coming through such a channel, would be entitled to our confidence. It is not to be supposed that Aristotle would desire Callisthenes

* Grote's Greece, vol. iii. p. 389.

to ask such a question, if he had not himself thought it capable of a satisfactory answer; and Callisthenes would scarcely have sent it to the prince of philosophers without a remark on its want of authority, had he conceived it to be in any respect unworthy of credence. We are justified, therefore, on these grounds, in regarding it as a truthful statement; and still more valuable is it when we connect it with the degree of knowledge which we have reason to think the immediate descendants of Noah would receive from their great progenitor.

We conclude, therefore, that the Tower of Babel was completed so far as to be used as an Observatory, as early as the year 2234 b.c., or about one hundred years after the deluge; and that it was presided over by scientific men, set apart for the purpose of observing and recording the motions of the heavenly bodies, and the phenomena connected with them. "The Chaldæan order of priests," says Mr. Grote, "appears to have been peculiar to Babylon, and other towns in its territory, especially between that city and the Persian Gulf. The vast, rich, and lofty temple of Belus, in that city, served at once as a place of worship, and an astronomical Observatory;—and it was the paramount ascendancy of this order which seems to have caused the Babylonian people generally to have been spoken of as Chaldæans; though some writers have supposed, without any good proof, a conquest of Assyrian Babylon by barbarians called Chaldæans, from the mountains near the Euxine."*—"We make out nothing," he adds, "distinct from Strabo respecting the Chaldæans, except that they were the *priestly order* among the Assyrians of Babylon, as they are expressly termed by Herodotus."

If the Tower of Babel had its college of intelligent

* Vol. iii. p. 387.

priests, whose astronomical observations were commenced within so short a period after the Flood, may we not equally suppose that the enlightened men to whom was confided the care of the Great Pyramid, and the interpretation of its uses as a practical standard of measures and weights, to be appealed to by all mankind, were at the beginning equally well instructed? They soon degenerated, no doubt, because they speedily lost their presiding chiefs, the Shepherd Kings, and probably afterwards had their numbers filled up by the Egyptians, who were inferior, not only to the sons of Joktan, all of whom had departed into Arabia, but even to the Chaldæan priests of the Tower of Babel. Mr. Grote very fairly infers this inferiority "from the fact that Ptolemy, though living at Alexandria, never mentions the Egyptians as astronomers, and cites no Egyptian observations; while he cites thirteen Chaldæan observations in the years B.C. 721, 720, 523, 502, 491, 383, 382, 245, 237, 229: the first ten being observations of lunar eclipses, the last three of conjunctions of planets and fixed stars."* This seems to be an important observation; but we must bear in mind, that there was an essential difference between the characters of the men who presided over the Tower of Babel, and those who were called to preside over the Pyramids. The founders of the Tower of Babel were, from the first, astronomers and astrologers. The founders of the Pyramids were, at the beginning, mathematicians and geometricians. Their successors long after founded a school for geometry at Alexandria, which has been renowned throughout all the world for the ability of its teachers. But with this school, the

* P. 387.

Egyptians never surpassed their original instructors,
the Arabians, in mathematical knowledge. With the
decay of transmitted information, their claims to intellectual distinction appear to have gradually ceased;
and though much mathematical knowledge was preserved through many centuries, it gradually lost its
vitality when it depended for its existence on the innate
energies of the native population.

### 139.

The original Tower of Babel resembled in its construction, we may fairly suppose, the subsequent Tower
of Belus, as described by Herodotus and other writers.
The latter was composed of eight several towers, as
they were called, rising one above another, the lowest
being a stade in length and breadth, and the whole, as
Strabo relates, being a stade in height.

"Herodotus saith, that the going up to it was by
stairs, on the outside, round it; from whence it seems
most likely that the whole ascent to it was by the
benching-in, drawn in a sloping line from the bottom to
the top, eight times round it; and that this made the appearance of eight towers above one another." Prideaux
has here added the words, "in a sloping line"; but the
description would be more correct if these words were
omitted, as they are not found in Herodotus.

Prideaux proceeds as follows: "For such a benching-
in, drawn in a slope eight times round in manner as
aforesaid, would make the whole seem on every side as
consisting of eight towers, and the upper tower to be
so much less than that next below it as the breadth of
the benching-in amounted to. These eight towers, being
so many stories one above another, were each of them
75 feet high, and in them were many great rooms, with

arched roofs, supported by pillars; all which were made parts of the temple, after the tower became consecrated to that idolatrous use. The uppermost story of all was that which was most sacred, and where their chiefest devotions were performed. Over the whole, on the top of the tower, was an Observatory, by the benefit of which it was that the Babylonians advancèd their skill in astronomy beyond all other nations, and came to so early a perfection in it as is related."

The height of the tower was equal to its breadth and length at bottom; and this measure was a stade or furlong, according to Strabo. The highest tower, which formed a chamber of a cube in measure, was provided with a large handsome couch, and near it was a table of gold. The ascent was from the outside, by means of a range of steps, conducted in succession along the sides of each of the towers till the top was reached.

A Greek stade was equal to 606 English feet, or 400 cubits. The height of each tower, accordingly, was 50 cubits. The length and breadth of the lowest tower was 400 cubits; of the second, 350; of the third, 300; of the fourth, 250; of the fifth, 200; of the sixth, 150; of the seventh, 100; and of the eighth, 50. These are measures of proportion, merely, in which there can be no error. Assuming, then, the stade to have been the measure of 600 feet, each tower would be 75 feet high; and if each step of the ascent was 9 inches in height, 100 steps would be equal to 75 feet. Nine inches is the height of each step in a tower of great antiquity, called the Tower of Ramleh, which Dr. Robinson met with on the great caravan road from Egypt to Damascus, in the part between Hebron and Jerusalem.*

* Robinson's Travels in the Holy Land, Vol. iii. p. 28.

As an Observatory, the highest chamber would command an extensive view over so vast a plain as that of
Shinar; but this could scarcely have been the end for
which it was constructed. To an astronomer, the ele-
vation of a chamber 600 feet above the plain would be
of little value. He could see no more of the stars
there, than on the ground below. Knowing, then, that
the use to which the tower was applied, by the information which Callisthenes obtained, was the making of
astronomical observations, we should conceive it to be
far more likely that a tower of this height was erected
as a means of observing the motions of the heavenly
bodies; and that it was so constructed as to contain in
the centre of all the towers a square or tubular shaft, of
about a stade, or 400 cubits, in height, through which
the stars might be observed, even at noon day. To
form this shaft, 600 feet high, would be, in the language
of Scripture, to make a tower "whose top may reach
unto heaven." If we suppose that the descendants of
Ham were so simple as to imagine that by the contrivance of placing one tower above another, each
smaller than the one it stood upon, they could reach
heaven, we impute to them a degree of folly of which
we see no signs in the earliest ages. They could not
make a well of any depth in that marshy ground; but
they could build a tower, which would serve the same
purpose as a well, to those who looked upwards through
the middle of it.

"From the bottom of deep narrow pits, such as a
well, or the shaft of a mine," says Sir John Herschel,*
" such bright stars as pass the zenith may even be dis-
cerned by the naked eye; and we have ourselves heard

---

* Astronomy, p. 63.

it stated by a celebrated optician, that the earliest circumstance which drew his attention to astronomy was
the regular appearance at a certain hour, for several
successive days, of a considerable star through the shaft
of a chimney." Such a shaft was formed, as we conceive, through the middle of the Tower of Babel. Of
similar construction was probably that well of Syene,
from the bottom of which the sun was said to be seen
at Midsummer-day, which caused that place to be
deemed within the tropics. That this was a well sunk
to a great depth in the earth would be unlikely, from
the difficulty of making such a well, at any time, in any
country, as well as from the extraordinary inconvenience
which would attend the use of it. That it was rather
an upward well, constructed in a tower, is far more probable, into the bottom of which any one could walk on
level ground, and enjoy all the advantages of which the
view up such a well was capable. Now there was a
famous *tower* at Syene, as we find from the following
passages in Ezekiel : " Behold, therefore, I am against
thee, and against thy rivers ; and I will make the land
of Egypt utterly waste and desolate, from the *Tower of
Syene*, even unto the border of Ethiopia."\* " They
also that uphold Egypt shall fall; and the pride of her
power shall come down; from the *Tower of Syene* shall
they fall in it by the sword, saith the Lord God."†
The marginal reading in both these passages supplies,
as an alternative, if it be thought preferable, " from
*Migdol* to Syene"; but *Migdol* means a *tower*, and the
inference is therefore the same : the tower was probably
one which contained a well, a kind of natural telescope,
like the shaft of a chimney, through which the stars

* Ezek. xxix. 10.         † Ezek. xxx. 6.

might be seen. Syene was one of two places, Alexandria being the other, from which Eratosthenes, in the third century B.C., is said to have determined the length of a degree of the meridian, by ascertaining the sun's position in the ecliptic in each place on Midsummer-day at noon.

The Tower of Babel had a base equal in extent on each side to its height. It was a building designed to last for many ages, and, in fact it did so. We can now build a chimney almost as high as this Tower without giving it any collateral or extraneous support. At Warrington, in Lancashire, a chimney has been built, of the height of 450 feet, self-supported on its own gradually tapering foundation. The height of the Great Pyramid is only 36 feet more than this; and, at the utmost that of the Tower of Babel did not exceed the height of this chimney more than 150 feet. But our buildings now are not intended for all time, as theirs were.

It is scarcely worth while to allude to the opinion of those who imagine that the Tower of Babel was built as a place of refuge for mankind in the event of another deluge. Its inadequacy for such a purpose could not fail to strike the minds of men of the dullest apprehension, many of whom would remember when, about one hundred years before, the waters had covered the highest mountains. Had they been afraid of another visitation like that, they would not have left the neighbourhood of Mount Ararat to dwell in the plain of Shinar; nor would they have thought a tower 600 feet high, built on such a plain, could avail to save them.

## CHAPTER XXIX.

*The Great Pyramid alluded to in the Book of Job — The meaning*
*of the "Morning Stars"— The meaning of the "Sons of God."*

### 140.

THE earliest allusion to the Great Pyramid is in the
Book of Job. After Elihu had offered himself
"to speak on God's behalf," in answer to Job, and had
shown that the Almighty is not to to be judged of by
man, for "we cannot find him out: he is excellent in
power, and in judgment, and in plenty of justice: he
will not afflict;"—"Then the LORD (Jehovah) answered
Job out of the whirlwind, and said:—

" Who is this that darkeneth counsel by words without
knowledge? Gird up now thy loins like a man; for I
will demand of thee, and answer thou me.

" Where wast thou when I LAID the FOUNDATIONS of
the earth? declare if thou hast understanding.

"Who hath laid the MEASURES thereof, if thou
knowest? or who hath STRETCHED THE LINE upon it?

" Whereupon are the FOUNDATIONS thereof FASTENED?
or who laid the CORNER-STONE thereof?

" When the MORNING STARS sang together, and all the
SONS OF GOD shouted for joy." (xxxviii. 1—7.)

In this sublime passage, the Creation of the Earth is
described in language borrowed apparently from the

building of the Great Pyramid. An earthly type is employed to represent a heavenly reality. This is the use of types, and without their aid, we could not express, nor even conceive of operations so far above man's power of comprehension, as the works of creation.

As the FOUNDATIONS of the Great Pyramid were LAID in the limestone rock on which it was built, so are the *foundations* of the Earth mentioned here; but in another place in Job, we are told that the Almighty "hangeth the Earth upon nothing" (xxvi. 7).

As the MEASURES of the Great Pyramid were determined by means of a LINE which was STRETCHED UPON IT, so are these terms applied in the Book of Job, to show that the Earth itself was made, as it were, by *measure*; and that a *line*, in the hand of the Almighty, was the means by which this measurement of the Earth was effected.

"Whereupon are the SOCKETS thereof MADE TO SINK," is the marginal reading for "whereupon are the *foundations* thereof *fastened?*" and it is the more literal rendering. Dr. S. Lee, in his new translation of the book of Job, explains *made to sink*, by "*have been impressed;* i.e., so as to have formed a sort of *shoe* or SOCKET;" and he refers to Exodus xxxvi. 24, for a parallel passage, where the sockets of the posts of the Tabernacle are described. It is remarkable that the word *socle*, a SOCKET, is the very term made use of by the French philosophers in 1801, when they speak of that indentation at each extremity of the Great Pyramid, in which the corner-stones, which formed the casing-stones at the angles, had been orginally laid before the casing was destroyed. Thus we see that the Earth is mentioned as having had its foundations sunk as into a *socket*, because the Great Pyramid was so imbedded; but in no other way could any term like this have been considered appropriate.

" Who laid the CORNER-STONE thereof?" We cannot suppose such an idea as a *corner-stone* to have any propriety, unless we regard the Earth under the figure of a PYRAMID; but, viewed under this figure, the description is attended with singular advantages. The Hebrew word for *corner*, is פִּנָּה *pinnah, angulus, extremitas,* (Buxtorf). It is found in Proverbs vii. 8, representing the " *corner* of a street." In Judges xx. 2, and 1 Sam. xiv. 38, it is used to describe the " *chiefs* of the people;" that is, the single person at the *head* or *extremity* of a body of men. In Job i. 19, where the *four corners* are spoken of, it is applied to a *house*.

The word *pinnah* is to be understood, in all cases where a *single object* is denoted by it, as specifying some object which *alone* has the pre-eminence—that which admits of *no equal;* and it is only when it is used with reference to a *house*, or to any other building having more corners than one, that the *plural term* can be employed: in which sense all the corners are equal, and no one of more importance than another.

A Pyramid is different from all other buildings in this respect—that it combines the two senses just mentioned. It may be spoken of as having *four equal corners*, and as having *also one chief corner-stone*. Herein it differs from a house, and from every other form of building. When, therefore, the question is asked, "Who laid the CORNER-STONE thereof?" we are constrained to regard it as having reference to a PYRAMID; and they who suppose it to relate to the corner-stone of a *house*, or of a *temple*, must be mistaken.

The placing of the *corner-stone* on the *top of the Pyramid* completed the structure. The adoption of this form of expression typifies, consequently, the *completion of the Creation of the Earth,* "when the MORNING-STARS sang together, and all the SONS OF GOD shouted for joy."

"As *men* were not then in existence," says Dr. Lee, "we necessarily have the *angels of God* joining in one universal chorus with the *morning stars.*" Dr. Wells, in his Paraphrase, renders this verse as follows: "Where wast thou when the morning-stars sang together, that is, when the *bright stars* first appeared to proclaim, as it it were, my praise, and all the sons or *angels of God* shouted for joy at the stars' first appearing?" Grotius understands by the "morning-stars" the *brightest of all the stars.* He quotes Abenesdra, as being of opinion, that the *planets* are meant, and that they are also alluded to in Ps. cxlviii. 4: "Praise him, all ye *stars of light.*" The Septuagint Version renders the "sons of God," by the *angels of God,* which reading, Grotius thinks, is confirmed by the 6th verse of the 1st chapter of Job: "Now there was a day when the *sons of God* came to present themselves before the Lord." The same figure is employed by Micaiah, in his address to the king of Israel: "I saw the LORD sitting on his throne, and all the host of heaven standing by him on his right hand and on his left" (1 Kings xxii. 19). It is by the use of types such as these, representing what is supposed to have taken place in kings' palaces, that we are enabled to conceive of things which are said to have been done in heaven. For want of types derived from earthly things, St. Paul could not convey to the minds of the Corinthians any idea of what he had seen when "he was caught up into the third heaven, and heard unspeakable words, which it is not possible for a man to utter" (2 Cor. xii. 4).

We read of some persons who were called, even on earth, the "*sons of God.*" In Gen. vi. 2, it is said: "The *sons of God* saw the daughters of men that they were fair: and they took them wives of all which they chose." On this occasion we see, for the first time, a distinction made among the descendants of Adam: some of them are called the *sons of God*, while others are, by implication, called the *sons of men.* After Seth was born, the only two families of the sons of Adam on the earth, were those who derived their descent from Cain, and those who derived it from Seth. We read of the latter, that "to him also was born a son, and he called his name Enos: then began men to CALL UPON the name of the LORD;" or, as the marginal reading expresses it, "then began men to CALL themselves BY the name of the LORD." Whatever may have been the cause, or whatever the time, when the name of the *sons of God* was first given to any of the sons of Adam, we shall be justified, from this passage, in concluding that it was restricted to the race of *Seth*, in contradistinction to whom the race of *Cain* were called the *sons of men.*

Soon after, a mixed race sprang up, when "the *sons of God* came in unto the *daughters of men*, and they bare children unto them, the same became mighty men which were of old, men of renown." For then "GOD saw that the wickedness of man was great in the earth, and that every imagination of the thoughts of his heart was only evil continually. And it repented the LORD that he had made man on the earth, and it grieved him at his heart. And the LORD said, I will destroy man whom I have created from the face of the earth; both man and beast, and the creeping things, and the fowls of the air; for it repenteth me that I have made them.

But Noah found grace in the eyes of the LORD"
(Gen. vi. 5).

Though Noah was a "just man," and Noah " walked
with God" (vi. 9), it cannot be doubted that one of his
children was not entitled to be called a son of God.
This was Ham, whose descendants built the City and
Tower of Babel — when the Lord came down to see the
City and the Tower which the *children of men* builded.
It does not appear probable that those sons of Noah,
who might be called the *sons of God*, were concerned
in the building of the Tower of Babel.  Bochart observes, on the contrary, that "neither Peleg, nor
Joktan, still less the thirteen sons of the latter, were
engaged in the building of the City and Tower of Babel.
Nor was Noah, nor Shem, nor Arphaxad, nor Salah,
nor Heber, to whom the covenant belonged."* Bochart
thinks that all those were excepted who were privileged
to partake of the *covenant,* and that to them only the
name of the *sons of God* was given.

After the coming of our Lord Jesus Christ, a *new
covenant* was entered into ; and they who partake of
it are, in like manner, said to be the *sons of God.*  They
are " the *children of God,* being the *children of the resur-
rection.*"† " For as many as are led by the *Spirit of
God,* they are the *sons of God.*"‡ " For ye are all the
*sons of God* by *faith in Christ Jesus.*"§  They who do
not become the *sons of God* by faith in Christ Jesus, are
accordingly the *sons of men,* the same as Cain and his
descendants.

We have, therefore, some reason to believe, that if
there were any *sons of God* who shouted for joy at the
completion of the Great Pyramid, they may have been

* Vol. i. p. 37.                    † Luke xx. 36.
‡ Rom. viii. 14.                   § Gal. iii. 26.

those descendants of Noah who had entered into covenant with God,—a covenant which God first made with
Adam; which Abel ratified for himself, by his offering
of the lamb as the required sacrifice; which Seth and
Enos renewed in their own persons, and perpetuated in
their line; until, in the person of Noah and some of
his successors, it was again entered into after the Flood,
and has never since been wholly lost sight of, or forfeited.
The *sons of God* may thus have become an appropriate
term, soon after the Deluge, for describing all those
persons who were engaged in constructing the Great
Pyramid.

*Noah, Shem,* and *Japheth,* with that mysterious being
*Melchizedek,* the king of Salem and priest of the Most
High God, constituted, if we are right in our conjecture, the chief of those *sons of God* who, as luminaries,
appeared in the early morning of the new world, having
outlasted the darkness of the preceding night, when
" every living substance was destroyed which was upon
the face of the ground, both men, and cattle, and the
creeping things, and the fowl of the heaven; and they
were destroyed from the earth: and only Noah remained alive, and they who were with him in the ark."

They may, we think, be not improperly designated
as *morning stars* also, because they survived the ruin of
the old world, and became harbingers of the new creation. The same name is applied to those who will
make their appearance with Christ on the morning of
that day, when " the new heavens and the new earth
shall appear, wherein dwelleth righteousness." With
reference to that time, Jesus says, " I am the bright
and *morning star;*" and " To him that overcometh I will
give the *morning star.*" In that day, " Many of those
who sleep in the dust shall awake, some to everlasting

life, and some to shame and everlasting contempt. And they that be wise shall shine as the brightness of the firmament; and they that turn many to righteousness as the *stars* for ever and ever." Under the same figure, it may not be improper to remark, that Balaam pro-phesied of CHRIST before his appearance in the flesh : " I shall see him, but not now : 1 shall behold him, but not nigh : there shall come a *star* out of Jacob, and a sceptre shall rise out of Israel" (Numb. xxiv. 17).

## Chapter XXX.

*The Great Pyramid alluded to in the Book of Psalms — The Great Pyramid referred to in Zechariah — The Great Pyramid referred to in the New Testament — A further Reference, in the Book of Job, to the Great Pyramid.*

### 141.

THE second instance of a reference to the Great Pyramid in the Scriptures is found in the 118th Psalm, verse 22 : "The stone which the builders refused is become the HEAD STONE of the CORNER. This is the LORD's doing, and it is marvellous in our eyes." The Septuagint translation is as follows: λιθον ὁν απεδοκιμασαν οὑτος εγενηθη εις κεφαλην γωνιας. "This stone, which they refused, is become the HEAD OF THE CORNER." No other form of building, than that of a Pyramid, would enable us to realise the idea contained in these lines. The HEAD of the corner, or the HEAD-STONE of the corner, is plainly not that square stone which is placed at any of the *four corners* of a building, but that ONLY CORNER-STONE which has the pre-eminence — that which forms its apex or its chief angle. In the actual building of the Great Pyramid, this CHIEF CORNER-STONE would be neglected by the builders till the very last. It would stand in the way, and be REJECTED till it was actually wanted; and then they who had observed it long before, and wondered, in their ignorance of the plan of the building, what purpose it was intended to serve, would find it raised all at once

to be the central point and crown of the whole edifice.
When it is added, "This is the LORD's doing; it is
marvellous in our eyes," the words may be spoken with
respect to the plan, when men were convinced the design was from the Lord; or it may be a remark made
reverentially, with respect to the future employment of
this figure as a type of the Lord Jesus.*

The Jews have always regarded this passage as a
prophecy relating to the Messiah. At the time of its
introduction into the PSALMS, it seems to have become
a proverbial saying. More than a thousand years had
then passed away since that *corner-stone*, after having
been rejected, was actually placed at the head of the
angle of the Great Pyramid; and so afterwards became
the type of the Messiah. Like this stone, at the end of
another thousand years, our Lord himself was *rejected*,
till he was raised to be the HEAD of his body, the
CHURCH, that in all things he might have the pre-
eminence. This prophecy is applied to our Lord in
Matt. xxi. 42; Mark xii. 10; Luke xx. 17. Peter also
says, in Acts iv. 11: " This is the STONE which was set
at nought of you builders, which is become the HEAD
of the CORNER. Neither is there salvation in any other;
for there is none other name under heaven, given
among men, whereby we must be saved." And again
(1 Pet. ii. 4): "To whom coming, as unto a LIVING

* That this was a *triangular* stone (and not a square one) in
the opinion of the dwellers at Jerusalem in later times, is shewn
by *Belon*, when he speaks of a stone in the valley of Jehoshaphat
near Jerusalem, in the following terms: "Quelque peu au dessous
en la mesme encoigneure est une *pierre triangulaire*, qu'ils dient
estre celle de laquelle l'Escriture Saincte à fait mention au
Pseaume; *Lapidem quem reprobaverunt aedificantes*" (p. 251,
edit. 1555).

STONE, DISALLOWED indeed of men, but chosen of God, and precious, ye also, as LIVELY STONES, are built up a spiritual house, an holy priesthood, to offer up spiritual sacrifices, acceptable to God by Jesus Christ. Wherefore also it is contained in the Scripture, Behold I lay in Zion a CHIEF CORNER-STONE, elect, precious; and he that believeth on him shall not be confounded. Unto you therefore which believe he is precious: but unto them which be disobedient, the STONE which the builders DISALLOWED, the same is made the HEAD OF THE CORNER, and a stone of stumbling, and a rock of offence, even to them which stumble at the word, being disobedient: whereunto also they were appointed." St. Paul, adverting to the same figure of a Pyramid, in words which cannot otherwise be fitly appropriated, says (Eph. ii. 19): "Now, therefore, ye are no more strangers and foreigners, but fellow-citizens with the saints, and of the household of God; and are built upon the FOUNDATION of the *apostles* and *prophets*, JESUS CHRIST himself being the CHIEF CORNER-STONE, in whom all the BUILDING, fitly framed together, GROWETH unto a holy temple in the Lord: in whom ye also are builded together for an habitation of God through the Spirit." The FOUNDATION is laid upon the *apostles* and *prophets;* and so our Lord says, on Peter's confession of him as the Son of God: "Upon THIS ROCK I will build my church, and the gates of hell shall not prevail against it" (Matt. xvi. 18). But that which forms the *foundation* is different from the CHIEF CORNER-STONE, in whom all the BUILDING, *fitly framed together,* at last GROWETH UP, and is united, as it were, in the one top stone called the CHIEF CORNER-STONE, binding all the living stones together into " an habitation of God through the Spirit."

## 142.

There is, apparently, a further reference in the Old Testament to the CORNER-STONE, as connected with the building of the GREAT PYRAMID. It is contained in Zechariah iv. 7; "Who art thou, O GREAT MOUNTAIN? before Zerubbabel thou shalt become a plain: and he shall bring forth the HEAD-STONE thereof with shoutings, crying, Grace, grace unto it!" Dr. Lee, speaking of "Who laid the corner-stone thereof; when the morning stars sang together, and all the sons of God shouted for joy?" observes :—"In Zech. iv. 7, we have *shouting* and *rejoicing* in a similar manner, on laying this CORNER-STONE, and there it is styled הָאֶבֶן הָרֹאשָׁה, PRINCIPAL or HEAD-STONE. Similar exultation is manifested on a similar occasion mentioned in Psalm cxviii. 22—25, where Christ as the Head of the Church is manifestly meant." We are probably correct, therefore, in conceiving that the expressions made use of in Zechariah, "GRACE, GRACE unto it," were similar to those which were shouted by the SONS OF GOD, when the CORNER-STONE was laid upon the Great Pyramid: and if, beyond this, we have only our imagination to help us, when we endeavour to form some conception of that HYMN OF PRAISE which was raised to heaven when the MORNING STARS sang together, and all the SONS OF GOD shouted for joy, we may console ourselves with the reflection, that it was a theme to which no words of man, if they had been recorded, would have been able to do justice.

## 143.

Our Lord Jesus Christ gives us the fourth illustration of the Great Pyramid in Scripture, when he describes the CORNER-STONE in these terms, "Whosoever shall fal on THAT STONE shall be BROKEN: but on whomsoever

N 5

it shall FALL, it will GRIND HIM TO POWDER.   If we only picture to ourselves an immense piece of rock, roughly shaped into the form of a PYRAMID, having, accordingly, *five sharp angles,* lying ready for use at the proper time, as the CHIEF CORNER-STONE of the structure, among the square-shaped stones, which were first to be wrought into the horizontal lines of the edifice, we shall see at a glance, that upon such a pointed rock it would be impossible for any human being to FALL without being "BROKEN."   Let us next imagine the same mass of rock in its gradual progress up the successive steps of the Great Pyramid to the summit, what imminent danger there would be, especially near the top, lest it should fall back to the bottom; and if so, how certainly it might be said, that "on WHOMSOEVER it should FALL, it would GRIND HIM TO POWDER."   The illustration is perfect, if we regard the CORNER-STONE as the TOP-STONE OF A VAST PYRAMID; but it has no propriety if we restrict our notion of it to a flat stone, however bulky, which might be built into the *foundation* or *superstructure* of a *house* or *temple.*

### 144.

One more passage occurs in the Book of Job, which carries our thoughts to the GREAT PYRAMID.   It is in the 19th chapter, the 23rd and 24th verses.   "Oh that my words were now written!   Oh that they were printed in a book! that they were graven with an iron pen and lead in the rock for ever!"   Dr. Lee gives, as the more literal translation, "Oh that my words were now written!   Oh that they were graven in a book! were cut with an iron tool, and with lead in the rock for ever!"   "With *lead* (he says) to be infused and so to fill up the cavities thus engraven, for the

purpose of preserving the writing from erasure by de-
composition, which might otherwise take place from the
action of the sun on the edges of the stone exposed to
it. According to Ibn Mocri, as cited by H. A. Schultens
in his edition of some of the Proverbs of Meidani, it
was customary with the ancient Arabs of Yemen, to
inscribe their precepts of wisdom on the rocks in order
to preserve them."

Inscriptions on rocks are often found, we know, of
very great antiquity, but they are usually cut on the
*perpendicular faces* of the rocks, into which incised
letters it would be impossible to pour melted lead. The
engravings, alluded to in Job, are of a different kind
from these; they must have been made on the *horizontal surface* or *inclined plane* of a rock, to allow of
molten lead being poured into the letters, for the purpose described. Now this condition would be actually
capable of fulfilment on the sloping face of the Great
Pyramid; and as there was anciently an inscription
carved upon it, according to the testimony of Herodotus, we deem it probable, from these words in JOB,
that those incised letters, of which it consisted, would
be of great magnitude and deeply cut, to make them
visible on so large a surface, having their hollowed
spaces filled up with lead, in order to give *perpetuity* and
*perspicuity* to the words so written " with an iron pen."
On the yellowish surface of the Great Pyramid, the
words so written would be as strongly marked, and as
legible by the contrast, as our words are, when they
are written with a blacklead-pencil on a sheet of
yellowish writing-paper.

CHAPTER XXXI.

*Origin of the Arabian Language— Origin of the Arabian Numerals
— Inscription on the Great Pyramid — Its probable Import.*

145.

THE third of the sons of Joktan, in the order in
which their names are recorded in Scripture, appears to have had, like his two elder brothers, some
peculiar claims to distinction.  Bochart says of him,
that, " in the opinion of Epiphanius, HAZARMAVETH was
the *inventor of the Arabian language,* though the Arabians
themselves refer it to *Joktan.*"  The Arabian language
could scarcely have been invented before the future
colonists were settled in the country ; and the son was,
in that case, more probably the inventor than the father.
Besides this, the Hebrew language would, in all likeli-
hood, be that of Joktan, since he was one of the sons
of Eber.  It would also be the language of his own
sons while they were in Egypt.  For though we are
told the " language was confounded" of those who were
engaged in building the city and Tower of Babel, so
that they could not " understand one another's speech,"
it does not appear that the builders of the Great
Pyramid had to encounter any such difficulty.  Afterwards, when they were settled in their respective coun-
ties, the Arabian language was introduced; for the
sons of Joktan are then described as having their dwelling in Arabia, "from Mesha, as thou goest, unto Sephar

a mount of the East, after their families, after their *tongues*, in their lands, after their nations."

But if the *language* of the sons of Joktan underwent no change till they were all located in Arabia, we have great reason to think that the *Arabian numerals* were invented while the sons of Joktan were yet in Egypt. As all other nations of antiquity made use of the letters of the alphabet for their numerals, it would naturally occur to them, that if either Joktan or Hazar-maveth were the inventor of the Arabian numerals, the same person was also the inventor of the Arabian language. In this respect, the remark of Epiphanius is interesting, as having some reference to the truth.

### 146.

The Arabian numerals at present in use consist of the following figures: 1, 2, 3, 4, 5, 6, 7, 8, 9, 0, the last being sometimes called *zero*. If these were the signs, or if any others, to the same effect, were employed in the Inscription on the Great Pyramid — and it is not supposed that any other than Arabian numerals were at that time in existence, since the letters of the alphabet had not then been invented — what proof, it may be asked, have we to offer that any of these were the numerals made use of in that inscription? We answer, that our proof is unquestionable. Among the hiero-glyphics in Egypt, the invention of which preceded that of alphabetic writing, three of these identical signs are found; viz., 1, 2, 3. Number 4 is represented by a sign like a *pot-hook*; 5, by the figures 2 and 3 placed side by side; 6, by 3 and 3 in like manner; 7, by the signs for 4 and 3 close together; 8, by two fours; 9, by a figure like the letter *q*: *zero*, or the cypher 0, is not met with. The authorities for all these figures may be seen in Dr. Thomas Young's " Rudiments of an Egyptian Dictionary," into which work they are copied from the hieroglyphics arranged by himself, and published by the Royal Society of Literature, in 1828 ; as also from the discoveries of Champollion, published in " Kosegarten, de prisca Ægyptiorum Litteratura Commentatio prima. Weimar, 1828."

The form and power of the figures 1, 2, 3, being the same in these old documents as they are found to be in our own language, are decisive proofs of the *existence* of the Arabian numerals in Egypt at a period co-eval with, if not anterior to, the use of hieroglyphics. The fact of some of the numerals being placed *in pairs,* side by side, to represent the numbers 5, 6, 7, 8, and the omission of the sign *zero* altogether, are proofs equally strong that the Arabian numerals had then been so long known in Egypt, that the memory of their proper power of *denary* increase, by position before another figure, was become in the interval utterly forgotten. Yet the mechanical reading of the interpreter was right, though he was ignorant of the principle on which it rested. The three kinds of proof combine to form an evidence irresistible that the Arabian numerals, consisting of nine single figures and zero, in all their present power, existed at the time the Great Pyramid was constructed, namely, about 4,000 years ago, much the same as they now exist in the most refined languages of modern times.*

The following table exhibits the *power by position* of the Arabian numerals, as it was originally understood ;

* The entire set of *numeral characters* is said to be found on the *mummy bandages* in Egypt. They are represented in *Büttner's Comp. Tables.* (See *Notes and Queries, May* 1, 1858, p. 355).

though we may doubt whether, in the earliest ages, it
was ever carried to so great an extent : —

| Trillions | Billions | Millions | Thousands, etc. |
|---|---|---|---|

987,654·321,087·654,320·543,298

By the introduction of a decimal point, the *enumeration*
of the above figures is much simplified.

### 147.

Let us now consider in what form the *inscription* on
the face of the Great Pyramid would probably be presented, if it were meant to exhibit the measure of the
*diameter* or *circumference* of the Earth, in figures which
might be supposed to represent the cost of the *radishes,*
*onions,* and *garlic,* consumed by the men who built the
Pyramids (§ 76).

When Herodotus saw the inscription, which was
about 1700 years after it had been made, he was evidently unable to decypher it ; and even the interpreter
who read over the figures to him, could not tell for
what purpose they had been put there, though it seems
he could repeat the figures correctly, according to the
above table, as far as they went. As he conceived
them to have reference to a sum of money, and knew
that, according to the money in use at that time, in
many different countries, 6000 drachmas constituted a
*talent* ; as also that the talent consisted of 60 *minæ,* or
pounds, of 100 drachmas each ; we may assume that he
saw and read over the smaller numerals first ; and then,
finding 1600 of these sums of 6000 recorded at the foot,
he took for granted that the whole amount had reference to the cost of the food of the labourers for those
articles, the radishes, onions, and garlic, whose symbols
or hieroglyphics he fancied he saw attached to the

respective lines of figures (§ 76). He erred in his application of the numbers, but he may have been correct in his reading of the numerals. Let us now endeavour to discover whether these same figures which he read over can, by any possibility, be so understood as to have presented to the minds of those who founded the Pyramids, and placed the inscription there, a record of the measure of the present or former Earth, as they estimated it.

The *diameter of the present Earth*, when taken at the Pyramids, is equal, as we have seen, to 500,000,000 English inches; and the measure of the English inch was then fixed, as a means of preserving to the end of time a record of that measure.

The *diameter of the former Earth* was 497,664,000 English inches; but this measure may also be represented by 48,000,000 royal spans, each equal to 10·368 English inches.

If the inscription related to the *former Earth*, the figures seen by the interpreter would represent the *diameter* without any difficulty; thus —

DIAMETER OF THE FORMER EARTH.

| IN ROYAL SPANS. | *Equivalents*<br>*In English Inches.* |
|:---:|:---:|
| 5 = 1″ | 51·840 = 1″ |
| 100 | 100 |
| —— | —— |
| 500 = 1′ | 5184 = 1′ |
| 60 | 60 |
| —— | —— |
| 30,000 = 1° | 311,040 = 1° |
| 1600 | 1600 |
| —— | —— |
| 48,000,000 | 497,664,000 |

The inscription, as here presented, begins with a well-known measure, viz., the *royal span* of 10·368 English inches, also called the *foot of Pliny*, of which there are 883 in the side of the Great Pyramid. It is the half of the royal cubit, and the quarter of the Karnak cubit. Yet it is evident that the *figures* seen by the interpreter, when applied to this number, make up the exact number of royal spans (or English inches) in the diameter of the former earth. Can this have been by accident? If not, what a strong confirmation it affords of the opinion we have expressed, that the inscription related to the measure of the Earth.

But the inscription may have had reference to the *circumference of the present Earth*. In this case, if we commence with the *inches of the Pyramid foot*, the following is the appearance which it would present:—

CIRCUMFERENCE OF THE PRESENT EARTH.

| IN PYRAMID INCHES. | *In English Inches.* |
|---|---|
| 150 = 1″ | 163·635 = 1″ |
| 100 | 100 |
| 15,000 = 1′ | 16,363·5 = 1′ |
| 60 | 60 |
| 900,000 = 1° | 981,810 = 1° |
| 1600 | 1600 |
| 1440,000,000 | 1570,896,000 |

Thus, in the case of the *circumference of the present Earth*, as also in that of the *diameter of the former Earth* the *figures* which Herodotus saw, and which the interpreter made vocal to him, were those which, when applied to a well-known measure of space, with which the founders of the Pyramids were familiar, would exactly express both these numbers, according to the numerical power of the Arabian figures; amounting, in the former instance, to 48,000,000 royal spans, or 497,664,000 English inches; and, in the latter, to 1440,000,000 Pyramid inches, or 1570,896,000 English inches — the Pyramid *inches* being those of the Pyramid *foot*, which is equal to 1·0909 of the English foot.

In either inscription, it is probable that a *deeply-incised line* was carved at the commencement, represent-ing, in the first instance, the length of 5 royal spans, or 51·840 English inches, as the *standard for the measure of the diameter;* and in the second, the length of 150 pyramid inches, or 163·635 English inches, as the *standard for the measure of the circumference* — the one line being about three times the length of the other.

It may be thought, that some other measures could be found, of great antiquity, which might be arranged so as to bring out somewhat similar results; but we have been unable to discover any other measures which have that property; and we believe there are no other. By adopting the measure of Thales and Anaximander, who divided the circumference into 400 parts, instead of 1600, we obtain a convenient scale for the inscrip-tion, if it recorded the circumference of the present Earth, and one which may have been engraven on the face of the Great Pyramid; but it does not tally so completely with the figures read by the interpreter. In this case, the deeply-cut line, at the head of the inscrip-tion, would be equal to 50 pyramid feet, or 54·544 English feet — according to the following state-ment:—

CIRCUMFERENCE OF THE PRESENT EARTH.

| INSCRIPTION IN PYRAMID FEET. | Equivalents in English Feet. |
|---|---|
| $50 = 1''$ | $54\cdot5445 = 1''$ |
| 100 | 100 |
| $5000 = 1'$ | $5454\cdot45 = 1'$ |
| 60 | 60 |
| $300,000 = 1°$ | $327,267\cdot0 = 1°$ |
| 400 | 400 |
| 120,000,000 | 130,906,800 |

If this inscription had been found on the face of the Great Pyramid, it would not be surprising, since the division of the circumference into 400 degrees was so early recognized. And here, moreover, the numbers, which are respectively attached to the *seconds*, *minutes*, and *degrees*, are very nearly the same as those which would now be assigned to them in the latitude of the Pyramids — as may be seen from the following figures in the *Table of Constants* :—

CIRCUMFERENCE OF THE PRESENT EARTH.

| IN GREEK FEET. | Equivalents in English Feet. |
|---|---|
| $100 = 1''$ | $101\cdot01 = 1''$ |
| 60 | 60 |
| $6000 = 1'$ | $6060\cdot6 = 1'$ |
| 60 | 60 |
| $360,000 = 1°$ | $363,636 = 1°$ |
| 360 | 360 |
| 129,600,000 | 130,908,960 |

But without in any degree departing from the strict line of our argument, we may safely conclude, that if

any inscription had been placed on the face of the
Great Pyramid—and we know that something of the
kind was seen there by Herodotus—it would probably
relate either to the *diameter of the former Earth,* or to the
*circumference of the present Earth.* The founders would
naturally desire to preserve a memorial of that earth
which had been destroyed, that it might be compared
with the new earth, from which they perceived it to
differ; and, for this purpose, the diameter would be
more interesting than the circumference. But it was
still more to be expected, that they would desire to
record the measure of the new earth; and, for this purpose, the circumference would be more interesting than
the diameter. They knew, also, that the same formula
could not serve for both purposes; and that, if the
*diameter* of the former earth were to be exhibited, it
was necessary that it should be accompanied with the
*circumference* of the present earth. The same numbers
would, in this case, suffice for either object. Thus,
without making any alteration in the figures read over
to Herodotus by the Interpreter, we see that they
might have been applicable to either object, or to both,
commencing in each case with a well-known measure
of length, taken from the Great Pyramid, and recognized as a measure of length by the founders of the
Pyramids.

## CHAPTER XXXII.

*Arabian Numerals preceded Alphabetic Writing — Origin of Alphabetic Writing — Claim on the part of the Hindoos to the earliest use of Arabian Numerals — Conclusion.*

### 148.

IT is remarked by Astle, in his "Origin and Progress of Writing," that "Men, in their most rude and uncivilized state, have the use of *numbers*; and therefore (he says) we shall not be surprised to find *numeral characters* in use among the Mexicans, and other nations, *before they were acquainted with letters :* the former were first invented, because they were *first necessary to mankind.*"*

The truth of this remark cannot be doubted. If we look into the earliest Books of the Old Testament, we shall find that the word, *to write*, does not once occur in the Book of Genesis; but the word, *to number*, is frequently met with. It is first employed in Gen. xv. 5, with reference to Abraham : " Look now toward heaven, and tell (*number*) the stars, if thou be able to *number* them : and the LORD said unto him, So shall thy seed be." Again, in xvi. 10 : " I will multiply thy seed exceedingly, that it shall not be *numbered* for multitude." Again, in xli. 48, with reference to Joseph, when he was appointed by Pharaoh over all the land of Egypt : " He

* Astle, 4to, p. 181.

gathered up all the food of the seven years, which were in the land of Egypt, and laid up the food in the cities : the food of the field, which was round about every city, laid he up in the same. And Joseph gathered corn as the sand of the sea, very much, until he left *numbering.*" Here the numbers must have been recorded, and carried to a very great extent. If the largest corn measure, the chaldron, were employed, the numbers would amount to millions of millions — far exceeding the numbers supposed to be recorded in the inscription on the Great Pyramid.

But as, in the English language, we not only have the verb, *to count*, but also the noun, *account*, which is sometimes used by us in the larger sense of a *history*, as well as in the more limited sense of a *bill*, or *reckoning*, so it was with the Hebrews. The same word, סָפַר *çaphar*, which means *to number*, in the previous quotations, is, with a change of the vowel points, used for a *book, bill, letter*, or *register* ; as סֵפֶר *çepher*, in Gen. v. 1 : " This is the *book* (or *account*) of the generations of Adam." Again, in Ex. xvii. 14 : " Write this for a memorial in a *book*, and rehearse it in the ears of Joshua." In Exod. xxxii. 32, also : " And if not, blot me, I pray thee, out of thy *book* which thou hast written. And the Lord said unto Moses, Whosoever hath sinned against me, him will I blot out of my *book*."

We have, moreover, in the English language, the noun *accountant*, formed from the verb *to count;* and again, in this respect, the Hebrew language agrees with ours. The participial form of the verb, *çaphar*, is used for a *writer*, or *scribe*, or *one who numbers* or *counts;* as in Isa. xxxiii. 18, " Where is the *scribe ?* where is the receiver ? where is *he that counted* the towers ?"

In the Book of Job, the word *çaphar* is found in the first two senses of *to number* and a *book;* but not in that

of a *writer* or *scribe*. When Job says (xix. 23), "Oh
that my words were now *written;*" and (xxxi. 35),
"That mine adversary had *written* a book," he introduces
a totally different word from *çaphar,* and one which has
no connexion with *numbering,* viz., כָּתַב *kathav.* The
same word is also rendered *write* in Ex. xvii. 14, where
it first occurs in the Old Testament.

### 149.

The first mention of the word *kathav,* to *write,* is
coincident, in point of time, with the first use of *alphabetic writing.* The discovery of the art of writing,
either by express revelation from the LORD to Moses,
or by the power of that spirit which was given to the
latter, took place on Mount Sinai, at the period when
the LORD called Moses up to him in the Holy Mount.
"And Moses came and told the people all the WORDS of
the LORD, and all the JUDGMENTS; and all the people
answered with one voice, and said, All the WORDS which
the LORD hath said, will we do. And Moses WROTE
(*kathav*) all the WORDS of the LORD, and rose up early
in the morning, and builded an altar under the hill,
and twelve pillars, according to the Twelve Tribes of
Israel. And he sent young men of the children of
Israel, which offered burnt-offerings, and sacrificed
peace-offerings of oxen, unto the LORD. And Moses
took half of the blood, and put it in basons; and half
of the blood he sprinkled on the altar. And he took
the ACCOUNT (*çephar*) of the COVENANT, and READ in the
audience of the people: and they said, All that the
LORD hath said will we do, and be obedient. And
Moses took the blood and sprinkled it on the people,
and said, Behold the blood of the COVENANT, which
the LORD hath made with you concerning ALL THESE
WORDS" (Ex. xxiv. 3—8).

The art of *alphabetic writing* is here perfected. The *words* are *written*; they are *written* in an *account*; they are the *words* of a *covenant*; they are *read* to all the people; and the people, on their part, *ratify the covenant*, by saying, "All that the LORD hath said will we do, and be obedient." The occasion was a most extraordinary one; and, if any event could be said to *require* so wonderful an inauguration, in order to give it due distinction in the eyes of mankind, it was this great event of *entering into covenant with God*, which covenant, in *words*, without the aid of writing, could not have been entered into between the LORD and his chosen people. This memorable event took place in the year, B.C. 1491 —about 670 years after the completion of the Great Pyramid. From this time, having its beginning at Mount Sinai, *kathav*, to *write*, is continually met with, to the end of the Old Testament; but it never occurs before the period here mentioned; and, from this time to the close of the Hebrew Scriptures, no other word than *kathav* is ever used in that sense. It was invented to express the *art of writing* at the same time that the *art of alphabetic writing* was discovered.

But *çaphar* still retained its former signification of *to count*, an *account*, and a *scribe*; and the new word did not displace the old in its application to any of these senses. Even in our own language we make a similar use of the word; for we not only employ in these several senses the *English* words *to count*, *to recount*, an *account*, and an *accountant*; but we have adopted the *Hebrew* word *çaphar* itself, in its proper signification of *to cypher*. We speak of the *art of cyphering* as if it were synonymous with the *art of arithmetic*; and when we style one of the ten figures more essentially *a cypher*, it may have been originally done to show the importance

of that *figure* without which the Arabic system of notation would be incomplete, though, when standing alone,
that *cypher* has no value. Even when the Greek alphabet was formed, which was subsequent, of course, to the
formation of the Hebrew, since it has adopted Hebrew
names for the Greek letters, the use of the *commencing
cypher* of the Arabian system of notation, was not quite
unknown nor unrecognised, though its power *after*
another figure was even then forgotten. The Greek
numerals are these:—

| 1 | 2 | 3 | 4 | 5 | 6 | 7 | 8 | 9 |
|---|---|---|---|---|---|---|---|---|
| $a$ | $\beta$ | $\gamma$ | $\delta$ | $\epsilon$ | $\varsigma$ | $\zeta$ | $\eta$ | $\theta$ |
| 10 | 20 | 30 | 40 | 50 | 60 | 70 | 80 | 90 |
| $\iota$ | $\kappa$ | $\lambda$ | $\mu$ | $\nu$ | $\xi$ | $o$ | $\pi$ | $\jmath$ |
| 100 | 200 | 300 | 400 | 500 | 600 | 700 | 800 | 900 |
| $\rho$ | $\sigma$ | $\tau$ | $\upsilon$ | $\phi$ | $\chi$ | $\psi$ | $\omega$ | $\partial$ |

The inference we draw from these numerals is, that
as the Greeks used the letter $\iota$, to represent the number
10, which number, among the Arabian numerals, was
denoted by the cypher 0 after the letter or numeral 1;
so they (the Greeks) were compelled to invent a letter
to serve for their first numeral; and this they did by
combining the cypher 0 with 1, which two figures stood
next each other, in the order of the Arabian numerals,
and thus formed the letter $a$, which stands for 1, without
interfering with their number 10, because they saw that
the cypher, placed *before* 1, does not add to its power.

## 150.

To call these numerals *Arabian*, is to assume that
*Arabia* was the country in which they took their rise, or
that the *Arabians* were the people by whom they were
invented; but the Hindoos possess an earlier title, it s

said, though even *they* lay no claim to the discovery. "In no case," says Dr. Peacock, "is the original invention of the notation by *nine digits and zero*, referred to by any of their authors; but it is always stated to be one of the *benefactions of the Deity*, which is the best proof of its possessing an antiquity antecedent to all existing records."* This testimony to its extreme antiquity, when joined to the evidence which we have obtained from the inscription on the Great Pyramid, and to the use of the Arabian numerals before the art of alphabetic writing had been discovered, after which the inventors withdrew into *Arabia* and settled there,—produces a chain of evidence in favour of that country, which ought to satisfy our minds that they have been rightly named *Arabian numerals*. All Hindoo and Arabian *authors* are of modern date compared with the period assigned to the Pyramids. The first *Arabian* who wrote upon Algebra, and made use of this mode of computation, is said to have been *Mohammed ben Musa*, who flourished about the end of 9th century. The use of Arabian numerals became general amongst *Arabian writers* about the middle of the 10th century. "In the 11th century, the *Moors* were not merely in possession of the southern provinces of Spain, but had established a flourishing kingdom, where the favourite sciences of their eastern ancestors were cultivated with uncommon activity and success; and from that quarter, and from the Moors in Spain, they chiefly appear to have been communicated to the Spaniards and other Europeans."† Italy was the next country to receive the Arabian numerals. They are not met with in England before the 14th century. The earliest example is thus mentioned:—"In the manu-

---

* Peacock's Arithmetic, p. 412.     † Arithmetic, p. 413.

script library of Corpus Christi College, Cambridge, there is a Table of Eclipses from 1330 to 1348, to which is also subjoined a *Table of the Arabic Numerals*, which is extremely interesting from its great antiquity."* The following are the forms which, in that work, are given to these numerals:—1, 2, 3, Ϟ, ᒋ, 6, ᴧ, 8, 9, 10. This is the earliest instance of the use of the Arabian numerals in England, and these are their current characters at that time.

Let us now consider the claims put forth on behalf of the *Hindoos*. There are two works on Arithmetic, Mensuration, and Algebra, called *Lilávati* and *Vija-ganita* (§ 77), which enjoy the highest reputation in Hindostan; they are the productions of *Bhascara*, who lived about the middle of the twelfth century. *Bhascara* frequently quotes *Brahmegupta*, who lived in the early part of the seventh century, portions of whose works, containing treatises on Arithmetic and Mensuration, are still extant. *Brahmegupta* refers to *Arya-bhatta*, "who flourished at least as early as the fifth century, and probably at a much earlier period;" and who "is considered the oldest of their uninspired and merely human writers," the subject of part of whose works was Algebra and Arithmetic.†

" From these facts," says Dr. Peacock, " which appear to be established upon very satisfactory evidence, it appears that Hindoo Algebra and Arithmetic are at least as ancient as Diophantus, and preceded, by four centuries, the use of those sciences among the Arabs."

But, on the other hand, we have the deliberate opinion of Professor Leslie, expressed to this effect, that, as a nation, the Hindoos were incapable of availing

---

* Peacock's Arithmetic, p. 418.     † Arithmetic, p. 412.

themselves to the full of the discovery which had been introduced to their knowledge. "I am sorry," he observes, "after all the pains I have taken, at not being able to come to a more definite conclusion relative to the origin of our present numeral characters. There is strong ground to suspect that the Hindoos obtained the knowledge of those figures from Upper Asia. The humble attainments of this people are not entitled to claim any very high antiquity. The expedition of Alexander the Great into the East opened a channel of learned intercourse; but, according to the testimony of his generals, Megasthenes and Nearchus, the people of India were at that period entirely ignorant of letters; nor had they acquired any skill in Arithmetic about the time of Arrian and Philostratus. The Sanscrit *alphabet* is asserted by Anquetil to have been formerly distributed into three classes, which, as in other languages, were employed to denote the successive ranks of *units, tens,* and *hundreds.* And Croze contends, that the followers of Zoroaster, on the Malabar coast, continued long afterwards to represent *numbers* by means of *letters.* This application of the alphabet has, no doubt, for some ages, given place among the Hindoos to the simpler and more perfect system of digital characters. At what epoch such a mighty change was effected it would be difficult to conjecture.

"The oldest treatise on Arithmetic possessed by the Hindoos, the *Lilávati,* remounts no higher than the eleventh century of our era. This famous composition, to which the vanity and ignorance of that people claim a divine original, is but a very poor performance, containing merely a few scanty precepts couched in obscure memorial verses. The examples annexed to these rules, often written probably by later hands in the margin, are generally trifling and ill chosen. Indeed, the *Lilávati* exhibits nothing that deserves the slightest notice, except the additions made by its Persian commentators. The Hindoos had not the sagacity to perceive the various advantages to be derived from the denary notation. They remained entirely ignorant of the use of decimal fractions, with which their acute neighbours, the Chinese, have been familiarly acquainted from the remotest ages. Their numerical operations are unnecessarily complicated, following closely the procedure which the application of an *alphabet* had obliged the Greeks to employ."*

The only way in which the recovery of the Arabian numerals can be accounted for, after the lapse of about 2000 years, during which the inventors had been occupying various parts of Arabia Felix, is by supposing, that among the greater part of the descendants of the thirteen sons of Joktan, the right use of the *nine figures and zero* had been forgotten; and that when their language became a *written* one, many of them adopted the Hebrew and Greek mode of notation by the letters of the alphabet. But some of them may have retained the ancient system; and from them it again took its rise, and spread over all the civilized world. Hence we may conceive how it happened, that the Hindoos were possessed, at so early an age, of the numeral *proportion* which the *circumference of the earth bears to its diameter*, contained in the *Vija-Ganita* (§ 77 and § 79). The Arabians are very likely to have preserved some record of this measurement: if not, we must suppose that the inscription on the Great Pyramid contained it, and that some of the priests who were driven out of Egypt by the inva-

* Leslie's Philosophy of Arithmetic, pp. 225, 226.

sion of the Romans in the first century after Christ, or
by the Persians and Arabians in the seventh century,
carried with them the knowledge of this measure, and
communicated it to the people among whom they took
refuge.  Professor Leslie says, that the word " *cifer*, or
more properly *sipher*, as appropriated to the digital
characters, is an *Arabic* word, introduced by the Saracens into Spain, signifying *to enumerate*" (p. 112).  Dr.
Peacock adopts the same notion, observing also, " The
use of the *zero*, or *cypher*, so important and so essential
to this species of arithmetic, has led to a more compre-
hensive meaning of the term, all the digits being designated by the general term of *cypher*, and the verb *to
cypher* having the same signification as *to calculate*, or
*work with figures*" (p. 420).  But we have shewn, that a
much earlier use of these terms, in the sense here stated,
is to be found in the *Hebrew* language, and in the first
book written in that language; in which language also
the term *zero* (גֶּרַע) is met with, which signifies a *seed*,
and is applied, as a coriander seed, to describe that
" small round thing" which lay on the ground, called
*manna*.*  If the Arabian word *cypher* were at that time
in use, in the same sense in which the Hebrew word
*çaphar* was employed in the Book of Genesis, it would
go far to prove that it was invented at the institution
of the Arabian system of notation on the founding of
the Pyramids.  It would be a strong confirmation also
of the opinion we have expressed, that *Arabia* was the
country to which the founders withdrew after the Pyramids were completed, and that they took with them
that celebrated *system of notation* which to this day bears
their name.

* Exod. xvi. 14, 31.

### 151.

Let us now briefly recapitulate some of the principal points of agreement brought forward in the course of this inquiry. Are they to be considered accidental coincidences? or do they prove, that the Great Pyramid was built by a scientific people, to whom some geometry was known, and, in particular, to whom the dimensions of the earth were known, with what would be now called tolerable accuracy?

It is certainly a most extraordinary coincidence, that the face of the casing stones should present so nearly that angle, with relation to the base of the Great Pyramid, which would have been given to it, had it been constructed at the present day to represent the *proportion* which the diameter of a circle bears to its circumference. The angle of the face is that of 51° 50′, while modern science would prescribe for it that of 51° 51′ 14″. Yet we must acknowledge this approximation to be the result of accident, unless we are prepared to admit, that the founders of the Great Pyramid were acquainted with the dimensions of the earth, and that they may have endeavoured to perpetuate a record of its proportionate measures, by making the perpendicular height of the Pyramid as compared with the perimeter of its base, equal to the radius of a circle as compared with its circumference.

But we are still more convinced that this angle was not produced without design, by the following evidence from an authority which cannot be controverted. Herodotus makes a statement which can have no meaning, unless it be that which we are now attributing to it. He says that each face of the Great Pyramid is equal in content to the square of the height. Now this is

o*

true when the angle of the face is equal to 51° 49′ 46″;
and the angle of the casing stones was very nearly this,
being 51° 50′, as taken by Mr. Brettell, which exceeds
the former measure by 14″ only. According to the
remark made by Herodotus, we conclude, therefore,
that the angle of 51° 50′ must have been intentional;
and if so, the coincidence cannot have been accidental.
We see, by this observation of the historian, how
nearly the scientific knowledge of the founders of the
Great Pyramid equalled that of modern mathematicians, and in what degree it was less precise. Instead
of the angle of 51° 51′ 14″, they gave to their casing
stones that of 51° 50′; and instead of 51° 49′ 46″ for
the square of the height, they supposed that of 51° 50′
to be correct. The medium is 51° 50′ 30″. The estimate of 51° 50′ is wonderfully exact, considering the
age in which it was made. The content of each face of
the Great Pyramid, with a base line of 764 feet, and a
sloping height of 618, is 236,076 square feet; and the
content of the square of the perpendicular height (486
feet), is 236,196 square feet. No other angle than one
between 51° 51′ 14″ and 51° 49′ 46″ could be devised,
of which the same thing which is here recorded by
Herodotus might be predicated.

That this was the angle intended to be realized by
the founders of the Great Pyramid, is further confirmed by the following proofs. The foot of Diodorus
Siculus, and of Drusus (1·0909 English feet), is contained 700 times in the side of the base of the Great
Pyramid. Supposing it to be contained 120 millions
of times in the measure of the circumference of the
earth, that measure would be equal to 130,908,000
English feet,—equal, therefore, to 1,570,896,000 inches.
If this last measure be doubled, the figures amount to

3,141,792,000. Now it is well known, that the *proportion* which the diameter of a circle bears to its circumference, is expressed by the figures 1 to 3·1415927 ; but these figures differ from those last mentioned only by the substitution of 5 for 7 in the *fifth* place. What is the reason of this remarkable agreement? Is it accidental? or does it imply design? We should be at a loss to shew how the figures originated at all, if it were not for the actual measure of the circumference of the earth in *English inches*. This supplies us with a reason for the higher number, which, in later times, and by the aid of more exact knowledge, was reduced to the lower number as the true proportion, without any reference to actual measure. Accordingly, the larger number is the earlier, since it was the result of some actual measure. But does this number represent the circumference of the earth in the latitude of the Great Pyramid? We reply that it does. The degree in lat. 29° is 363,676, and in lat. 30°, 363,724, as calculated by Pinkerton. Jomard makes the degree proper to Egypt 363,532, and 363,684. Cassini says, it was equal to 75 Roman miles ; and as each mile was 4848·5 English feet, according to our estimate of the Roman foot in this inquiry, the degree was 363,637·5. The Pyramid measure of the circumference of the earth 130,908,000, divided by 360, makes each degree equal to 363,636 English feet, or one foot and a half less in the degree than that of Cassini.

With this further proof, that an actual measurement of the earth had been made by the founders of the Great Pyramid, it would be absurd in us to speak of the agreement of these numbers as accidental. Let us rather inquire how it happens, that the numbers which in the present day indicate *proportion* merely, should at

the building of the Great Pyramid be so nearly those
which represented the actual measurement of the earth.
By this means, we shall probably arrive at the *origin of
numbers*. The *proportion* of the diameter of a circle to its
circumference is now represented by 1 to 3·1415927;
and it appears that, at the building of the Great Pyramid, the actual diameter of the earth was indicated by
1 when its circumference was represented by 3·141792.
These numbers were doubled, to shew the *proportion* of
the fractional numbers to 1. The half of each is,
therefore, the real measure, which allows for the diameter 500 millions of inches, while the circumference
is equal to 1570,896,000 inches. But these are English
inches. We conclude, therefore, that the English inch
was *invented at this early period* to express 500 millions
in the diameter; and its preservation to the present
time, affords indisputable evidence that the measure of
the earth, both in its diameter and its circumference,
was made originally by the founders of the Great Pyramid, who must have had for this purpose that mathematical knowledge which we have in these pages ascribed
to them.

It is probable, that as the measure of the earth after
the deluge was so early ascertained, that of the former
earth had been estimated in like manner. We have
some reason to suppose this, from the fact, that the
measure of the ark was made in *sacred cubits*, each
being equal to 24·8832 English inches. Of these sacred
cubits, there would be 20 millions in the diameter of
the earth, if it were estimated as equal to 497,664,000
English inches, instead of 500 millions, as at present.
In royal cubits of 20·736 inches each, the diameter of
the former earth, according to this estimate, would be
equal to 24 millions; and in miles of the Pyramid

foot of 1·0909, which exceed our present mile by *one-eleventh* part, as that pyramid foot exceeds our English foot in the same proportion, the number of miles in the diameter of the former earth would be 7200. These round numbers favour the notion, that the former earth had been measured, before that of the present earth was undertaken. But if this were true, we might expect that, before the latter measure was completed, the old measures would be still made use of in the construction of the interior parts of the Great Pyramid.

Now, we have evidence of the use of these former measures in the interior of the Great Pyramid, as well as in the Temple of Solomon, which was constructed by cubits of the " first measure," that is, by the cubit of Karnak. We have this *antediluvian* measure also preserved in the construction of that *vessel of porphyry*, which stands on the floor of the king's chamber in the Great Pyramid. Its contents are equal, in cubic inches, to the cube of 41·472 inches, the cubit of Karnak, viz., to 71,328 cubic inches. Its capacity was equal to that of the Hebrew vessel, called the *laver*, in the Temple of Solomon. It contained also 128 (Greek) *hecteis*, and 128 (Roman) *modii*, and 128 (English) *pecks* of wheat, in which latter form it has come down to our own times—our *chaldron* being a measure of capacity only recently discontinued. A *quarter* of wheat is equal to 8 bushels, which, as its name implies, is the *fourth* part of some larger measure: this was the *chaldron*. Thirty-two bushels of wheat, in the reign of Henry III., would fill a vessel containing 71,680 cubic inches, exceeding by only 10 pints the contents of the Pyramid coffer. Six hundred years ago, this measure of the bushel was said to be that of the ancient standard of England; and yet we see that it formed a component part of the measure of the Pyramid coffer, which was itself the cube of the Karnak cubit, a cubit in use before the Flood. Instances of agreement such as these cannot be accidental.

In the reign of Geo. IV., the present imperial measures were established, according to which, 32 bushels would fill a vessel containing 70,982 cubic inches. Here the measure of the chaldron falls as far short of the contents of the Pyramid coffer, as the measure of Hen. III. exceeded it, viz., by 10 pints. An average of the two would give the true measure of the Pyramid coffer. This may be deemed an accidental agreement; but either extreme exhibits a most extraordinary conformity with the original measure after the lapse of 4000 years. The Pyramid coffer, and the English chaldron, alike contain 2500 lbs. troy of water, or 2000 lbs. avoirdupois of wheat; equal to 32 bushels, reckoning each bushel to weigh 62½ lbs.

When so many evidences of the scientific knowledge of the founders of the Great Pyramid present themselves, these facts cannot be disregarded. The difficulty may be great in supposing a people to have been in existence at that early period, who were capable of executing a work of so vast a magnitude on purely scientific principles; but is it not also probable, that to some individuals God may have given the knowledge, even at that early age of the world, for which we are now contending? How could Noah have built the Ark, if he had not been divinely instructed as to its fabrication? And might he not have been equally instructed in the knowledge requisite to form the Great Pyramid? Both these wonderful works are based on *measures*, and the latter structure shews a knowledge of those measures which were in use before the Flood, as well as of those which were afterwards established, implying, therefore, an acquaintance with antediluvian things. How could the Arabian numerals, and the knowledge by which they were so arranged as to increase ten-fold in power by change of position, have been discovered so soon after the Deluge, if the same system had not existed before, or if divine assistance had not been granted at so early a period after that event? Even after these figures had once been known, the majority of mankind, for at least 3000 years, remained ignorant of their use, and never again hit upon the arrangement as a discovery.

To Moses, the art of writing by means of alphabetic characters was revealed on Mount Sinai; and all that the ingenuity of the most intelligent nations could invent afterwards to supply the place of *numerals*, was to arrange the *letters* of the alphabet in triple sets, for the purpose of representing *units*, *tens*, and *hundreds*. Moses, we are told, was *admonished of God*, when he was about to make the *Tabernacle*, which was to serve as the example and shadow of *heavenly* things; "for, See, saith he, that thou make all things according to the *pattern* shewed to thee in the Mount."* There is an originality in the character of these early revelations, which shews them to have had a higher source than that of man's present intelligence, great as it may seem. Our modern discoveries are rather *inferential*, consisting chiefly in the application of things known to purposes previously unknown. Of this kind is the invention of the art of printing, as well as the employment of alphabetical numeration. I would not detract from the importance of modern discoveries; but I think they seem to benefit mankind less than the communications of the art of

* Heb. viii. 5.

ship-building, of the Arabian system of numeration, of
geometry, or the means of measuring the earth, and of
the art of alphabetic writing :—

"So thoughts beyond *their* thought to those high bards
    were given."

In regard to the Great Pyramid, it was the happy
discovery of the *two casing stones*, when all were thought
to be destroyed, which at once changed *conjecture* into
*certainty*. We now, probably, know all that we shall
ever know respecting the origin and purpose of the
Great Pyramid, and all that we require to know. What
vague generalities was Mr. John Greaves obliged to be
contented with ! He could only arrive at this conclusion,—"That each side of the Pyramid, computing it
according to Herodotus, contains in length 800 Grecian
feet, and in Diodorus Siculus' account, 700 ; Strabo
reckons it a furlong; that is less than 600 feet, or 625
Roman ; and Pliny equals it to 883 : but that of
Diodorus Siculus, in my judgment, comes nearest to
the truth." We now find, that all these seemingly
different measures, when properly understood, are equal
to each other, and mean the same thing. The various
lengths assigned to the side of the base by the *moderns,*
agree within a few inches, though they appeared before as far asunder as 693, 728, 746, and 764 feet. The
perpendicular height is now found to be exactly 500
*Italian* feet (of ·972 English); the perimeter is equal
to 3150 *Roman* feet (of ·9697). The *Grecian* foot is
1·0125 ; the *Ptolemaic,* 1·0101 ; the foot of *Drusus,* or
*Diodorus Siculus,* 1·0909 ; and that of *Pliny,* which is
properly a *span,* 10·368 inches. Twice this last number
is the *royal cubit* (20·736) ; and twice this number is
the *Karnak cubit* (41·472 inches). Lastly, the *geometri-*

*cal foot,* or span, mentioned by mathematical writers in the beginning of the sixteenth century, belongs to this system (9·8175 inches). Twice this measure is the *oriental cubit* (19·6356 inches) : and two of these oriental cubits form the *Pyramid meter,* which is the *forty-millionth* part of the circumference of the earth, in the latitude of the Great Pyramid (39·2724 inches), a measure differing from the *French metre* only *one-tenth* of an inch in 40 inches, but the better fitted for an universal standard of international measures, since it forms an integral part of that ancient system which binds all the nations of the earth together in one common bond of reciprocal measures of *length, capacity,* and *weight.*

By the knowledge derived from the angle of the casing stones, and the length of the base of the Great Pyramid, all those measures of proportion which seem arbitrary in the *Table of Constants,* are found to be no longer so. That the figures "1296000" should represent the *circumference* of the earth ; " 3437·74677," the *radius* reduced to *minutes;* and " 206264·8," the *radius* reduced to *seconds;* is no mystery when these figures, as *Ptolemaic feet,* are multiplied by 1·0101 English feet. The circumference then becomes equal to 130,908,000 English feet, — the radius reduced to minutes, is 347,246·240 English feet, and the radius reduced to seconds, is 20,834,805·600 English feet, all being actual measures made according to the standard of the Great Pyramid.

The measures of the earth before the Flood are no less certainly established. Before the Great Pyramid was completed, those measures which were employed in the construction of its interior might be supposed to be derived from the measures of the former earth; and such they are now proved to have been. To these measures we owe the *sacred cubit,* by which the ark was constructed, the *Karnak cubit,* by which the Pyramid coffer was constructed, and the primitive mile of 5760 English feet, which exceeded by *one-eleventh* part our present English mile.

When we speak of a *pint* of water or wheat, we shew by the etymological connection of that word with a *pound,* that a *pint in measure* is a *pound in weight.* A *pint of wheat* is a *pound of wheat.* The Pyramid coffer contains 256 gallons of wheat, each gallon weighing 10 lbs. troy. It also contains 256 gallons of water, each gallon weighing 10 lbs. merchant's weight, or avoirdupois. The troy pound is equal to 5760 grains troy : the merchants' weight was equal to 7200 grains, but it is now reduced to 7000·grains. In England, 32 grains of wheat, of middle size, are equal to 24 grains troy.

If the intention of the founders of the Great Pyramid had been to construct a building which should remain unimpaired for thousands of years, they would naturally do all that has been done, to insure to this edifice that perpetuity. They would form it of the most lasting materials, and cover it over with casing stones of still greater hardness, capable of receiving a high polish. They would make the casing stones of great bulk, and of nearly equal size throughout : and it appears, from what Herodotus says, that each contained in superficial measure not less than 30 square feet. They would join them together with the thinnest cement of extreme tenacity, so as to prevent, if possible, the insertion of any instrument which could tend to their separation. They would lay the lowest tier of casing stones on a perfectly smooth pavement of the same hard material. They would carry up the structure to a sharp point, that

neither the elements, nor man, should obtain a lodg-
ment on the top, which might tend to the disintegra-
tion of the chief stone of the angle.  If a standard of
measures of *length* were intended to be by this means
provided, the length of the base of the building would
suffice for it.  If the angle of the face with the base
were requisite to be taken into account, it could be
easily ascertained.  If a vessel of any kind were to be
added as a standard of measures of *capacity*, it would
be placed in the inside, in some well-constructed room,
duly ventilated; access to which might be obtained
under circumstances of considerable difficulty.  This
vessel of capacity would be formed of one block of the
hardest kind of material, such as porphyry or granite,
in order that it might not fall to decay.  The way to
this chamber from without would be rendered easy of
discovery by those to whom the secret was revealed,
but would not, probably, be obvious to common ob-
servers.  Strabo says, that about midway up in one of
the sides was a moveable stone, which, when it was displaced, revealed the indirect passage that led to the
inmost chamber of the building.*  After the Great
Pyramid had existed for about 3000 years, it appears
to have been divested of its marble coating by the
ravages of the Saracens, who employed the materials in
building some parts of the city of Cairo.  This is said to
have been done by order of Almamon, the Caliph of
Babylon, about the middle of the ninth century, or
1000 years ago.

* Εχει δ' εν ὑψει μεσως πως των πλευρων λιθον εξαιρεσιμον·
αρθεντος δε συριγξ εστι σχολια μεχρι της θηκης.—Lib. vii. p. 1161,
Casaub. Amst., folio, 1707.

## 152.

The author has finished his investigation, the result of much thought and labour for many years. It would have been easy to make it a larger work; but he was desirous to present his observations to the reader in the briefest form compatible with the development of the entire argument.

It does not supersede any other theory; for none has ever gained possession of the public mind. The notion that the *Pyramids of Gizeh* were the *sepulchres of kings* has never been advanced to the dignity of a theory. His view does not rest, for its favourable reception, on any discoveries to which the writer alone has had access. His hopes of success with the reflecting reader, are founded on the universality of the knowledge of the facts to which he calls attention, and which, on that account, require no proof. His translations are generally made in the words of others, because he wished every part of his argument to be based on the firmest foundation; and when he desired to rest any portion of it on a different rendering, he has been careful to quote the original, or to refer to it in such terms as would be equally satisfactory.

The writer could not have added any value to his work had he visited the Pyramids himself, and made any of the measurements on his own responsibility. He has, on the contrary, higher satisfaction in thinking that nothing depends on his own unsupported authority. The most agreeable of all his duties has consisted in the opportunity, which this Essay has afforded him, of referring to the statements of other writers on the subject of the Pyramids, in whose observations he has met with the strongest evidence of truth. This is so much the case, that instead of showing that their remarks were at variance with each other, as many have attempted, he has had nothing more to do than to record the testimony of every author *in the sense in which he meant it to be taken*, in order to produce a chain of evidence of the most indisputable character, all tending and needful to the understanding of the purpose for which the Pyramids of Gizeh were constructed.

---

*Note on the quotation from Jonathan, at page 230.*

I am indebted to the Rev. Robert Payne Smith, sub-librarian at the Bodleian, Oxford, who was consulted by a friend about the Chaldee quotation from *Jonathan*, at p. 230, for the following correction :—" דמשח ית ארעא באשלין, *qui mensurabat terram cum funiculis* — ' he who measured the Earth *with cords.*' The words are the same as those in *Bochart*, but they are differently arranged, and Bochart has translated them, as it would seem, incorrectly ; but his word *finibus* is, possibly, a mistake for *funibus.*" — The Hebrew word for *a cord,* חֶבֶל, is also a measuring *line,* in Zech. ii. 1, " Behold a man with a measuring *line* in his hands"; as well as in 2 Sam. viii. 2 ; Psa. lxxviii. 55 ; and in other places.

# APPENDIX.

## ADDITIONAL SCRIPTURE MEASURES OF LENGTH.

*Measures of Noah's Ark—Measures of the Tabernacle—Measures of Solomon's Temple and Palace—Measures of the Giants—Measures in Ezekiel.*

### 153.

*In the Sacred Cubit of* 2·0736 *Feet, or* 24·8832 *Inches.*

|  |  |  | Eng. Feet. |
|---|---|---|---|
| NOAH'S ARK* . . . . . . | 300 cubits in length | = | 622·080 |
| ———— . . . . . . | 50 „ „ breadth | = | 103·680 |
| ———— . . . . . . | 30 „ „ height | = | 62·208 |
| The window of the Ark . . | 1 „ „ „ | = | 2·073 |

The window extended, probably, the whole length of the Ark, along the roof, and acted as a ventilator, being covered over by a ridge-roof.

The waters rose upwards of 15 cubits above the highest mountains, or 31 feet English. This would allow the Ark to be sunk, by its contents, half its height into the water, and yet to float clear of the highest mountains.

### 154.

We are not told in the Sacred Scriptures by what

---

* The *hull* of the Great Eastern Iron Ship is 680 feet long, 83 feet broad, and 60 feet high from keel to deck.

measure Moses was instructed to make the *Tabernacle* in the wilderness, and the various articles it contained. It may have been made by the *sacred cubit,* but it is not unlikely to have been by the *cubit of Karnak.* We give, therefore, both estimates in the following table:—

### *The Measures of the Tabernacle.*

| | Cubits. | In the Karnak Cubit. English Feet. | In the Sacred Cubit. English Feet. |
|---|---|---|---|
| The Ark of the Tabernacle— | | | |
| ————— in length . . . | 2½ | 8·640 | 5·1840 |
| ————— in breadth . . . | 1½ | 5·184 | 3·1104 |
| ————— in height . . . | 1½ | 5·184 | 3·1104 |
| The Mercy Seat of pure Gold— | | | |
| ————— in length . . . | 2½ | 8·640 | 5·1840 |
| ————— in breadth . . . | 1½ | 5·184 | 3·1104 |
| The Table of Shew Bread— | | | |
| ————— in length . . . | 2 | 6·912 | 4·1472 |
| ————— in breadth . . . | 1 | 3·456 | 2·0736 |
| ————— in height . . . | 1½ | 5·184 | 3·1104 |
| | | Inches | Inches. |
| The Border round it, 1 span (or palm) | | 10·368 | 12·441 |
| | Cubits. | English Feet. | English Feet. |
| Ten Curtains of the Tabernacle— | | | |
| ————— in length . . . | 28 | 96·634 | 58·0608 |
| ————— in breadth . . . | 4 | 13·824 | 8·2944 |
| Five Curtains, coupled together . | 20 | 69·120 | 41·4720 |
| Five Curtains, coupled together . | 20 | 69·120 | 41·4720 |
| Eleven Curtains of Goat's Hair— | | | |
| ————— in length . . . | 30 | 103·680 | 62·2080 |
| ————— in breadth . . . | 4 | 13·824 | 8·2944 |
| Five Curtains, coupled together . | 20 | 69·120 | 41·4720 |
| Six Curtains, coupled together . . | 24 | 82·944 | 49·7664 |
| The Boards of the Tabernacle, standing up— | | | |
| Each Board, in length . . . . . | 10 | 34·560 | 20·3760 |
| ————— in breadth . . . . | 1½ | 5·184 | 3·1104 |

| | Cubits. | Karnak Cubit. English Feet. | Sacred Cubit. English Feet. |
|---|---|---|---|
| Twenty Boards on the South Side . | 30 | 103·680 | 62·2080 |
| Twenty Boards on the North Side . | 30 | 103·680 | 62·2080 |
| Six Boards on the West . . . . | 9 | 31·094 | 18·6624 |
| Two Boards for the Corners . . . | 9 | 31·094 | 18·6624 |
| Eight Boards for the Four Corners | 12 | 41·472 | 24·8832 |
| The Altar of Burnt-offering— | | | |
| ———— ———— in length . . . | 5 | 17·280 | 10·3680 |
| ———— ———— in breadth . . . | 5 | 17·280 | 10·3680 |
| ———— ———— in height— . . . | 3 | 13·368 | 6·2208 |
| The Court of the Tabernacle— | | | |
| Hangings for the South Side, length | 100 | 345·600 | 207·3600 |
| ———— ———— North Side „ | 100 | 345·600 | 207·3600 |
| ———— ———— West Side „ | 50 | 172·800 | 103·6800 |
| The Breadth of the Court, on the East | 50 | 172·800 | 103·6800 |
| Hangings on one Side the Entrance | 15 | 51·840 | 31·1040 |
| ———— on the other Side . . . | 15 | 51·840 | 31·1040 |
| ———— for the Gate of the Court | 20 | 69·120 | 41·4720 |
| The Court, in length . . . . . | .100 | 345·600 | 207·3600 |
| ———— in breadth, everywhere. | 50 | 172·800 | 103·6800 |
| ———— in height . . . . . | 5 | 17·280 | 10·3680 |

| | Span. | Inches. | Inches. |
|---|---|---|---|
| The Breastplate of Judgment— | | | |
| ———— ———— in length . . . . | 1 | 10·368 | 12·441 |
| ———— ———— in breadth . . . | 1 | 10·368 | 12·441 |

| | Cubits. | English Feet. | English Feet. |
|---|---|---|---|
| The Altar of Incense, in length . . | 1 | 3·456 | 2·0736 |
| ———— ———— in breadth . | 1 | 3·456 | 2·0736 |
| ———— ———— in height . . | 2 | 6·912 | 4·1472 |

The horns of the Altar of Incense were included in this height, which would probably reduce the flat part half a cubit.

The Ark of the Tabernacle had a crown, or cornice of gold, about it, by which the Mercy-seat was kept in its place (*Scott*).

A crown, or cornice of gold, was also round the Table of Shew-bread, and another round the border of it.

The span of the sacred cubit is equal to half a cubit, or 12·441 inches.

In describing the breadth of the border round the Table of Shew-bread, and the length and breadth of the Breastplate of Judgment, the word employed in the Hebrew is *zereth*, a span; but as a *span*, in the cubit of Karnak, is equal to 20·736 inches, the Latin Vulgate more properly translates this word by *palmus*, because a *palm* of the cubit of Karnak is equal to 10·368 inches, and that was probably the measure intended. A *span* is the more correct term, if the actual length be regarded, and not its relation to the scale of the cubit; but a *palm* is the more correct, if we attend to the proportion which it holds in the scale. Either word will be right, if it be rightly understood. The *palm* of the *cubit of Karnak* is the *span* of the *royal cubit*.

We cannot, however, be certain whether the cubit of Karnak (the cubit after the first measure, as it is called in 2 Chron. iii. 3) was the cubit by which the measure of the Tabernacle and its furniture was estimated. It may have been the sacred cubit which Moses referred to. In that case, the preceding calculations will require to be reduced as low as they are stated in the second column.

### 155.

The following measures are those of the cubit of Karnak, or " cubit of the first measure."

#### SOLOMON'S TEMPLE.

| | Cubits. | Cubit of Karnak. English Feet. |
|---|---|---|
| The Temple of Solomon, in length . . . . | 60 | 207·360 |
| ———————————— in breadth. . . . | 30 | 103·680 |
| In this breadth the houses for the Priests are included, 5 cubits on each side . . . | 5 | 17·280 |

| | Cubits. | Cubit of Karnak. English Feet. |
|---|---|---|
| The Temple of Solomon, in height . . . . | 30 | 103·680 |
| The height was also 120 Karnak palms . . | | 103·680 |

*\*\** *The breadth of the Temple was the breadth of Noah's Ark.*

| | Cubits. | Cubit of Karnak. English Feet. |
|---|---|---|
| The Porch before the House of the Temple, was, in length, according to the breadth of the House . . . . . . } | 20 | 69·120 |
| Its breadth before the House . . . . . . | 10 | 34·560 |
| The nethermost Chamber, against the wall . | 5 | 17·280 |
| The middle Chamber, resting on the wall. . | 6 | 20·736 |
| The third Chamber, resting on a higher part | 7 | 24·192 |
| The height of each Chamber . . . . . . | 5 | 17·280 |
| The House, or Temple before the Oracle . . | 40 | 138·240 |
| The Oracle was, in length . . . . . . . | 20 | 69·120 |
| —————————— in breadth . . . . . . | 20 | 69·120 |
| —————————— in height . . . . . . . | 20 | 69·120 |
| Two Cherubim in the Oracle, each in height. | 10 | 34·560 |
| The Four Wings of each Cherub, in breadth each | 5 | 17·280 |
| ——————————————————— together . . | 20 | 69·120 |
| The Altar of Brass, in length . . . . . . | 20 | 69·120 |
| ———————————— in breadth. . . . . . | 20 | 69·120 |
| ———————————— in height . . . . . . | 10 | 34·560 |
| The Pillars of *Jachin* and *Boaz*, in height . | 18 | 62·208 |
| Also said to be 35 cubits high, each cubit . | | 1·780 |
| The Pillars, in compass, each . . . . . . | 10 | 41·472 |
| The Chapiters of Molten Brass, in height . . | 5 | 17·280 |

## 156.

*The following Measures are those of the Royal Cubit, or Cubit of Memphis.*

### SOLOMON'S PALACE.

| | Cubits. | Royal Cubit. English Feet. |
|---|---|---|
| The House of the Forest of Lebanon, in length | 100 | 172·800 |
| ———————————————————— in breadth | 50 | 86·400 |
| ———————————————————— in height . | 30 | 51·840 |

| | Cubits. | Royal Cubit. English Feet. |
|---|---|---|
| The Porch of Pillars, in length . . . . . | 50 | 86·400 |
| —————————— in breadth . . . . . | 30 | 51·840 |
| The Stones of the Foundation of the Palace. | 10 | 17·280 |
| Other stones of the foundation . . . . . | 8 | 13·824 |
| The Molten Sea, from brim to brim. . . . | 10 | 17·280 |
| ——————— in height . . . . . . . | 5 | 8·640 |
| ——————— in compass. . . . . . . | 30 | 51·840 |

The Knops, 10 in a cubit, each 2·073 inches.

The thickness of the Molten Sea was a Palm, 5·184 inches.

| | Cubits. | English Feet. |
|---|---|---|
| Ten Bases of Brass, each, in length . . . . | 4 | 6·912 |
| —————————————— in breadth . . . | 4 | 6·912 |
| ——————————————— in height . . . . | 3 | 5·184 |
| Each Base had Four Brazen Wheels, in height | 1½ | 2·592 |
| Ten Lavers of Brass for each Base, each Laver | 4 | 6·912 |
| The Brazen Scaffold, on which Solomon stood and kneeled at the Dedication of the Temple, was, in length . . . . | 5 | |
| ———————————— in breadth . . . . . | 5 | |
| ———————————— in height . . . . . | 3 | |

This scaffold, it may be observed, was, in all its proportions, equal to the original Brazen Altar which Moses
had made for the Tabernacle (§ 154). The word *scaffold*
is, in Zechariah xii. 6, rendered " *hearth*." It stands in
all other places for " *laver*." Solomon is said to have
made this scaffold, in 2 Chron. vi. 13.

## 157.
### *Measures of the Giants.*

| | Royal Cubits. Eng. Feet. |
|---|---|
| The iron bedstead of Og, the King of Bashan (the last of the Giants), was, in length, 9 cubits, "after the cubit of a man". . . . . . . . . . . . . | 15·5 52 |
| ———————————————— in breadth, 4 cubits . . . . | 6·912 |
| Goliath of Gath was, in height, 6 cubits and a span . . | 11·232 |
| An Egyptian of great stature was, in height, 5 cubits . | 8·640 |
| The gallows of Haman was, in height, 50 cubits . . . | 86·400 |

## 158.

### The Measures in Ezekiel.

Some of the measures in Ezekiel are made by a "measuring reed of six cubits long, by the cubit and hand-breadth"; that is, the *sacred cubit*. A reed is therefore 12·4416 English feet.

The rest of the measures are probably made, as some of them certainly are, in the cubit of Karnak, or "cubit of the first measure." But the *Altar* (xliii. 13) is measured by the *sacred cubit*.

*The following Measures in Ezekiel represent the Cubit of Karnak in English Feet.*

| Cubits. | | Eng. Feet. | Cubits. | | Eng. Feet. | Cubits. | | Eng. Feet. |
|---|---|---|---|---|---|---|---|---|
| 1 | = | 3·456 | 10 | = | 34·560 | 20 | = | 69·120 |
| 1½ | = | 5·184 | 11 | = | 38·016 | 25 | = | 86·400 |
| 2 | = | 6·912 | 12 | = | 41·472 | 30 | = | 103·680 |
| 3 | = | 10·368 | 13 | = | 44·928 | 40 | = | 138·240 |
| 4 | = | 13·824 | 14 | = | 48·384 | 50 | = | 172·800 |
| 5 | = | 17·280 | 15 | = | 51·840 | 60 | = | 207·360 |
| 6 | = | 20·736 | 16 | = | 55·296 | 70 | = | 241·920 |
| 7 | = | 24·192 | 17 | = | 58·752 | 80 | = | 276·480 |
| 8 | = | 27·648 | 18 | = | 62·208 | 90 | = | 311·040 |
| 9 | = | 31·104 | 19 | = | 65·664 | 100 | = | 345·600 |

THE END.

Made in the USA
Coppell, TX
27 February 2022